Trail of Tears

Trail of Tears

Julia Coates

Landmarks of the American Mosaic

 GREENWOOD

AN IMPRINT OF ABC-CLIO, LLC
anta Barbara, California • Denver, Colorado • Oxford, England

Copyright 2014 by ABC-CLIO, LLC

All rights reserved. No part of this publication may be reproduced, stored in a retrieval system, or transmitted, in any form or by any means, electronic, mechanical, photocopying, recording, or otherwise, except for the inclusion of brief quotations in a review, without prior permission in writing from the publisher.

Library of Congress Cataloging-in-Publication Data

Coates, Julia.
 Trail of tears / Julia Coates.
  pages cm. — (Landmarks of the american mosaic)
 Includes index.
  ISBN 978-0-313-38448-6 (hardback) — ISBN 978-0-313-38449-3 (ebook)
1. Trail of Tears, 1838–1839—Juvenile literature.   2. Indians of North America—
Southern States—Relocation—Juvenile literature.   3. Cherokee Indians—
History—Juvenile literature.   4. Cherokee Indians—Relocation—Juvenile
literature.   I. Title.
 E99.C5C668   2014
 975.004'97557—dc23   2013029453

ISBN: 978-0-313-38448-6
EISBN: 978-0-313-38449-3

18 17 16 15 14   1 2 3 4 5

This book is also available on the World Wide Web as an eBook.
Visit www.abc-clio.com for details.

Greenwood
An Imprint of ABC-CLIO, LLC

ABC-CLIO, LLC
130 Cremona Drive, P.O. Box 1911
Santa Barbara, California 93116-1911

This book is printed on acid-free paper ∞

Manufactured in the United States of America

Contents

Series Foreword

THE LANDMARKS OF THE AMERICAN MOSAIC series comprises individual volumes devoted to exploring an event or development central to this country's multicultural heritage. The topics illuminate the struggles and triumphs of American Indians, African Americans, Latinos, and Asian Americans, from European contact through the turbulent last half of the 20th century. The series covers landmark court cases, laws, government programs, civil rights infringements, riots, battles, movements, and more. Written by historians especially for high school students, undergraduates, and general readers, these content-rich references satisfy thorough research needs and provide a deeper understanding of material that students might only be exposed to in a short section of a textbook or a superficial explanation online.

Each book on a particular topic is a one-stop reference source. The series format includes

- Introduction
- Chronology
- Narrative chapters that trace the evolution of the event or topic chronologically
- Biographical profiles of key figures
- Selection of crucial primary documents
- Glossary
- Bibliography
- Index

This landmark series promotes respect for cultural diversity and supports the social studies curriculum by helping students understand multicultural American history.

Preface

NATIVE AMERICANS are noticeably absent from most histories of the United States. Appearing briefly in historical accounts of colonial times, Indians are presented as having aided the first colonists, or impeded their sociopolitical developments, or levied bloody attacks on their settlements. Always deemed marginal players to the central story of the European immigrants and their descendants who are described as those who built the American nation, American Indians have never warranted more than a few paragraphs in most texts used in American classrooms.

However, chances are that Indian Removal and the Trail of Tears were the subjects of at least one of those paragraphs. Americans who know nothing about Indians or Indian history may be able to correctly identify this event, although they often cannot provide any additional information or insight about it. The story of the forced removal of tens of thousands of Indians from their homes and homelands, and the deaths of thousands along the brutal marches that ensued is one that many Americans recall and an injustice they deplore.

This work brings depth to the story of Indian Removal in a way that is easily accessible for students and the general public. As a reference work, it will aid students to place this historic federal policy into the broader context of events and issues within the United States, but especially within the process of political and cultural responses offered by one of the most prominent Indian nations impacted by the policy, the Cherokees. Through a chronology that succinctly outlines the chapters to follow, biographies of the most significant historic figures of the era, primary documents, and an annotated bibliography, readers will not only have a strong introduction to the subject, but will also begin to comprehend the significance of the ongoing dialogue in contemporary times between the United States and the tribal nations within its borders.

I wish first to acknowledge two Cherokee scholars of their own history. Principal Chief Chad Smith of the Cherokee Nation provided an opportunity for me to contemplate and internalize this subject for years through teaching the Cherokee Nation history course that he originated. Tribal Councilman Jack Baker has shared information from his primary research that brings to life families and practices of the time period. Although not directly involved with this project, Theda Perdue, Anna Smith, Duane King, and Brett Riggs have provided detail and illumination over many years that have greatly changed my initial understanding of the preremoval and removal era. My cherished friendships with Kimberlie Gilliland, Andrew Sikora, Tom and Sally Lewis, and Cathy Monholland have supported me through a myriad of difficulties that impacted the timely delivery of the manuscript. To all, my profound gratitude.

Most especially, I have been profoundly influenced by the literally hundreds of hours that I have spent in conversation with Cherokee screenwriter Shane Smith on the subject of removal. His understanding of the humanity shared by all peoples that renders this a universal story lifts its telling from abject tragedy to highest inspiration. It is my most fervent hope that this work also reflects the enlightenment that he has shared with me.

And to my family, who for so many years have patiently supported an overworked daughter and sister who doesn't get to see them as much as she would like to, I love you.

Introduction

MANY GENERATIONS in the past, a people inhabited an island somewhere to the south of the present day United States. This small group lived on their island, surrounded by salty, undrinkable water, yet ventured out by canoe to gain great familiarity with the waters and the other islands around them. But after years and years of idyllic existence, their island started to tremble and shake and the day came when it began to spew forth fire. As these strange and unfamiliar events unfolded, the people collected themselves in their canoes and set out on the waters, escaping the terrifying changes that were occurring to their land. One by one the canoes left the shore, each loaded with islanders, until all were at last on the water. As they rowed further out to sea, the people in the last canoe turned to look back at their island, and in that moment, they saw it shattered by an explosion of fire. They continued to paddle away from it and eventually the horizon was empty, as if their homeland had never existed.

So begins a version of an old Cherokee story about a great migration over many centuries and vast areas of water and land—a migration made by a people who later came to be known as "Cherokees." This trek brought them at last into the southern Appalachian region of the present-day United States, but only after days, if not weeks, at sea, followed by a journey spanning many generations across broad areas of unknown territory, once land had been encountered again. As with all ancient stories, this one is flexible and has been shaped and reshaped by countless generations of Cherokees, as well as in the records made by outsiders to the society.

Many versions of the story exist, therefore, and the particular details are debated by Cherokees today. General agreement is found upon several points, however: once they reached land, the people who later came to be known as the Cherokees migrated in a northerly direction, crossing several rivers, until they began to encounter "white water"—snow, sometimes described as a "wall of ice." Most accounts suggest their migration turned to the east at that time, crossing a very large river, the "Long Man" as Cherokees recount it today, almost certainly the Mississippi. The tale acknowledges contact and interactions with other tribes by these travelers, and some versions even suggest significant adaptations of their own Cherokee culture and language based in these encounters with Mississippian-era Mound Builders. Finally, the Cherokees took a southern turn and migrated into the region generally regarded as their homeland—areas along the rivers of the western Carolinas and eastern Tennessee.

Several accounts of the story told by ceremonialists and traditionalists claim that originally there were 12 traveling groups, or 12 canoes, or 12 clans, but that as time went on they were reduced or coalesced into only 7. The story is thus explanatory of the origins of the seven clans by which the Cherokee people organized themselves for social and political action for centuries to follow.

But perhaps the most interesting aspect of the story is not in the story itself, but in the fact that a tale of ancient migration and of adaptation to new places and new peoples is told as part of the Cherokees' history of themselves. One can only speculate as to how the national character of the Cherokee people was shaped by the need to incorporate the new that the people were encountering—new experiences, technologies, and environments—while maintaining a sense of continuity and identity rooted in a different place and a different origin.

It is even more fascinating to speculate when one understands that this migration story is not generally known among the people of the Eastern Band of Cherokees, the group that remained in North Carolina after the removal from the southeast in 1838 of the majority of the Cherokee Nation. The story only survives among the people of the Cherokee Nation, the descendants of those who were forcibly removed from their homelands in the 1830s to what is today the state of Oklahoma. For those in North Carolina, who remained in the place where even archaeologists agree they had inhabited for at least 1,200 years, it has been important to strengthen and solidify their claims and connections to the homeland as contemporary struggles to defend land rights have developed. But for those Cherokees in Oklahoma, whose ancestors were forced to migrate in 1838–1839, although strong feelings for the former homelands still exist, it has been important to emphasize the qualities of adaptability and continuity in new places that the old migration story teaches. That, after all, has been their more recent reality as well.

The Trail of Tears, as the forced Cherokee migration of 1838–1839 is known in American history, is not as much a story about the journey itself as about the events leading up to it. The removal of tribes whose homelands were in the eastern and mid-western regions of an expanding United States was first promoted as federal policy after the 1803 Louisiana Purchase, during the administration of President Thomas Jefferson. In the two decades immediately following, tribes from the Ohio Valley and Great Lakes regions were forcibly removed to lands west of the Mississippi River—areas in present-day Kansas, Nebraska, and Iowa—apparently without much awareness on the part of the American public. The pressures to remove had increased greatly on the southern tribes by the late 1820s, but these "Five Civilized Tribes," as they were coming to be known, employed legal and political strategies to resist the attempts to wrest them from their lands. The Seminole Nation, located in the swamplands of Florida, also engaged in military resistance against the United States, resulting in the costliest war for the United States to that date.

But the Cherokee Nation, which offered not only the greatest legal and political resistance to removal but also whose efforts brought the policy to the consciousness of the American public, is most associated with the Trail of Tears. When the editorials of Elias Boudinot, the editor of the *Cherokee Phoenix*, the first newspaper to be published by an Indian nation, began to be reprinted in major daily newspapers in the northern United States, knowledge of the cause of the Cherokees was widely disseminated. Through the advocacy of missionary societies in New England, whose missionaries worked among the Cherokees, reform-minded Americans rallied to support them. And when Georgia, in its attempt to rid the state of Indians, began passing laws that appeared to circumvent the U.S. Congress and Constitution, federalists throughout the country were drawn into opposition to Indian removal. The Cherokees cultivated public sentiment and the states' rights question in ways that split the House of Representatives and foreshadowed the conflict of the American Civil War 30 years before that event. They then went on to bring their grievances to the Supreme Court, which ultimately upheld their rights, thereby forcing an American president to perhaps betray his own constitutional requirements in order to take Cherokee lands and remove them.

The story of the Trail of Tears is usually told as a tragedy, as certainly it was. Tragic stories are frequently populated by villains and victims, one entity who acts upon another, and the story of Indian removal as it has been popularly told in recent years is no exception. But the emphasis that has typically been placed on the internal divisions within the economic and political strata of Cherokees during the era obscures the true perfidy. The various Trails of Tears occurred as a result of betrayals of treaties and its own constitution on the part of the federal government. Had it adhered to its own governing principles, the removals of Indian tribes could never have been legally achieved by the United States.

For the most part, the people who suffered on the Trail of Tears were not the powerful and influential members of Cherokee society, and they certainly weren't the president and Congress of the United States. The thousands of uncelebrated Cherokee subsistence farmers, who had left behind small cabins and a few utilitarian possessions, were those who trudged the almost 900 miles in icy rain. Their voices are largely silent in the documentary record, and even their names are scattered about and relatively hidden in the accounts. But this is their story most of all. And when the focus shifts to place them at the center, the few records that do chronicle their experiences reveal stories of everyday heroism, valor and courage, pride and humility, and persistence most of all. Yes, they would lose their land, but in their refusal to relinquish the things that made their lives meaningful—family, community, culture, faith, and their nation—their story becomes larger, one that belongs to *all* peoples. In the end, the lesson of the Trail of Tears is not one of division, betrayal, or tragedy, but of triumph.

Chronology

1721   First treaty signed between the Cherokees and the British colonial government in South Carolina includes land cession.

1738–1739   Smallpox epidemic results in a 50% population loss among the Cherokees leaving only 10,000 still living.

1747–1751   War between the Cherokees and the Creeks leads to British embargo of the Cherokees.

1753   Grand Council meeting at Chota (TN) at which the Cherokees designate the first principal chief, Old Hop, chosen by the Cherokees themselves.

Smallpox epidemic results in one-third loss of Cherokee population, bringing the Cherokees back down to approximately 10,000 in number.

1755–1763   The French and Indian War, in which the Cherokees allied with the British.

1755   Second treaty signed between the Cherokees and the British colonial government of South Carolina includes more extensive land cession.

1759–1761   Series of British attacks results in the destruction of about 40% of the Cherokee towns in North and South Carolinas, despite the fact that the Cherokees are allied with them by treaty.

1763–1775   Five treaties between the Cherokees and British colonial governments result in the loss of almost 57,200 square miles of territory, about 46% of their original territory.

1775–1784   The American Revolutionary War, in which most Cherokees wanted to remain neutral, but Cherokee warriors allied with the British.

1776   Cherokee warriors are defeated in their attacks on American settlements on the Holston River in Tennessee.

1777   Two treaties with American colonial governments in South and North Carolinas result in additional land cessions and ultimately the relocation of some Cherokee towns to northeastern Alabama.

1779–1781 In a series of military campaigns, Americans destroy about 80% of Cherokee towns.

1782   Smallpox epidemic among the Cherokees results in a one-third loss of population, bringing the total population to about 9,000.

1783   Treaty with American colonial government in Georgia results in a land cession.

1784–1791 Warrior confederation comprised mainly of Cherokees, the Chickamauga Cherokees, emerges from Revolutionary War and continues to skirmish with American frontiersmen despite an official peace agreement between the Cherokees and the United States.

1785   The Treaty of Hopewell is the first treaty between the Cherokees and the United States. It involves land cessions in Tennessee.

Late 1780s Cherokee settlements in east central Tennessee are abandoned as a result of conflict with American frontiersmen.

1788   Commerce Clause of U.S. Constitution states that only the Congress has regulatory authority over Indian affairs

1790   Trade and Intercourse Act requires that any transfers of Indian lands must go to the United States.

1791   Chickamauga Cherokees are defeated by frontiersmen.

Treaty of Holston is the first time the Cherokees state their nationality in a legal document. It involves land cessions in Tennessee and North Carolina.

1792   Chickamaugan leader Dragging Canoe dies.

1794   About 500 Chickamaugans and their families emigrate to northeastern Arkansas.

1801   First Christian mission (Moravian) to the Cherokees.

1802   *Articles of Agreement and Cession between the United States and the State of Georgia* (the Georgia Compact) are passed by Congress.

1803   The Louisiana Purchase. Indian Removal from eastern lands to areas west of the Mississippi River becomes federal policy.

1807   Cherokee leader Doublehead is killed by members of the National Council, the first time a chief was killed under a relatively new edict proclaiming death for anyone who ceded Cherokee land without permission from the entire National Council.

1808   First written statute of the Cherokee Nation establishing law enforcement and empowering it to deal with certain crimes.

1809   About 1,000 Cherokees from the Lower Towns immigrate to (present-day) north central and northwestern Arkansas.

1810   An agreement by the seven Cherokee clans to abolish "blood law" within the Cherokee Nation, to be replaced with penalties established by statute.

1811   New Madrid earthquake destroys Chickamaugan Cherokee villages in northeastern Arkansas and Missouri bootheel area; many relocate slightly westward to rejoin with those who had immigrated in 1809.

1813   Red Stick (Creek) warriors attack American settlements in Alabama.

1814   At the Battle of Horseshoe Bend, Andrew Jackson raises volunteer army to retaliate against the Red Sticks; he is joined by Cherokees in the effort, who took action that saved the battle.

1816–1817   Despite their service in Jackson's army, the United States demands and coerces two additional cessions of land from the Cherokees.

1817–1819   Emigrations of about 3,000 Cherokees, known as "Old Settlers," from lands that had been ceded by treaty to Arkansas territory.

1817   Cherokees pass the Act of Reform, which restructures the Cherokee governing system into a more centralized system that more closely resembled that of the United States.

1818   Buck Oo-watie, later known as Elias Boudinot, starts at the American Board of Commissioners for Foreign Missions (ABCFM) school at Cornwall, Connecticut.

1819   John Ridge, Boudinot's cousin, also begins at the ABCFM school in Cornwall.

1819   Reserves for the Oconluftee Cherokees, later known as the Eastern Band of Cherokee Indians, were granted in ceded lands in western North Carolina.

1820   Electoral districts and judicial districts are established in the Cherokee Nation as elaboration of the legislative and judicial branches was undertaken.

1821   The Cherokee syllabary, the writing system of the Cherokee language, is revealed and demonstrated by its inventor, Sequoyah (George Guess).

1823   *Johnson v. McIntosh* decision rendered in the Supreme Court, a part of which applies aspects of the European Doctrine of Discovery to Indians in the United States and denies their ownership of their own lands, acknowledging only their occupancy rights.

1824   John Ridge marries Sarah Northrup, causing unrest in the town of Cornwall, Connecticut.

1824–1827   Conservative Cherokees' rebellion against the development of constitutional government, called "White Path's Rebellion."

1826   Elias Boudinot marries Harriet Gold, resulting in their being burned in effigy by the citizens of Cornwall, Connecticut. The ABCFM school closes permanently as a result.

1827   First constitution of the Cherokee Nation ratified.

1827   Creeks ousted from Georgia as a result of betrayals by one of their chiefs.

1828   First edition of the *Cherokee Phoenix* is printed, the first newspaper to be published by an Indian nation.

1828   Western Cherokees sign treaty that cedes land in the Indian Territory to the Cherokee Nation and provides for the removal of the western Cherokees from their Arkansas reservation to lands in the Indian Territory several hundred miles to the west.

1828   Andrew Jackson elected president of the United States.

1828–1829   Gold was discovered near (present-day) Dahlonega, Georgia.

1829   First Georgia Harassment Law passed.

1829   *Georgia v. Corn Tassels* case that opens the door for the Cherokee Nation to challenge Georgia's harassment laws in the Supreme Court.

1830   Second Georgia Harassment Law passed, which included provisions for the establishment of the Georgia Guard.

1830   Indian Removal Act passed in Congress.

1830–1832   Choctaws sign the Treaty of Dancing Rabbit Creek and their removal to the Indian Territory follows.

1831   *Cherokee Nation v. Georgia* decision is rendered by the Supreme Court. The Cherokees lose on a technicality of their inability to establish the court's original jurisdiction, but the merits of the issue remain unexamined.

1831   Missionaries of the ABCFM are arrested by the state of Georgia. Most acquiesce to the state laws, but two, Samuel Worcester and Elizur Butler, force a state trial.

1832   *Worcester v. Georgia* is filed with the Supreme Court in February and a decision is rendered in March that strikes down Georgia's assertions of jurisdiction over the Cherokee Nation and upholds the Cherokee Nation's territorial boundaries and sovereignty within.

1832   Elias Boudinot resigns the editorship of the *Cherokee Phoenix* after Principal Chief John Ross and the National Council forbid him from printing his arguments in favor of removal after the federal nonenforcement of the Supreme Court victory. Elijah Hicks is appointed editor.

1832   Georgia harassment of the Cherokees increases as a result of President Jackson's indication to the state that he will not enforce the Supreme Court's decision. The state refuses to release the imprisoned missionaries.

1832   November: South Carolina passes its Nullification Ordinances, bringing the conflict between states' rights advocates and federalists to a head. As fears that the country will be divided escalate, pressures on the missionaries to accept state pardons increases.

1832   November: Andrew Jackson is reelected president.

1833   January: The missionaries acknowledge "wrongdoing," accept pardons from the state, and are released.

1833   Significant numbers of Cherokees remove to the Indian Territory after losing their homes and property to the Georgia Guard and Georgia lottery winners.

1834   *Cherokee Phoenix* ceases publication as a result of Boudinot's resignation and mounting pressures from the removal crisis.

1835   February: John Ross leads a delegation to Washington, D.C. ostensibly to negotiate a treaty, but most likely as a stalling tactic to prevent other unauthorized individuals from negotiating a treaty of removal with U.S. commissioners.

1835   Spring: As Ross negotiation crumbles, John Ridge approaches U.S. commissioners with an offer to negotiate a treaty. Ridge is entirely unauthorized to do so, but the commissioners work with him and others to develop a treaty.

1835   Principal Chief John Ross and his family are evicted from their home at the Head of Coosa and reoccupy an old cabin in southeastern Tennessee that had been built by Ross' grandfather.

1835   Summer: The Ridge Party calls several councils at John's home at the Head of Coosa to try to persuade Cherokees to enter into a treaty. Most are poorly attended, except one in July, when Cherokees attend primarily to vote down a federal overture to pay the annuity per capita, rather than to the Cherokee government.

1835   October: At the annual National Council meeting in the fall, U.S. commissioner Schermerhorn tries to present a treaty to the people, but is thwarted by the Ross government. The council votes down the proposed treaty.

1835   December: Chief Ross takes a delegation to Washington, D.C. under the pretext of negotiating a treaty, but mainly to forestall the treaty meeting that has been called by Schermerhorn for the end of the month at which, it is feared, a treaty not sanctioned by the Cherokee government will be signed.

1835   December 21–28: A group of 300 Cherokees meet to revise and sign a removal treaty, the Treaty of New Echota.

1836   Cherokee petition of protest received by the U.S. Senate.

1836   May: Treaty of New Echota is ratified in the Senate by a difference of one vote.

1836   November: Martin Van Buren elected president.

1836–1837   Many Treaty Party families immigrate to the Indian Territory, allowed to take their slaves and most of their personal property, and with relatively few deaths.

1836–1838   Federal troops occupy the Cherokee Nation, at first to quell Indian uprisings, but discovering no such tendencies among the Cherokees, later giving their protection to Cherokees suffering from the abuses of the Georgia Guard.

1837   March: Martin Van Buren inaugurated president of the United States.

1837   Fall: General John Wool court-martialed for interfering with the activities of the Alabama militia as empowered under state law. Wool was acquitted, but resigned in disgust with the orders he anticipated he would be given to enact the roundup of Cherokees for removal.

1838   April: Stockades are erected in the Cherokee Nation in preparation for removal.

1838   May: Federal roundup of Cherokees begins.

1838   June: Three detachments, totaling about 2,800 Cherokees, are sent west on a water route. Drought hampers their progress and there is much suffering. Reports of high death rates among the Cherokee are communicated to the military commanders and tribal leadership.

1838   June: Removal is halted as drought conditions set in. Cherokees are transferred out of the stockades and into internment camps.

1838   July: Cherokees are allowed to take over the management of their own removal. Congress allocates additional monies as the expense of holding Cherokees in camps throughout the summer eats up the previously allocated funds.

1838   August: Cherokees begin to be transferred from the camps to departure points.

1838   September–October: Twelve detachments leave the Cherokee Nation heading north and then west on the Trail of Tears.

1838   October: Oconoluftee Cherokees are officially exempted from the roundup and removal after their cooperation in tracking escaped Cherokee fugitives who had killed federal soldiers.

1838   December: Last detachment leaves the Cherokee Nation.

1838   December: Detachments are trapped for three weeks by blizzards in southern Illinois, and many Cherokees die throughout.

1839   January: First detachment of Cherokees arrives in the Indian Territory.

1839   January–April: Additional 12 detachments arrive in the Indian Territory.

1839   June: Leadership of the Treaty Party is executed in simultaneous extralegal strikes. The event sets the Cherokees into civil war.

1839–1846 Cherokees experience internal warfare resulting in hundreds of killings as Ross Party and Treaty Party supporters vie for power within the Cherokee Nation.

1839   July: The Act of Union, the organic document of the modern Cherokee Nation, was passed, unifying the western Cherokees and those who had just arrived from the removal as one government.

1839   September: A superseding Cherokee Constitution to govern over the Cherokee Nation in the Indian Territory was ratified.

1843   An election for chief is held, throughout which internal violence escalates. John Ross is reelected by a significant majority.

1846   August: Under threat of permanent division, the United States coerces dueling parties within the Cherokee Nation into a peace agreement and treaty, with concessions to the Treaty Party but also an acknowledgement of the Ross government as the sole elected leadership of the Cherokee Nation. With this treaty, the removal era and its aftermath closes, and the Cherokees enter into a Golden Age (1846–1861) of peace and prosperity.

ONE

A World Unbalanced

On May 31, 1838, on a night as he awaited the soldiers who would be coming to forcibly remove him from his home, the Reverend Steven Foreman—a Cherokee citizen, a member of the Cherokee National Council, and one of the first ordained Cherokee Christian ministers—penned the following in a letter from his home in southeastern Tennessee:

> From the date of my letter you will perceive that I am still in the Cherokee Nation East . . . . How much longer we shall be permitted [to] remain here on our own lands, to enjoy our rights and privileges, I do not know. From the present aspect of affairs, we shall very soon be without house and home.[1]

One can imagine Reverend Foreman perhaps seated on the porch of his cabin on Candy's Creek in southeastern Tennessee, looking out at dusk on the hills surrounding him, knowing that the mountains that contained the center of the Cherokee world lay only a short distance away, and realizing that these were among the last moments he would ever rest his eyes on this adored land. Foreman's love for his homeland was unquestionably matched by every one of his countrypeople. The Great Smoky Mountains had defined the Cherokees and their culture for countless generations. Although ancient stories told that their people had originally inhabited an island home somewhere to the south, their presence in this Appalachian region dated from at least 1,000 years earlier, and perhaps much longer. They had integrated themselves deeply into these mountains, the rivers and streams that cut through the valleys were the people's lifeblood as well, and the animals and the flora had become part of their families. In later eras, when others came among the Cherokees and intermarried with them, the Scotsmen in particular understood that the heart of the Cherokees beat in these

1

mountains, for it had not been so very different for them in the land from which they originated. The people and the mountains, the mountains and the people, they were one.

Some Cherokees had ventured out of the mountains of the Carolinas to settle on the plateau to the west, between the Tennessee and the Little Tennessee Rivers. More recently, others had been driven south and west by American frontiersmen into northern Georgia and northeastern Alabama. But even there, the presence of the mountains and the Cherokees who remained within them was always in sight, or at least in the mind's eye. The mountains were ancient and worn, the rivers had cut many paths through them, and small caves were scattered throughout. But the Cherokees knew that much more was hidden in these mountains and rivers as well. Their world was filled with opposing forces and one needed to know how to manage them as one journeyed through the mountains and onto the rivers, as one journeyed through life.

Who knew when one might come upon the Great Uktena sunning itself in a valley? This magnificent serpent had a large crystal embedded in the center of its forehead that was said to convey great powers to the one who held it. One might die in trying to take it from the Uktena, or in simply defending oneself from this creature that aggressively guarded it. Taking it was a task best left to the medicine people who might actually know how to use the crystal. Surely the one who obtained it would have tremendous ability to heal, but also to harm, should they be so inclined.

Who knew what mysterious beings might appear from the caves? Many had reported seeing the Little People in these mountains, small likenesses of the Cherokees themselves, but who were faintly malevolent. It was best to avoid them and their trickery, unless one was a medicine person, in which case these cunning individuals might have much to teach, if one was able to gain their trust. Some Cherokee warriors had also reported instances when the Nunnehi, apparitions of Cherokees from ancient times, had manifested on the ridgetops at the height of a battle. Often at a moment when it seemed the Cherokee warriors were bested, these beings materialized to help turn the tide. Usually, the other side did not know who or what had struck them, only that they had been immediately disoriented and disabled.

Who knew what awaited them in the rivers? Although Cherokees "went to water" every morning, immersing themselves at the edges of the cold streams to sing and smoke tobacco in their long-stemmed pipes as they opened their day with prayer and ceremony, and although they traveled easily by canoe on the surface of the waters, venturing into the depths of the waters was risky. Under the rivers lay the openings to the world below, and many malicious forces seeped through the cracks of the riverbed, lying in wait for the unsuspecting victim who ventured in too far.

This was the world of the Cherokees. It was a world where nothing was separate from anything else. The positive was embedded in the negative; the negative contained aspects of the positive. It was secretive and shrouded. It was to be honored, but also to be feared if one did not respect both its order and its chaos. Living in this world was a matter of managing its contradictions, keeping the opposing forces in a balance and keeping oneself in balance. This was the way to have a good life.

When the Reverend Steven Foreman looked out on the mountains for the last time, it was not merely to cherish a final look at the scenery. Although he had become a relatively acculturated man and had, like many of his countrypeople, adopted some of the practices of the Europeans and Americans who had occupied their lands, this good Christian minister was still a Cherokee. He intuitively knew that the mountains, and all that was in them, conveyed the lessons of how to be a Cherokee, how to manage oneself in the world, and how to be balanced and have a good life. If the Cherokees were no longer a part of these mountains and no longer had relationships with the beings within them, who would they be?

* * * * * * * * * * *

The Great Smoky Mountains form the border between North and South Carolina to the east and Tennessee to the west. More than a thousand, and maybe several thousand, years ago, in the region around the intersection of what are today these three states, new inhabitants pushed into this difficult, unoccupied territory and established permanent settlements. Their neighbors, peoples who spoke other languages and lived by different social organization, had many names for the newcomers. The one that came to be commonly used, "Cherokee," may be a Choctaw term in its origins. As stated by the 19th-century anthropologist James Mooney, "There is evidence that it is derived from the Choctaw word *choluk* or *chiluk*, signifying a pit or cave, and comes to us through the so-called Mobilian trade language, a corrupted Choctaw jargon formerly used as the medium of communication among all the tribes of the Gulf states, as far north as the mouth of the Ohio" (1900, reproduced 1982, 15, 16). The "Cherokees" may thus have been, in the view of their neighbors, "the people who live in caves."

But they had a different concept of themselves and their domain, and used the term "Ani Giduwagi," a term roughly translated from their own language as "the people who are on top" as they perceived their mountain homes to be.

The Cherokees had many neighbors. To their east, in what is today South Carolina, were the Yamassee and the Catawba, smaller tribes that were often raided by the Cherokees. To their south, in areas that are today southern South Carolina, southern Georgia, and southern Alabama, was the militarily powerful Muscogee Creek Confederacy, an amalgamation of many tribal and cultural groups that had been assimilated either willingly or by force into the confederation, and with whom the Cherokees were alternately in alliance or at war. To their west and north lay vast expanses of territory, in what are today Tennessee and Kentucky, which were not permanently inhabited by anyone but were traversed and utilized not only by the Cherokees, but also by many tribes, including those from north of the Ohio River such as the Shawnee, Delaware, Wyandot, and Miami, as well as the Chickasaw and Choctaw from western Tennessee and northern Mississippi. These vast areas were the great hunting grounds, teeming with deer and other animals, and in the hunting season of late fall and winter, men from many tribes were occupied in the woods in pursuit of food and hides for their villages.

The Cherokee villages were located in regions extending from what are today western South Carolina, into the high mountains of western North Carolina, and rolling down into the valleys and hills of southeastern and east central Tennessee. Much of the region was rugged and "capable of supporting human life only in marginal patches of fertile fields and sheltered caves [and its] geography dictated a dispersal into many towns connected only by narrow, often dangerous paths" (Reid 1970, 7). Although a somewhat shifting number, the Cherokees averaged about 65 villages of only a few hundred inhabitants each. In addition, some small settlements of perhaps 30 people often lay just outside the villages' borders—little "suburbs" that were socially and politically attached to the larger village. Exact Cherokee population figures before the arrival of Europeans are unknown, but the various methods for estimating population indicate a population of at least 30,000.

The inhabitants of Cherokee towns were connected by a shared language, shared ceremonial practices, and a system of kinship through clans. The clan was their basic social unit. Among the Cherokees, seven matrilineal clans defined who was related to whom. Historian Theda Perdue explains, "According to the principle of matrilineal descent, people belonged to the clan of their mother: their only relatives were those who could be traced through her. . . . Children were not blood relatives of their father or grandfather; a father was not related to his children by blood" (1998, 42). The clans identified who had obligations and responsibilities to whom, as well as from whom one could expect assistance. They insured that Cherokees could journey between the towns and always find connections, a place to get a meal, companionship with clan relatives, and a place to spend the night. They also guaranteed that everyone had support—elders, children, women, and men. According to law professor John Philip Reid, it would not be an exaggeration to say that "clan membership was the single most important aspect of a Cherokee's life" (1970, 38). Perdue agrees, "Clans helped them live upstanding lives through instruction, support, and protection. Clans enabled Cherokees to place themselves in the world and establish appropriate relationships with the rest of the cosmos. Cherokees grounded their sense of self in the clan, and individual identity melded into clan affiliation" (1998, 59). Since the clans were matrilineal, women were considered to be the heads of clans and they had ultimate authority over the children, the household, and the agricultural fields belonging to the clans of each town. Although discussions about the household and the fields generally included all the adult members, both men and women, women made the final decisions in these domains.

Women's dominance in agriculture, where they were responsible not only for working the fields but also for distribution of the harvest, as well as the foods that were gathered from the woods and orchards, meant that they dominated in the tribe's economic realm. Although men hunted deer and other game to supplement the diet, it was the beans, squash, pumpkins, and especially the corn that were grown by the women that comprised the majority of the food supply. Because of the powerful influence of women in some of the most important spheres of Cherokee society, the Cherokees of the pre-European contact era have been defined as an "egalitarian" people. There was equality between men and women, and each had the same degree of influence and freedom of action in the overall society.

While women dominated in the household and the agricultural sector, men were dominant in other arenas. Their foremost occupations were in hunting and warfare. While hunting may not have been a primary economic role in old Cherokee society, it was an important activity for men nevertheless and took them from the village for weeks or even months at a time in the late fall and winter. Warfare was sporadic and not an ongoing activity, but certainly defense of the towns and the families within them was the domain of men. Although women sometimes went along on the hunt or with war parties, they primarily did so to skin and butcher animals and process the meat, or to load and hand off weapons, rather than as hunters or warriors themselves.

Because these various occupations were strongly identified either with women or with men, "a person's job was an aspect of his or her [gender], a source of economic and political power, and an affirmation of cosmic order and balance" (Perdue 1998, 18). Since their agricultural labor conceptually associated women with their primary crop, corn, a figure called "Selu" emerged in Cherokee story. "Selu" is the word for corn in the Cherokee language, and in the stories, Selu is the Corn Woman—the premier woman of the Cherokees. She represents one side of the balance of the Cherokee world—femininity and the proper occupations for women. She is powerful, more powerful than the stories' hunter figure, Kanati—who is her husband. Kanati represents the other side of the balance, masculinity and proper masculine occupations, but it is Selu who gives life to the Cherokee people, both in the children and the food she brings forth from her body and the bounty that she supplies to the family.

As stated by Perdue, the Cherokees "conceived of their world as a system of categories that opposed and balanced one another." The Selu and Kanati stories teach about this deepest of cosmological ideas in which "women balanced men just as summer balanced winter, plants balanced animals, and farming balanced hunting." The roles of women and those of men were not the same and, in the Cherokee conception, should not be the same, but should be of equal influence and importance. As with everything in their world, "peace and prosperity depended on the maintenance of boundaries between these opposing categories, and blurring the lines between them threatened disaster," and the Selu and Kanati stories also indicated the ills that would befall a people who transgressed the categories (1998, 13).

In addition to hunting and warfare, men dominated in government. This was perhaps their most influential sphere, but even here their authority was truly representative rather than absolute. Each Cherokee town was autonomous and self-governing. No town exercised authority over any other, but regional coalitions often formed to enact policy within their particular area. But one region of towns did not necessarily agree with towns from other areas, as their interests might differ. In this highly decentralized system, there was no recognizable overarching political connection, such as a "nation."

Within each town, a council of approximately 10–14 men provided a sense of order and represented Cherokee political and governmental affairs. Townspeople selected representatives to serve on the town's council, which was comprised of two political societies. One, which has been styled as a "white" society or white government, called so because white is the color that represents peace in the Cherokee world, was the portion of the council that was predominant most of the time, that is, when the Cherokees were at peace. Its members were generally older men with strong recognized skills in facilitation, mediation, and diplomacy. The other side of the council was styled as the "red" society or government, red being the color of success in the Cherokee world. The men who served in this body were the wartime leadership. They stepped to the forefront when the Cherokees were in a situation of widespread, prolonged warfare. But even then, they did so only because the white society allowed it. The white society was still the more authoritative side of the town council. The men who were selected to serve in the red government tended to be a bit younger and were acclaimed for their skills as military strategists, as well as their proven bravery and combat experience.

Overall, the Cherokee council exhibited a broad range of leadership of different age groups and different skill sets. Some of these representatives, who were later called "chiefs" by the British and Americans, represented their towns at various times, and others at other times. The system continued within the towns the highly decentralized style of government that distributed authority over many, rather than investing it in one or a few.

It may seem strange that in such a strongly egalitarian society as that of the Cherokees, all of the chiefs were men. But these men were not the only "leaders" in the society, they were more precisely a group who enforced and enacted the consensus of the entire town within its boundaries and also represented it to the outside world. Leadership, however, came from all quarters—adult men and women who spoke with equal authority, whose words were considered equally by the others, and who participated in very spirited discussions of the issues facing the town as they came together each evening in the town's council house. Only after the entire town had reached consensus did the council act as they were directed. Although they might facilitate and influence the discussion, the council did not in and of themselves make the ultimate decisions.

As stated by Reid, "the town was one of the two legal institutions to which the Cherokees applied the doctrine of collective responsibility. The second was the clan" (1970, 32). Cherokee clans regulated some of the most serious transgressions that might occur in Cherokee society. A system of law that came to be known as "blood law" functioned under the purview of the clans. Blood law has often been called "the law of revenge," but from a Cherokee perspective, revenge may have had little to do with it, although it is understandable how it seemed so to outsiders to the culture. Blood law dealt primarily with killings that might take place in Cherokee society, but its principles also extended to some other transgressions, such as theft. Derived from a complex cosmological basis, blood law attempted not to find justice for the victims of such transgressions, but to restore balance to a world and society that had been unbalanced by the act. Blood law is sometimes referred to as "clan law" as well, since it was enforced by the affected clans. They were the only authority that had the right to be involved—those clans of the victim and the perpetrator.

For instance, if a person had been killed by someone of another clan, the clan and family of the victim were obligated to see that the situation was balanced before their loved one could move on to the next world. But the clan of the perpetrator actually had the greater obligation since they were the offending clan. The balance was regained by the killing of someone from the clan and family of the perpetrator, usually the perpetrator himself, but another clan relative would be acceptable as well if the victim's clansmen could not strike at the perpetrator. Since clans were matrilineal, that usually placed at some risk the brothers and maternal uncles of the wrongdoer. Sometimes instead, a captive could be given to the victim's family by the offender's family to be adopted into the victimized clan to "replace" the lost family member. Or sometimes a killer might flee to the Cherokees' sanctuary town, Chota, located in east central Tennessee, where he remained protected. Some historic sources speculate that the perpetrator desired to remain in Chota until the next Green Corn Ceremony—a large religious event that rebalanced the entire world and nullified all transgressions. But others find those sources to be unreliable and suspect that fleeing to Chota was an attempt to delay in order that another form of restitution could be negotiated. In either case, the offender could afterward return to his town secure in the knowledge that no one would attempt any longer to take his life. However, according to Reid, a killer who exercised this option "became safe from the avenger of blood—but his clan kin did not. Unless a settlement was quickly arranged, a manslayer could not remain in Chota without sacrificing a relative, perhaps his brother, to pay the blood price for which he was responsible" (1970, 112).

Any of these scenarios might be employed to rebalance the world and Cherokee society, even when the killing was accidental. Through a complex understanding of relationships that focused on collective, rather than individual, obligations and responsibilities of the clans to each other, the Cherokees kept order in their society through intricate social pressures that drew everyone into the duty of conducting themselves well so that others would not suffer the consequences of their actions. But for Europeans viewing these practices as outsiders, the occasional killings not of the perpetrator, but of other clan members led to an interpretation of blood law based on revenge.

For centuries, the Cherokees enjoyed clear understandings of how to place themselves in the world, in towns, in clans, and in families. They lived by a body of knowledge of oppositions, balance, obligations and indebtedness to each other, and collective responsibility. It was a system where everyone knew what their relationships were to the others, what their roles in family and society were, and what was expected of them, indeed what was *required* of them, in order that all would survive and prosper. It was a society where everyone had a place, none were forgotten, and all were secure, as long as nature and their neighbors cooperated.

By the mid-1600s, the Cherokees had new neighbors. To the south and the west of their territory, peoples who came from across the great waters were moving through the land, in search of riches and resources, and promoting their religious beliefs. Although the Cherokees had had some earlier contact with these peoples—the French and particularly the Spanish—it was a people to the east, the British, whose intentions seemed more permanent. They were developing cities along the coastline and some of their families had begun to venture westward into areas that were inhabited by several tribes, establishing homesteads and small settlements. In this century, the first of these strangers to reach the Cherokee towns came from a city the strangers called Charles Town, located on the easternmost seaboard of an area they claimed and named "Carolina." The Cherokees had no reason to be particularly suspicious of these people, and in the manner of their culture, after initial observations, extended their hospitality to them.

The strangers brought many fascinating new objects and tools, and being a people who were not only open and adaptive to other peoples, but also to new technologies, the Cherokees were intrigued by the many items they encountered. Woven cloth was useful since it was far more pliable than the hides they'd been using as clothing, and the women wanted it, since it would render much easier the task of making clothing. There were blankets for warmth that would be more convenient to carry as one traveled. There were brass pots and kettles, which were far more efficient for conducting heat and cooking than the clay pots used by Cherokee women. There were new implements for the men, such as axes for chopping trees and hewing out canoes that made the work much faster and easier than the slow, burning process that had been previously employed. There were iron traps that were much more reliable for trapping animals. And of course, there were the large items—knives, horses, and guns—that would change their lives. For men who were hunters and warriors, the world and their work were very different after they acquired these items.

But it was an array of goods. Desiring everything from awls, scissors, beads and coins, needles and thimbles, mirrors and glassware, dishware, and cutlery, the Cherokees began to acquire the goods and technologies that would add ease and convenience to their lives. By the first decades of the 1700s, trading relationships between the Cherokees and British traders from Charleston were underway. Several decades later, an additional trading path between towns in east Tennessee and Williamsburg, Virginia, was developed. Very shortly, European goods had permeated the lives of the Cherokees. Cherokee hunters now worked the woods for longer periods of time, for the Europeans wanted deerskins in exchange for the desired goods. In Europe, on the verge of an industrial revolution, deer hide was fashioned into the belts that ran machinery, the containers that carried liquids, and the protective coverings for wheel rims. Many things that would later be made of plastic or rubber were made of deer hide in the 1600s and 1700s. The extreme demand for hides had resulted in the overhunting of deer on the European continent, and deer had been depleted and had become somewhat scarce. When Europeans began to explore the Americas, the abundance of deer, which they considered a resource, was regarded as a new trove of wealth and European traders began to employ Indian labor to hunt for them and enrich them through the trading relationships. Indians would supply Europeans with deerskins and in trade the Europeans would supply Indians with technology and its products. In this way, the Cherokees entered into the global economy.

Cherokee men began to hunt more extensively. With the guns they had procured, they could hunt more effectively than they had ever been able to in the past. And with the demand for deerskin on the part of the European traders, there was now a different reason to hunt, not simply to provide additional food to the families. Through their increased hunting, Cherokee men began to play a far greater role in the economic sphere of their society than ever before, and soon their role rivaled that of the women. But not only was the relationship between men and women changing, the relationships between the Cherokees and the animals also became unbalanced. The animals were no longer regarded as relatives to the degree they had been in the past, to be honored for their sacrifice and spared if not needed for basic survival. Now they were becoming a commodity.

As trade between the Cherokees and Europeans, the British in particular, increased, exposure to European diseases also escalated. The most dreaded of these diseases was smallpox, which typically killed about one-third of European populations whenever an outbreak occurred. In the Americas, where the disease had never been known before European contact, encounters with infected Europeans or trade goods such as blankets introduced the scourge, and initial rates of death approached 50 percent when epidemic first struck a tribe whose members had built no immunities.

The first epidemic to strike the Cherokees occurred in the 1690s, although not much is known about it. In 1738, however, historic records describe another outbreak about which much more is known. In an epidemic that lasted about a year-and-a-half into 1739, smallpox ran through the Cherokee towns in all regions, and then returned in a second wave. Over an 18-month span of time, roughly half of the Cherokee people died in the epidemic!

Additional smallpox epidemics struck the Cherokees in the 1750s and in the early 1780s as well, again killing about one-third of the people each time. While still very devastating, this was not as high a proportion as previously, since immunities had developed among those who had contracted the disease earlier but had survived. Although smallpox was the greatest threat, other diseases such as measles and whooping cough, also unknown in the Americas before European contact, had impacts as well. Throughout the 1700s, the challenge of simply surviving the threats posed by killer diseases constantly occupied the Cherokees as thousands of lives were lost over the decades, and it is hard to imagine the degree of social upheaval within the Cherokees that must have occurred as a result of the losses of life in this century.

The intensive trading relationship with Europeans led not only to exposure to European diseases, but also to reactionary shifts in the Cherokees' governing structures. The extremely decentralized nature of Cherokee government frustrated European officials who often could not understand with whom they should negotiate or how to secure a consistent agreement from dozens of politically autonomous towns. Over several decades, British colonial officials often ignored the proper representatives of Cherokee governments by designating different Cherokees to act as "chiefs," bestowing favor and privilege upon these persons and the towns they came from, despite the fact that these individuals had no sanction from the Cherokees themselves to act in this capacity. The impacts had significant ramifications for Cherokee governing structures. The men most often appointed by the British were warriors—a class of younger men whom Cherokees themselves would never have approved as their peacetime representatives. In this manner, the unity of red and white societies in each of the Cherokee town councils was undermined and warriors, who would normally never have asserted a greater degree of authority, increasingly challenged the councils' headmen. For the British, the primary motive was to make alliances with warriors, thus minimizing the threat that warriors posed to encroaching frontier settlers. But it was a tactic that also worked well in creating divisions within the Cherokees as tensions between the two sides of Cherokee town councils were encouraged and heightened by British actions. The British, and later the Americans, repeatedly employed the same strategy with dramatic results.

Through several decades, from the 1720s to the 1750s, warriors designated by the British were also influential in procuring and distributing the much-desired trade goods. Since the warrior chiefs selected by the British were from particular towns, those towns—Tenase, Tellico, and Hiwassee, towns in the valley and plateau regions west of the mountains—began to dominate among the Cherokees. Other towns began to compete with these towns for British favor, particularly Chota, which had long been regarded as a "mother town" of the Cherokees and was considered their ceremonial center since it was the site each year of the Green Corn Ceremony—the large spiritual gathering that rebalanced the entire world. Chota felt that its rightful position of importance among the Cherokees was being undermined by the British selections of representatives from other towns as "kings," "emperors," and "principal chiefs" of the Cherokees. The British ignored Chota's assertions, however, and continued to favor their own selected "chiefs."

Between 1747 and 1751, the Cherokees were engaged in prolonged conflict with the Creek Confederacy that strained their relationships with the British traders who were by then residing in some of their towns. Several of these traders were profiting by arming both sides in the conflict. The Cherokees, who knew that traders had manipulated them into a situation of indebtedness, hastily attacked and killed traders when they attempted to deny the Cherokees further credit to obtain guns and ammunition. South Carolina immediately implemented a trade embargo on Cherokee towns, despite the best efforts of the warrior chiefs at that time to prevent it. In the situation of embargo, Chota's status among the Cherokees rose even further as its headmen from the peacetime side of its council made outreach to the French to the west and Virginia traders based in Williamsburg, as it was geographically positioned to do best. Because Chota was able to procure some amount of goods from the French during the time of British embargo, it effectively demonstrated to many Cherokees that it could use its bidirectional trading ability—with the British in Williamsburg, but also the French to the west along the Mississippi River—to provide the Cherokees with a more secure trading situation.

Chota's leadership thus challenged the warrior leadership from Hiwassee, who worked vigorously to have the British embargo lifted in order that they were not replaced in the degree of influence they exerted among the Cherokees. After 10 months, the embargo was lifted, but for many Cherokees, Chota had already proven its greater value to them and was perhaps regarded afterward by both Cherokees and the British as the political capital of the Cherokees. The conflict with the Creeks ended in 1752 and in the years immediately following, Chota solidified its position of leadership among the Cherokees. By 1753, Chota had received the sanction of many Cherokee towns to represent their national interests and Old Hop, the headman of Chota, received the title of Principal Chief, this time bestowed by the Cherokees themselves rather than designated as such by the British. Old Hop served by the agreement and consensus of the Cherokee grand council, the convention of chiefs from all the towns, until his death in 1760. He was succeeded for the next several decades by headmen from Chota, firmly establishing that political leadership was now vested in this town, as well as it being a spiritual center.

In the years following, the Chota leadership consolidated its authority, including the establishment of regular meetings of chiefs from all the villages that became attached to the annual Green Corn Ceremony that took place at Chota. One of the Chota leadership's most interesting developments was to establish the grand council as an authoritative body that could exercise what have been called "coercive powers." Henceforth, the council asserted, it had the authority to issue edicts and regulate actions by Cherokee villages and individuals throughout their territory, particularly when it came to matters of trade and frontier conflicts. Chota's attempt at more centralized political authority may be seen, with the solidification of a principal chief selected by the Cherokees themselves and a grand council that met regularly and gave itself coercive authority, as the first step toward executive and legislative branches of the Cherokee government that would later be developed.

By 1755, the Cherokees found themselves wedged politically between the two great European powers that inhabited the American continent— Great Britain and France. As tensions between the two came to a head in that year, war erupted. Although most tribes allied with the French, the

Cherokees were divided regionally in their sympathies. Within Cherokee towns in the Carolinas, pro-British sentiment was strongest, since their trading relationships were almost exclusively with British traders out of Charleston. But towns in southeastern Tennessee and, to a greater extent, the east central Tennessee plateau were divided, with many favoring the French to their west. Nevertheless, the Cherokees entered into a treaty of alliance with their strongest trading partner, the British, at the outset of the French and Indian Wars.

However, the alliance was tense from the start. Within only a few years, Cherokee sentiment was shifting toward the French, as Britain neglected many of the provisions of the treaty. Promised trade goods had not been delivered to the Cherokees. Forts to defend the Cherokees against French attack had not been constructed. British settlers continued to encroach into Cherokee lands and launch attacks on Cherokee hunters and warriors. British soldiers killed and scalped Cherokees serving alongside them in order to collect the bounty Britain had placed on Indian scalps. By the late 1750s, after several years of tension, the relationship between the British and the Cherokees had deteriorated badly. Cherokees laid siege to a British fort in east central Tennessee, Fort Loudon, and forced its surrender. Thus humiliated, Britain sent colonial forces out of South Carolina to destroy Cherokee towns. In two campaigns conducted in 1759 and 1761, British forces burned to the ground over 25 Cherokee towns in the areas of western South Carolina and the mountains of North Carolina, about 40 percent of their settlements. Employing scorched earth tactics, not only were the structures of the towns destroyed by fire, but the fields, the woods, and the orchards around the towns that the Cherokees depended on for their food supply were burned. British commanders reported that their soldiers had "pull'd up all the Corn, cut down the fruit Trees, & burn'd the Houses" (French, in Perdue 1998, 97) and that the force had destroyed 1,400 acres of "Corne, pease, & beans, & has driven near 5000 Men, Women, & Children, into the Woods, where, if they do not make a proper Submission, they cannot fail of starving in the winter" (Amherst, in Perdue 1998, 97).

Under these conditions, the Cherokees entered into a peace agreement with the British, their ally, in 1762. They were able to return to the areas where their towns had been and rebuild, but it had been a punishing encounter with a new genocidal style of warfare that was commonly employed in Europe but that had never been used by tribes in their conflicts with each other. Many Cherokees were shocked by the severity of British actions and the attempts to eradicate the Cherokees completely. They began to question whether military defense was even feasible in the face of an aggressor who was willing to fight in this fashion.

In 1763, the French and Indian Wars ended with a British defeat of the French. With the expulsion of the French presence from the North American continent, trading relationships between the British and the Cherokees changed dramatically over the next 15 years. By mid-century, the Cherokees had already become heavily dependent on trade goods, and the time that many had spent as refugees during the war had been a pointed reminder to them that widespread knowledge of traditional technologies had already been lost. As long as a competitive situation between the British and the French had existed, the Cherokees had been able to satisfy their requirements for goods without tremendous detriment to their well-being. But "with the French and the Spanish effectively out of the colonial picture, the indigenous nations lost their bargaining position, which had been an effective means of gaining political and economic concessions from the Europeans" (Champagne 1990, 67, 68).

Between 1760 and 1775, colonists, in violation of British law, poured across the mountains and established settlements on Indian lands. In addition, the British continued to employ economic strategies that drove the Cherokees into indebtedness. Traders used variable exchange rates to insure that the Cherokees were always running behind in their obligations to traders. As the Cherokees were increasingly encroached upon and fell further and further behind in their debts, some chiefs began to cede land in payment of the artificially inflated debts. Previous to the war, during the many decades of their relationships with the British, the Cherokees had ceded only two pieces of land in South Carolina due to encroaching settlers. But in between 1768 and 1775, five cessions of land in what are today Virginia, West Virginia, Kentucky, Georgia, and Tennessee were made to British colonial governments. Amounting to more than 47,000 square miles, over one-third of the Cherokee land base was lost in this short period of time.

The divisions between headmen and warriors that had been fostered by the old British habit of establishing warriors as "emperors" and "kings" had contributed to intermittent defiance on the part of warriors toward Cherokee headmen which had flared at times through the decades. The challenges were especially pronounced when in 1775, Cherokee headmen ceded a huge tract, over 25,000 square miles, of land in Kentucky. Informally called "Henderson's Purchase," the sale had been to a consortium of British traders represented by a man named Richard Henderson. The Cherokee chiefs later contended that they believed they were making a lease of land, but the document had in fact read that it was a sale. Whether or not the headmen had been deliberately duped, the cession raised strenuous objections from warriors.

The internal conflict erupted the following year as the American Revolution was breaking out. In a war between British colonists who had enacted economic schemes on the tribes versus frontiersmen who had encroached onto their lands (and now calling themselves "Americans"), many Cherokees did not feel there was a good alliance to be made. Older Cherokees who remembered the devastation of Cherokee towns during the French and Indian Wars were reluctant to enter into another military conflict with an adversary who was clearly willing to use scorched earth and genocidal tactics against them. But younger warriors among the Cherokees, many of whom had experienced the ferocious attacks on Cherokee towns in 1759–1761 and the incessant encroachment into Cherokee lands of frontierspeople now calling themselves "Americans," wanted to employ their own particular skills on the side of the British. They chose this alliance for a variety of reasons, one of which may have been that many of their clanswomen had intermarried with British loyalists, or they were the sons of British officials and traders who had moved into Cherokee towns and society and were now urging the warriors toward that alliance. As the Revolutionary War broke out, the warriors were appealing to the headmen of the Cherokees to sanction their planned attacks against American settlements on the Holston River in Tennessee, called the Wautaugan settlements. Although several meetings occurred at which the warriors presented their strategy, Cherokee headmen were reluctant to approve such attacks, fearing that American retaliation would be severe. Finally, the division that had been fostered by the British for almost 40 years by that time was successful. Dissident warriors exploded into open conflict with the tribe's headmen, despite the lack of approval from the grand council.

Later that year, the warriors launched their assault. But the situation was more complicated than the warriors had anticipated. The settlements had been forewarned of the impending Cherokee attacks by some of the residents of the nearby town of Chota, some of whom had economic relationships, close friendships, and even intermarriages with inhabitants of the settlements. Having lost the element of surprise, the warriors were defeated by the Americans who were prepared in advance for the attack. Although the Cherokees of Chota had probably hoped the Americans would be grateful having been forewarned and, in Cherokee conceptions of balance, would thus have an obligation to the Cherokees, the Americans from the settlements did not seem to feel gratitude, but rather angry that the attacks had been conceived of at all.

After the defeat of the warriors at the Wautaugan settlements, American colonial governments demanded additional cessions of land from the

Cherokees. In 1777, two parcels of land in North Carolina and Tennessee were given up as part of the spoils of war. But even this was not enough. As Cherokee warriors continued to engage American settlers in skirmishes, American armies from Virginia, North Carolina, and South Carolina strategized to carry out attacks against Cherokee towns. The attacks began in 1779 and continued through 1781, as the Americans engaged in the familiar scorched earth style of warfare. Throughout these years, over 50 Cherokee towns were burned to the ground and it may be that as many as 12,000 Cherokees fled as refugees and were living in conditions of homelessness and starvation, just as they had 20 years earlier during the French and Indian Wars.

On the heels of this complete devastation, smallpox struck yet again. In addition to an earlier outbreak in 1780 that had occurred primarily in newer towns located around the region of present-day Chattanooga, Tennessee, that had been established by resistant warriors and their families, the epidemics resulted in an additional 2,500 deaths, bringing the total Cherokee population to less than 16,000, or about half what it had been a century earlier. In that same year, devastated by the attacks of American colonial militias, the Cherokees entered into a peace agreement with the Americans. As part of the agreement, additional lands in Georgia were demanded by the Americans, resulting in the Cherokees' 10th cession of land in 61 years. With this cession, the colonial treaty era ended, but the Cherokees had already lost slightly more than 50 percent of their territory before the United States officially came into existence. It is hard to imagine the level of turmoil and confusion experienced by the Cherokees as the Revolutionary War concluded. Their towns were destroyed, their people were dispersed and hungry, and disease had devastated them once again. They had always believed that they were in control of themselves and their world. If they maintained the delicate balances of their society, if they lived their lives as good people, and if they held faithfully to their spiritual beliefs and practices, all would be well. And for the most part, over many centuries of their existence, it had been. But as their entire society lay in ashes, the Cherokees began to wonder what had they done to cause this destruction to occur, for clearly their world had become unbalanced.

Note

1. From papers of the American Board of Commissioners for Foreign Missions (ABCFM), Houghton Library, Harvard University, ABC:18.3.1, V. 10, Item 205. Provided to the author by Cherokee Nation Tribal Councilor Jack Baker.

References

Brown, John P. *Old Frontiers, the Story of the Cherokee Indians from Earliest Times to the Date of Their Removal to the West, 1838.* Kingsport, TN: Southern Publishers, Inc., 1938.

Champagne, Duane. *Social Order and Political Change: Constitutional Governments among the Cherokee, the Choctaw, the Chickasaw, and the Creek.* Palo Alto: Stanford University Press, 1992.

Corkran, David. *The Cherokee Frontier: Conflict and Survival 1740–62.* Norman: University of Oklahoma Press, 1962.

Duncan, Barbara, ed. *Living Stories of the Cherokee.* Chapel Hill: University of North Carolina Press, 1998.

Faulkner, Coleela. *The Life and Times of Reverend Stephen Foreman.* Tahlequah, OK: Cherokee Heritage Press, 2006.

Hatley, Tom. *The Dividing Paths: Cherokees and South Carolinians through the Era of Revolution.* New York: Oxford University Press, 1995.

Kelton, Paul. *Epidemics and Enslavement: Biological Catastrophe in the Native Southeast 1492–1715.* Lincoln: University of Nebraska Press, 2007.

Milling, Chapman J. *Red Carolinians*, 2nd edition. Columbia: University of South Carolina Press, 1969.

Mooney, James. *Myths of the Cherokee and Sacred Formulas of the Cherokees*, from 19th and 7th Annual Reports Bureau of American Ethnology (1900 and 1891). Nashville: Charles and Randy Elder—Booksellers, 1982.

Perdue, Theda. *Cherokee Women: Gender and Culture Change 1700–1835.* Lincoln: University of Nebraska Press, 1998.

Reid, John Philip. *A Better Kind of Hatchet.* University Park: Pennsylvania State University Press, 1976.

Reid, John Philip. *A Law of Blood, the Primitive Law of the Cherokee Nation.* DeKalb: Northern Illinois University Press, 2006 (first published in 1970).

Rozema, Vicki. *Footsteps of the Cherokees: A Guide to the Eastern Homelands of the Cherokee Nation*, 3rd edition. Winston-Salem, NC: John F. Blair, 2013.

Thornton, Russell. *The Cherokees: A Population History.* Lincoln: University of Nebraska Press, 1990.

TWO

The Federal–Tribal Dance

Although it was entirely within their beliefs and worldview for the Cherokees of that time to take responsibility for their own devastation, their experience with colonial powers in the 1700s reflects patterns that were repeated many times, with many indigenous groups, and in many parts of the world. Deliberately creating and fostering political divisions within another society, employing economically exploitive schemes, even using disease as a weapon are all characteristics of the process of "colonization"— the attempt by a more powerful group to occupy and subjugate a less powerful people. But the Cherokees in the late 1700s did not have the benefit of hindsight. Their world was in shambles and their beliefs led them to look for the ways that they had contributed to their own devastation. Had they not led balanced lives, had they not maintained their ceremonies properly, had they failed in their responsibilities to their clan relatives? What had *they* done to cause their circumstances?

Many of the more conservative Cherokees suspected that the adoption of European and American technologies was to blame for their apparent ruination. By the first decades of the 1800s, prophetic movements rose among the Cherokees, exemplified best by the vision of an old seer called Tsali (Charlie). Reports of his unsettling vision spread rapidly among the Cherokees and led to vigorous cultural debates about its meaning. Tsali had seen himself dressed as the "conjurers" of previous generations would have been—in skins and hide, laden with nose rings and earrings, tattooed, and wearing a scalp lock. In itself, this was a potent image, but the most powerful aspect of it was not the conjurer, but rather the two snarling black wolves at each side, which he held by the scruffs of their necks. In the vision, the Creator, through Tsali, also snarled at the Cherokee people, commanding them to give up their European-style clothes and houses, cast off all of the foreign goods they had acquired, and kill the cats and other strange animals that had been given to them. He ordered those who would survive to follow him to the highest mountaintop, predicting a great storm that would destroy the world, sparing only those who would return to the purity of an older time and older ways. But when such a storm failed to materialize, the errant vision of the old conjurer only contributed to the loss of confidence in their medicine people that many Cherokees were feeling. Given the devastation they had experienced as a result of the Revolutionary War, as well as the deaths due to smallpox, the cultural confusion was widespread over many aspects of Cherokee society.

As a new government, the United States of America, came into existence, federal policies promoted further aspects of colonization. While American frontiersmen and settlers continued their encroachment into Indian lands, the United States developed corresponding legal mechanisms by which to take additional territory from the tribes. Gained through legislation and treaties that were primarily designed as real estate transactions, the federal occupation of additional Indian landholdings represented the strong expansionist tendencies of the early nation. As stated by historian Colin Calloway, "Like Europeans before them, Americans not only acquired the land but also established the legal framework by which they, and not the Indians, would own it" (2011, 220).

Colonization of native cultures became vital as well, as other agents of the first federal policy toward Indians, known as "civilization" policy, undertook to consciously encroach into tribal society with the goal of remaking Indians into peoples who would more resemble the new Americans in their values, language, religious practices, and economic activities. Federal officials, called "Indian agents," and missionaries became the vanguard of the new policy, as they attempted to coerce Indian men into farming and raising stock animals, to develop Indian women into housewives and textile producers, and to spread Christian doctrine among the tribes. More deeply, civilization policy insisted that Indians "had to sever their communal connections with the land, adopt the practice of owning private property, and assume Western European gender roles" (Johnston 2003, 39). If Indians could be made into people who resembled Americans and who held more Americanized values, what would be the problem of living alongside them and of Indians living among the larger American population?

Cherokee responses to these colonizing overtures were varied and complex. At a time when the visions of an older generation were in question, coupled with the Cherokees' noted tendency to be curious about and adaptive of new ideas and technologies, the tenets of the civilization policy may have seemed to some to be an opportunity to rebuild after the devastation of the Revolutionary War, a hand extended by the United States. But while the agents of colonization and the civilization policy measured their successes by the superficial appearances of Cherokee assimilation to American norms and values, later proclaiming the Cherokees a "civilized" tribe, Cherokee acceptance of the policy was probably understood quite differently within their society. They did not desire to be like Americans, but rather to be better Cherokees by melding the new ideas and technologies to their own society. They sought to reinforce and reaffirm their original rights in ways that the newcomers would understand and respect. They strove to maintain their social values even as their social customs changed. And thus the intricate, centuries-long interplay between federal goals and Cherokee aspirations began.

* * * * * * * * * * * *

When the Cherokees quit the Revolutionary War in 1783, it had been marked by a Cherokee land cession to an American colonial government in Georgia. In the same year, the Cherokees' ally, Great Britain, finally decided that its former colonial holdings in North America were not worth further expense and trouble. It is unlikely the Cherokees understood Great Britain as the global superpower of its era and therefore unlikely to "lose" the war to a ragtag bunch of revolutionaries. Instead, the Cherokees viewed the conflict as an intrafamily dispute. For decades, they had known these new "Americans" as British people too, although sometimes the more badly behaved members of that family who had been the most egregious trespassers into Indian lands on their frontiers. But with the American victory, the Cherokees realized the apparent permanence on the continent of the newly declared United States of America, and they struggled to maintain their own standing in light of this new development.

For the United States, its efforts to define its relationship with the tribes within its borders also encompassed an internal struggle between the newly established federal level of government and the individual 13 colonies, now becoming states within its overall system. Coupled with its desire to continue to colonize Indian landholdings, the U.S. Congress made early attempts to assert its dominance in relation to the states. As the preferred legal mechanism by which Indian lands could be transferred to the United States, the first treaties between the federal government and the tribes were significant documents by which it not only acquired Indian lands, but also denied the states the ability to exercise oversight of the tribes within their state borders. They indicate some of the first tensions between federalist and anti-federalist, or what would later be known as "states' rights," positions within the new nation.

The Treaty of Hopewell between the Cherokees and the United States was ratified in 1785, two years after the conclusion of the Revolutionary War. The treaty clarified the boundaries of remaining Cherokee land, but also reaffirmed that lands in Kentucky that had previously been taken, perhaps illegally, by the consortium led by Richard Henderson, would now revert to U.S. ownership. In short, the land would not be returned to the Cherokees, and all Cherokee areas that had been aggressively colonized by Americans would remain outside the jurisdiction of the tribe. Although the United States did not take additional land from the Cherokees by this treaty, the commissioners moved to solidify the goal of asserting federal preeminence over the state level of regulatory authority. Article IX is the most significant article of the Treaty of Hopewell, stating

> For the benefit and comfort of the Indians, and for the prevention of injuries or oppressions on the part of the citizens or Indians; the United States in Congress assembled shall have the sole and exclusive right of regulating the trade with the Indians and of managing all their affairs in such manners as they think proper.[1]

Although the article reads poorly, as though the Cherokees would be managed by the U.S. Congress, Congress initially interpreted this article as reserving the right to regulate by legislation the trading *relationship* between the United States and the tribes, not that it would regulate the tribes themselves. Although this treaty predates the ratification of the U.S. Constitution, this same language appears in the Commerce Clause of the Constitution, thus extending this federal regulatory authority over its relationships with all the tribes within the United States. This authority to Congress, called "plenary rights," has emerged as one of the foundational aspects of the existence of tribes within the federal framework, and "most litigation dealing with Indian matters revolves around the interpretation of this clause" (Deloria, Jr. and Wilkins 1999, 25). In this fashion, the federal Congress, in the original governing document of the United States, denied the ability of individual states to regulate commercial and other relationships with tribes within their state boundaries.

The Cherokees also sought to define aspects of their own legal and cultural existence through the treaty. Article III of the treaty establishes the Cherokees as a protectorate of the United States, desirable on the part of both the United States and the Cherokees as each sought to diminish

violence on the frontiers since Cherokee warriors and Tennessee frontiersmen continued to skirmish after the war. The United States hoped to
bring Cherokee warriors into alliance, and the Cherokees hoped the United
States would assert greater control over frontiersmen in its role as Cherokee protector. Both were disappointed in their hopes.

The Cherokees established relatively favorable jurisdictional terms in
the treaty, which acknowledged their authority over all persons within
their territory, except in the instance of a capital crime in which one party
was a Cherokee and the other was an American citizen (Articles V–VII).
It also allowed a "deputy" or delegate to be seated in Congress to represent the Cherokee Nation (Article XII). But the trade-off was a significant
concession. In Article VIII of the treaty, the Cherokees agreed to cease the
practice of blood law—their manner of restoring balance in the case of a
taking of a life, which outsiders consistently misinterpreted as "revenge."
From the American perspective, while many aspects of Cherokee social
beliefs and customs could be "civilized" more gradually, they insisted the
practice of killing apparently "innocent" people must stop, especially since
it sometimes impacted Americans. In the treaty, the Cherokees agreed to
halt their practice of blood law, but in actuality, the practice continued for
several more decades. Cherokee concepts of what constituted the foundations of law did not change as quickly as Americans might have liked.

Just as the colonizing relationship between the United States and the
Cherokees was being established by treaties, the civilization policy was
also implemented as part of the treaty relationship. By 1791, in the Treaty
of Holston between the Cherokees and the United States, American commissioners were advancing the tenets of that policy as part of the occupation of Cherokee lands by frontierspeople that both resulted from and
contributed to ongoing skirmish. Known as "Tennesseans," one of whose
leaders was John Sevier, later the first governor of that state, these frontiersmen were constantly challenged by a recalcitrant group of Cherokee
warriors known as "Chickamaugans," led by an effective Cherokee strategist named Dragging Canoe. As the skirmish had continued throughout the
late 1780s and into the 1790s, Cherokee towns in east Tennessee had been
abandoned, including their religious and political center of Chota. Settlers
continued to move into those areas and others, despite the fact that the
Cherokees had not ceded those lands.

While the boundary line established in the Treaty of Hopewell was
intended to contain all whites outside the Indian territories, ethnologist
Charles Royce asserts that "the boundary line . . . had been unsatisfac-
tory to both the Cherokees and the whites. On the part of the former,

the chief cause of complaint was the . . . [settlers'] evident disposition to encroach . . . at every opportunity. The whites were discontented because further curtailment of the Cherokee territory had not been compelled by commissioners" (1883, reprinted 2006, 32). Tensions were rising and fear of Cherokee reprisal stimulated negotiations. The Treaty of Holston was intended to alleviate the friction by forcing a Cherokee cession of land that was already occupied by whites and penalizing whites for further encroachment. Instead, "rewarding the squatters by purchasing from the Cherokees the land they had occupied illegally set a pernicious precedent. Intruders learned that they could get away with violating the boundaries that supposedly protected Indian lands" (Perdue and Green 2007, 28).

But as new Cherokee towns were being established in other regions within the remaining Cherokee territory, U.S. commissioners may have seen the perfect opportunity to insert principles and practices of "civilization" into Cherokee rebuilding efforts. In Article XIV of the Treaty of Holston, negotiated and signed mainly by warriors on the Cherokee side, Indian agents were established for the first time to spread "civilization" among the Cherokees:

> That the Cherokee nation may be led to a greater degree of civilization, and to become herdsmen and cultivators, instead of remaining in a state of hunters, . . . the United States will send . . . so many persons to reside in said nation . . . not exceeding four in number. . . . These persons shall have land assigned to them by the Cherokees for cultivation for themselves and their successors in office; but they shall be precluded exercising any kind of traffic.[2]

Although the Cherokees had long been primarily "cultivators," instead of primarily hunters, at least for the purposes of their own subsistence, the American ideal was that men should farm, rather than women. Many Americans regarded the hunting activities of Indian men as merely "sport," especially in relation to the hard work done in the fields by women. They felt it was time for Indian men to forego such "laziness" and get to work. Article XIV intended that the United States would establish the first Indian agents to the Cherokees, who would provide the agents with a bit of land they could use to instruct the Cherokees in a more Euroamerican style of farming in which fields were plowed in straight furrows, crops were separated from each other, and, most importantly, men controlled this crucial economic domain.

Traditionally, agricultural fields had belonged to clans, rather than individuals or families. The displacements of Cherokee population resulting from disease, frontier skirmishes, and outright warfare had already weakened the practice of living in extensive households that were built around networks of related clanswomen and their fields. Civilization policy represented a critical blow to the extended family, clan-based Cherokee household. The goal of turning men into farmers also had significant impacts on the residence pattern of Cherokees, as fields worked by clans began to transition to fields maintained by more "nuclear family" households—households formed, at least to outward appearances, around a married couple and their children, the Euroamerican norm.

Animal husbandry—raising stock animals—was another aspect of the civilization policy. While wealthier Cherokees had been acquiring domesticated animals for several decades, federal agents desired that subsistence farmers also have access to cattle and pigs. Cherokee men were more comfortable with this tenet of the policy. They accepted the stock animals, but they rejected the American notion that pastures should be fenced off and stock penned up. Instead, they allowed the cattle and pigs to range freely in the woods, often leading to the reversion of the pigs to a feral state. However, feral pigs and free-range cattle could be "hunted" as game. Both "white backcountry farmers as well as the garrison at Fort Loudon complained constantly about the loss of livestock to hunting parties. Because livestock usually foraged in the forest until late fall, the Native assumption that these animals were game was not implausible" (Perdue 1998, 120). Thus, "animal husbandry" as practiced by the Cherokees resulted in the reinforcement of old values. First, the refusal to fence lands reflected old Cherokee values of shared tribal resources, and second, the treatment of "stock" animals as "game" allowed the traditional male gender identity as "hunter" to remain viable among Cherokee men.

Civilization policy also decreed that once women were separated from their traditional agricultural work, they could be enticed into what Americans viewed as more appropriate occupations—becoming housewives and engaging in textile production for the household and the marketplace. Cotton cards, spinning wheels, and looms were provided to many women, and agents and missionaries stood ready to teach Cherokee women the domestic arts—the production of many of the items one might typically find in the Euroamerican frontier household.

Cherokee men and women had different reactions to these civilizing overtures. Generally, men were more reluctant to engage in the occupations coercively suggested to them, which they regarded as feminine occupations. But for women, the civilization program tended to reinforce the importance of their roles in society, as it focused on agriculture and domestic production. For them, the technologies and skills proposed to them opened new vistas. While Cherokee men may have initially felt excluded from the benefits of the civilization policy, in their usual fashion, they adapted new occupations derived from the skills learned by the women, particularly as merchants to the outside world of the products women were creating in increasing quantity. Since it had long been the role of men to interact with the larger world as both negotiators and defenders, "a new symbiotic relationship between men and women, reminiscent of traditional roles" thus emerged (Perdue 1995, 109). In Cherokee terms, it seemed natural to males to become the middlemen between the women who were the producers within their society and the consumers in the outside world.

But both genders were in opposition to the idea that Cherokee men should become farmers. Men saw it as women's work—not demeaning work, but work that so strongly defined the feminine gender that they could not conceptually become comfortable with it. Women also recognized that if they were no longer in charge of the production and distribution of the bulk of the people's food supply, their status and influence in Cherokee society would be reduced. In the balanced world of the Cherokees, agricultural production was the weightiest item on the women's side of the social scale. As both agriculture and marketing came increasingly under the purview of Cherokee men, women's influence in the society was diminished from what it had previously been, and the balance of the world was disrupted further.

While Cherokees were attracted to certain aspects of the civilization policy, they initially exhibited almost total disinterest in one particular component of it. Christianizing Indians was viewed by some Americans as a central necessity, while others viewed it as marginal to the policy's primarily economic goals. But Cherokees regarded it as entirely irrelevant to their own aspirations. While there had been some isolated conversions of Cherokees to Christianity throughout the 1700s, the ceremonial practices had retained preeminence, although they had become more localized in individual towns, particularly after Chota was abandoned. Few Cherokees saw any superiority of Christian beliefs over their own centuries-old practices, which had sustained their society in a worldview that they found both ethical and supportive. While some missionary groups sought entrance to Cherokee society, civilization policy did not provide any federal resources toward those efforts, as would later be the case under subsequent federal assimilation policies of the late 1800s. The Cherokees were initially uninterested in allowing the establishment of Christian missions within their territory, and the federal government did not mandate it.

However, among a new generation of Cherokees, the adult children of some of the first intermarriages between Cherokees and British colonists that had occurred throughout the 1700s, especially in the middle decades, some ideas emerged that radically reshaped their society. Although raised in Cherokee homes and towns, and entirely Cherokee in their allegiances and socialization, they had exposure through their European parents' (usually their father's) culture to a second language and the literacy that was associated with it. They also displayed the typical Cherokee interest in adapting these new possibilities to create better Cherokees. Seeing, as many Cherokees did, the apparent respect the United States gave to written documents such as treaties, constitutions, and statutes, many Cherokees began to believe that the development of a generation of Cherokees who could read, write, and speak English would provide them with another manner of defending their territory and their culture.

Cherokee leadership began seeking the education of their children in the English language. There were few possibilities for acquiring this type of education, but with the desire of Christian missionaries to gain entrance to Cherokee society in order to proselytize, the Cherokees brokered a deal. The Cherokees would allow the establishment of missions so long as there was a school attached to the mission that would provide education in and through the English language for the Cherokee children who attended.

The first missionaries to the Cherokees were Moravians, a Germanic denomination from Salem, North Carolina. In 1801, they established the first mission to the Cherokees at Spring Place, Georgia, on property that was utilized by James Vann—the wealthiest Cherokee of his time, a member of the Cherokee Council, and a plantation operator and slave owner. Other denominations followed, including the Methodists, Congregationalists, Presbyterians, and Baptists. Although the primary interest of the Cherokees was in education, rather than Christianity, the mission schools instructed the Cherokee children who attended using biblical scriptures to teach the English language. But not only was the English language transmitted, the stories and lessons of the Bible were also transmitted to the children, and as stories have always comprised an important part of Cherokee teaching techniques, the stories were repeated at home by the children to their families. The parents of the children attending mission schools realized that there were honorable values contained in this book and began to demonstrate an interest as well. In the first decades of the 1800s, the children who predominantly attended the mission schools were those of Cherokee political and economic leadership, and thus the first exposure to Christianity was among that segment of the tribe.

In typical Indian fashion, however, Cherokees did not seek to replace their own spiritual beliefs with Christianity, but merely to supplement them, as Christian teachings were often adapted to and meshed with long-standing Cherokee beliefs in a process known as "syncretism." And almost immediately, Cherokees experienced a disjuncture between what was taught in the Bible and the actions employed against them by a Christian nation. As one Cherokee, Yonaguska, stated, "It seems to be a good book; strange that the white people are not better after having had it so long" (McLoughlin 1994, 12). Although a central component of the civilization policy, Christianity was not aggressively promoted by federal agents and developed slowly among the Cherokees. It was decades later, after the American Civil War, before Christianity became the religious belief and practice of the majority of the Cherokee people.

The influence of the descendants of the first intermarriages between Cherokees and Europeans was felt in another important way as well. As it had been demonstrated to the Cherokees throughout the Revolutionary War and afterward that military engagement with Americans was probably no longer feasible, Cherokees looked for other methods to defend their territory and their right to manage themselves and their communities as they wished. Some Cherokees, again as a result of their exposure to ideas from their European parents' culture, began to conceive of a more unified political body, a legal and governmental apparatus that could defend their sovereignty and right of self-determination in ways the Americans would understand and respect. With the evidence of exactly such new political body emerging before them, the United States of America, the Cherokees questioned, why could not they do the same? Could they not also declare their own separate nationality with the same confidence exhibited by the United States in doing so?

The Treaty of Holston of 1791 declared Cherokee nationality for the first time. In its preamble, the treaty stated

> A Treaty of Peace and Friendship made and concluded between the President of the United States of America, on the Part and Behalf of the said States, and the undersigned Chiefs and Warriors, *of the Cherokee Nation* [emphasis added] of Indians, on the part and Behalf of the said *Nation* [emphasis added].[3]

Statements of Cherokee nationality were repeated throughout the remainder of the preamble and Article I of the treaty, and were consistently employed ever after by both the Cherokees and the United States. Representing their response to territorial colonization, these rising assertions of political nationality emerged among the Cherokees in the 1790s, at a time when population was shifting south and west from the areas of eastern Tennessee that had been ceded by the treaty, including the region of the former Overhill settlements such as Chota—the Cherokees' spiritual and political center since the mid-1700s. By the early 1790s, new towns had formed and towns from ceded areas had relocated into areas of northern Georgia and northeastern Alabama, regions where Cherokees had never had permanent settlements before, giving way to more regional designations—Lower and Upper Towns. New governmental meeting places had been chosen—Willstown in northeastern Alabama (generally identified with communities known as the Lower Towns) and Ustenali (or Oostanaula, generally identified with communities known as the Upper Towns), named for the river in northwestern Georgia near which it was located. The latter emerged in the second decade of the 1800s as the single capital of the Cherokee Nation.

In the early 1800s, the Cherokees established a body referred to as a "National" Council as part of their rising indigenous nationalist movement. Younger leadership insisted that the Cherokees must unify their consortium of self-governing, autonomous communities into one body, one voice, and one policy—a national government—if they were to have any hope of retaining their sovereign rights in the face of American expansionism. Although probably first conceptualized by the adult children of European and Cherokee intermarriages and parents, some Cherokees raised in entirely Cherokee households and worldview also joined the new effort. The critiques of the past and efforts for governmental restructuring were probably generational in their origins rather than based in racial or cultural characteristics. The new generation sought the way to be more politically effective Cherokees in the new federal situation, and in these years, "the Cherokees took a major step from being an ethnic nation to being a nation-state" (McLoughlin 1986, 109).

The process of nation-building did not occur rapidly or without internal conflict among the Cherokees. As always, the dilemma involved retaining Cherokee social values while melding them onto new structures. Throughout the first two decades of the 1800s, the Cherokees redesigned their government in ways that more closely resembled those of the United States, but still with an eye to incorporating tribal principles. The Cherokees certainly examined the structure of the Americans' tripartite system, with executive, legislative, and judicial branches, but the system perhaps did not seem terribly foreign to them since they had already centralized somewhat in the mid-1700s, creating what were the foundations for executive and legislative bodies. Although "the outward appearance and functioning of the political organization had changed greatly, it was still based on long-established patterns that were familiar to the average Cherokee" (Persico 1979, 92).

For instance, in the first decades of the 1800s, the Cherokees adapted their grand councils to better serve their needs. While the development of the Cherokee legislative branch has often been described as a "bicameral" system and also attributed to the United States' model, Cherokee conceptions of the adaptation were different. For centuries, the Cherokee towns had had a duality in their councils, mirroring old beliefs and respect for opposites, as peacetime and wartime governments had coexisted within the body. This system was institutionalized into the National Council of the Cherokee Nation in 1811 by the creation of a body within the Council, called the National Committee, emerging as a parallel to the old red or warrior governments of the 1700s. The Committee was not, strictly speaking, another side to the council, but rather a "cabinet" within the Council. The National Committee was initially comprised of nine individuals chosen from the councilors who would act in specific roles, such as the National Treasurer and the National Clerk. The men selected for the National Committee displayed interesting characteristics. Although not specifically mandated, most members of the National Committee spoke, read, and wrote English (although many who were chosen in this era were bilingual Cherokee speakers as well) and they tended to be those who had more acculturated attributes—American-style educations and experience in business and finance, for instance.

It may seem perplexing that the National Committee was the evolution of the "red," or warrior, side of the old town councils. The members of the National Committee, being the English-speaking members of the Council, tended to be those who traveled to Washington to negotiate with federal officials. They provided the legal language for the written Cherokee statutes, and they were those who developed the outline of the first Cherokee Constitution of 1827. How are men such as this derived from a warrior government? But by the first decade of the 1800s, Cherokees recognized that the "battle" had shifted. No longer was their fight a military engagement. Henceforth, their fight to maintain sovereignty and territory was a legal and political fight. And the men of the National Committee were the "warriors" on the front lines of that battle.

While the names of the men of the National Committee are often the most prominent in the historic record, they never acted without overall sanction from the majority of the National Council. The "symbiotic" relationship between men from very different segments of Cherokee society represented a "clear effort by strong . . . leaders to adjust tradition to current circumstances. It was no easy matter to convince a Council that had a majority . . . who spoke no English to graft all of these innovations onto traditional practices" (McLoughlin 1986, 284). But it may not have seemed that unusual to the Cherokees. In that body, which was dominated by more culturally traditional, monolingual Cherokee speakers, the selection of such individuals to serve on the Committee was a strategic balancing of opposites by the Council—an old Cherokee practice.

In the mid-1700s, the Cherokee grand council had declared that it had the power to issue edicts that were to be obeyed by all the Cherokee towns, but this avowal of centralized authority had been asserted primarily in relation to trade and foreign affairs. As the council continued to proclaim its presumed authority throughout the last decades of the century, increasing numbers of Cherokees began to accept it as an overarching lawmaking body, even as it began to dominate over internal affairs as well. In the first decade of the 1800s, the National Council began to codify its issuances. Although still relatively rare, the orders of the Council began to be written as statutes beginning in 1808. Written in English, a language the majority of Cherokees neither spoke nor understood, the written statutes were as much a signal to the United States of Cherokee governmental sovereignty as they were laws for the Cherokee people to live by. The most significant impetus for developing written statutes was "the identification and establishment of a new legal system with the goal of preservation of tribal lands. Even the religious, traditionally conservative fullbloods came to believe in the necessity of convincing white society of tribal progress in adopting new laws as *the* means to prevent removal from the native lands" (Strickland 1975, 162). The first written statute regulated law enforcement that had been established in the Cherokee Nation a few years earlier, a mounted police unit called the Cherokee Lighthorse. If there were going to be laws, there needed to be a system to enact them. The Cherokee councils of the past 50 years had recognized the dilemma.

The second statute passed by the Cherokee Council in 1810 was significant. It referenced an agreement that year by representatives of the seven clans of the Cherokees to abolish blood law within the Cherokee Nation. Although the United States had attempted for 25 years to coerce the Cherokees away from this system of law, they had never succeeded in dislodging this practice that was so deeply based in Cherokee world-view. But by 1810, the need to defend sovereignty and their land base had become paramount for the Cherokees, and if shifting their worldview was required in order to achieve those goals, then the Cherokees would shift. The 1810 law acknowledged several components of blood law that were adapted to more readily resemble American notions of law. First, the Cherokee clans accepted that outstanding imbalances were to be nul-lified, in other words, any killing that had not been handled to date by the practices of blood law would be addressed instead by statutory law of the National Council. Second, the Cherokee clans acknowledged that sometimes there were justifiable reasons for a killing (self-defense, for instance) and that these circumstances would now be taken into account. And third, the clan leadership agreed that "murder" could occur within a clan itself. Blood law had been based in the corporate nature of clans, rather than individuals, and if a clansman killed another within their own clan, there was no perceived imbalance, and thus no response, as clans were considered to be a self-regulating unit. By acknowledging that mur-der could occur within a clan, the law shifted the focus and responsibility to the individual, rather than the corporate clan unit. As the economic activities of the Cherokees and the need to defend culture, land, and sov-ereignty from American encroachment escalated in the early 1800s, the Cherokees elaborated a national government to counter such attempts. Although their governing structures had always been complex, the in-creasing complexity of the new system was more recognizable to the United States. But there was still much about it that remained thoroughly Cherokee in its values.

The United States remained focused on land acquisition. In the 1790s, there had been a need to acquire Indian lands as a way to pay Revolutionary War veterans who still had not been compensated by the United States for their service. Rather than monetary payments, which the United States had no ability to offer, it was thought that land could be taken from tribes and transferred to veterans as a way to give them a start in the new nation. In 1790, the United States passed complex legislation, the Trade and Intercourse Acts, which regulated a variety of commercial situations—regulations that were amended a number of times between 1790 and 1834—and which elevated and firmly established federal authority. Certain sections of the legislation and its amendments specifically addressed Indian lands. Section 12 of the 1802 Act, the first that did not have an expiration date, states

That no purchase, grant, lease, or other conveyance of lands, or of any title or claim thereto, from any Indian, or nation, or tribe of Indians, within the bounds of the United States, shall be of any validity, in law or equity, unless the same be made by treaty of convention entered into pursuant to the constitution.[4]

Reinforcing Congress's plenary power established in the constitution, this section of the Trade and Intercourse Acts decreed that if Indian lands are to be transferred by the tribe to another entity, the only entity that can be on the receiving end of the transfer was the United States. Therefore, a tribe could not legally transfer its land to an individual or a state. In this, the United States emulated laws passed by Great Britain in an earlier era—laws that had apparently been violated by Richard Henderson and his trading consortium in 1775. In other amendments, the act discouraged trespass onto Indian lands by establishing stiff monetary penalties for anyone who did. In anticipation that it would take Indian lands and then allocate them to veterans in payment, the United States had earlier been attempting to keep Indian lands unencumbered by previous claims. In continuing the restriction, the United States was anticipating westward expansion and settlement of its growing population.

Freed from the exploitive trading policies employed by Great Britain previous to the Revolutionary War, the rapid and massive cessions of Cherokee land stopped for the time being. During the 1790s, the Cherokees ceded only small acreages in Tennessee and North Carolina in 1798. But the United States was pressuring other sovereigns for land as well, and those sovereigns, the southern states, had motives of their own in relation to the Indian tribes remaining within their borders. In 1802, the two interests converged in federal legislation entitled the "Articles of Agreement and Cession between the United States and the State of Georgia." It is more commonly known as the Georgia Compact.

In 1730, Great Britain had included lands to the west—the present states of Alabama and Mississippi—in its charter to the colony of Georgia, and as late as 1802, Georgia was still holding those lands. The United States wanted to acquire those territories and begin the process of developing additional states, but Georgia had attempted to cede the lands to a land speculation company. Georgia agreed to turn over all of the land to the federal government if the United States would compensate the speculation company, but the state also extracted a promise from the United States that the federal government would extinguish Indian titles to lands that lay within Georgia's own state boundaries, thus giving Georgia legal jurisdiction over the individual Indians within its state.

Georgia required this guarantee from the United States since, under the terms of the Trade and Intercourse Acts, Georgia could not take direct ownership of Indian lands, which could only be transferred to the United States. In the Georgia Compact, the United States essentially agreed to act as Georgia's agent in the deal. The compact includes a preemption right—a first right of ownership of those Indian lands—to Georgia, once the United States has extinguished Indian title through treaties. While the Creek Confederacy had historically been more prominent in Georgia, by the time the compact was made, Cherokees were also beginning to establish settlements in Georgia, including their council meeting place in Ustenali. Ultimately, Cherokees claimed the northern third of the state of Georgia as part of their territory.

The lands that became the states of Alabama and Mississippi transferred from Georgia to the United States after the passage of the Georgia Compact. But the compact could not legally force treaties upon the tribes within Georgia, so the United States sought their voluntary compliance to land cessions. Although the United States was aggressive in its efforts, neither the Creeks nor the Cherokees were inclined to comply, and thus the United States' fulfillment of their side of the agreement with Georgia languished for years, much to Georgia's dismay.

The year after the compact was passed, a momentous event occurred in the United States. Although France had lost all of its territories on the North American continent in the French and Indian Wars of the 1750s and 1760s, it had reacquired vast territory in North America in 1800 as a result of its dominance over Spain in the era of Napoleon Bonaparte. France had forced cessions of Spanish territory in North America. However, in 1803, France sold the area to the United States, more than doubling the size of U.S. territory. The Louisiana Purchase gave impetus to a shift in federal policy toward Indians. While President Thomas Jefferson sent the famous expedition of Lewis and Clark to explore the new lands and make account of the tribes they encountered, tribes to the east of the Mississippi River— in lands already long occupied by Britain and the United States—faced increasing encroachment by Americans into their lands.

In these circumstances, a new theory emerged that drove Indian policy for the next decades. While civilization policy was not discarded, the Indians' lack of interest in many of its tenets coupled with the acquisition of the new lands led to a proposition on the part of policymakers that the removal of Indians from their eastern lands—where they were being encroached on by white settlers—to the new lands west of the Mississippi River would either (a) allow those tribes to continue in a preferred tribal way of life or alternately (b) would allow them the additional time it seemed they would need to develop the practices of "civilization" without also being subjected to the hostility of encroaching whites. The apparent incongruity of these two goals did not seem to trouble the minds of reformers who promoted Indian removal as a solution for both Americans and eastern tribes. Either proposition provided theoretical support for the true goal of acquiring additional Indian lands, and "three factors—the depletion of the game, the gradual transformation of the tribes, and the possibility of removal—formed a vague fusion in the white man's mind" (Sheehan 1973, 247).

Although not broadly enacted until later decades, the policy of Indian Removal was formulated under the administration of President Thomas Jefferson after the acquisition of the Louisiana Purchase. Within 10 years, removal was being quietly but coercively employed against tribes in the Ohio Valley and Great Lakes regions. Although the Americans living in those areas were certainly cognizant of the removals, the larger American public does not seem to have known or shown much concern that such practices were occurring. Removals of the southern tribes did not commence until more than a decade later, but the threat of the policy being implemented against them increasingly permeated Cherokee sensibilities as the years passed.

For almost the first 40 years of the 1800s, the Cherokees made rapid adaptations of their culture, society, and government as part of the continuing process of melding new ways with old values. Cherokees acquired new skills and became blacksmiths, gunsmiths, silversmiths, millers and miners, ferrymen, hostelry, and tavern operators. Some developing occupations led to great wealth in some families as Cherokees established entrepreneurial types of businesses and entered into contracts for goods with outside commercial enterprises, as well as bartered with other Cherokee producers. A few emulated white southern planters and developed plantations employing an African slave labor force to produce crops for the market. Most Cherokees remained subsistence farmers, producing their own crops, hunting and gathering for supplemental foods, producing their own textiles and clothing, and constructing their own dwellings and almost all of their household items. By the 1820s, Cherokee dependence lessened as the Cherokees became once again a relatively, economically stable and prosperous people.

The most important adaptations, however, occurred in the social realm. The initial Cherokee desire for education in the English language had compounded to a desire for education for its own sake. Soon after mission schools were established and Cherokees began to grasp the way that the strange markings on paper conveyed language, several Cherokees undertook finding the way to create a literate version of their own language. The breakthrough was achieved by a Cherokee named Sequoyah, who devised an 86-character written Cherokee language based in the combinations of sounds in the Cherokee language that comprised syllables, called a syllabary. The value of Sequoyah's invention was not immediately understood by all Cherokees. Intuitively, many realized that the syllabary stood "in a pivotal position—between the reinforcement of a hierarchy and its dismantling; between self-definition and external categorization; between independence and nationalism on the one hand and assimilation on the other" (Bender 2002, 25). In short, the syllabary perhaps presented the finest line yet for the Cherokees to attempt to walk between being better Cherokees and no longer being Cherokees at all.

But ultimately, after use of the syllabary was demonstrated to the National Council by Sequoyah and his young daughter in 1821, almost all Cherokees came to realize that the amazing feat opened up new possibilities for education and communication, particularly as they entered into an era of increasing federal pressure to remove from their southeastern homelands to lands west of the Mississippi River. The Cherokees first began to develop schools throughout the decade, thus taking control of their educational process. A native speaker of Cherokee could acquire use of the syllabary in about two weeks, thus becoming almost instantly literate—a process that made the adaptation of new ideas and philosophies more accessible to the everyday person. Although missionaries still worked among them, the burgeoning Cherokee school system proved to be the primary source of high educational attainment among the Cherokees throughout the remainder of the 1800s.

But even more importantly in the pre-Removal era was their establishment of the first newspaper ever printed by an Indian nation, the *Cherokee Phoenix*—named after the mythical Greek bird that rose from the ashes of destruction. As a metaphor, the Cherokees could not have found a better image to describe their own existence. The newspaper was developed as a bilingual edition, in order that it could be employed as a bilateral tool. Not only could they insure that their own people were well-informed about the actions of their leadership in relation to the removal issue, but in subsequent years, they used the English-language articles and editorials of the *Phoenix* as a potent force to sway public opinion and politicians in America. The newspaper became the most tangible symbol to Cherokees

Statue of Sequoyah by Daniel Horsechief (Cherokee) in front of the former Cherokee National Female Seminary, presently Seminary Hall, Northeastern State University, Tahlequah, Oklahoma. (Photo by Andrew Sikora)

and Americans alike of the "advancement" of the Cherokees. Sequoyah's invention had helped his people to "build their self-esteem and pride. Rather than believing that writing was an art or magic resting in the hands of colonists and their armies, Sequoyah understood that it was a relatively simple instrument that could help the members of his tribe communicate with each other" (Cushman 2011, 36).

As many Americans became cognizant of the "civilized" characteristics of Cherokee society, it appeared that the Cherokees had become the model of the policy. Soon, not only the Cherokees, but the others of the five large southeastern tribes—the Creeks, the Choctaws, the Chickasaws, and the Seminoles—were being referred to as the "Five Civilized Tribes." While the surface appearances of assimilation were obvious to Americans, more recently "an alternative narrative [that] forces reconsideration of Cherokee culture change, even in a period when it seemed so dramatic," has been developed (Perdue 1998, 113). Americans did not readily perceive the motivations for the adaptations of culture, society, and government in which the Cherokees had engaged, and they did not realize that under the surface, much about Cherokee life continued as it always had. But the Cherokees were learning what they needed to of Euroamerican society in order to convince Americans that they, too, were a sovereign people who held their own territory and could manage their own affairs, just as Americans did. The Cherokees employed the civilization policy as a way of resisting the removal policy.

Notes
1. See Primary Documents, Treaty of Hopewell.
2. See Primary Documents, Treaty of Holston.
3. See Primary Documents, The Treaty of Holston.
4. See Primary Documents, Trade and Intercourse Acts.

References
Bender, Margaret. *Signs of Cherokee Culture: Sequoyah's Syllabary in Eastern Cherokee Life*. Chapel Hill: University of North Carolina Press, 2002.

Calloway, Colin. *First Peoples: A Documentary Survey of American Indian History*, 4th ed. Boston and New York: Bedford/St. Martin's, 2011.

Cushman, Ellen. *The Cherokee Syllabary: Writing the People's Perseverance*. Norman: University of Oklahoma Press, 2011.

Deloria, Vine, Jr. and Clifford Lytle. *American Indians, American Justice*. Austin: University of Texas Press, 1983.

Deloria, Vine, Jr. and David Wilkins. *Tribes, Treaties, and Constitutional Tribulations*. Austin: University of Texas Press, 1999.

Horsman, Reginald. *Expansion and American Indian Policy, 1783–1812*. East Lansing: Michigan State University Press, 1967 (reissued in paperback, Norman: University of Oklahoma Press, 1992).

Johnston, Carolyn Ross. *Cherokee Women in Crisis: Trail of Tears, Civil War, and Allotment, 1838–1907*. Tuscaloosa: University of Alabama Press, 2003.

McLoughlin, William G. *Cherokees and Missionaries, 1789–1839*. New Haven, CT: Yale University Press, 1984 (reissued in paperback, Norman: University of Oklahoma Press, 1995).

McLoughlin, William G. *Cherokee Renascence in the New Republic.* Princeton, NJ: Princeton University Press, 1986.

McLoughlin, William G. *The Cherokees and Christianity, 1794–1870: Essays on Acculturation and Cultural Persistence.* Athens: University of Georgia Press, 1994.

McLoughlin, William G., Walter H. Conser, and Virginia Duffy McLoughlin. *The Cherokee Ghost Dance.* Macon, GA: Mercer University Press, 1984.

Mooney, James. *Myths of the Cherokee and Sacred Formulas of the Cherokees,* from19th and 7th Annual Reports Bureau of American Ethnology (1900 and 1891, respectively). Nashville: Charles and Randy Elder—Booksellers, 1982.

Perdue, Theda. "Women, Men, and American Indian Policy." In *Negotiators of Change: Historical Perspectives on Native American Women,* edited by Nancy Shoemaker. New York: Routledge, 1995.

Perdue, Theda. *Cherokee Women: Gender and Culture Change 1700–1835.* Lincoln: University of Nebraska Press, 1998.

Perdue, Theda and Michael D. Green. *The Cherokee Nation and the Trail of Tears.* New York: Viking Penguin, 2007.

Persico, V. Richard, Jr. "Early Nineteenth-Century Cherokee Political Organization." In *The Cherokee Indian Nation: A Troubled History,* edited by Duane King. Knoxville: University of Tennessee Press, 1979.

Royce, Charles C. *The Cherokee Nation of Indians* (Fifth Annual Report of the Bureau of Ethnology, Smithsonian Institution, 1883–1884). Whitefish, MT: Kessinger Publishing, 2006 (reprinted).

Sheehan, Bernard W. *Seeds of Extinction: Jeffersonian Philanthropy and the American Indian.* Chapel Hill: University of North Carolina Press, 1973. (reprinted, New York: W. W. Norton & Company, Inc., 1974).

Starkey, Marion L. *The Cherokee Nation.* New York: Alfred A. Knopf, 1946.

Strickland, Rennard. *Fire and the Spirits, Cherokee Law from Clan to Court.* Norman: University of Oklahoma Press, 1975.

THREE

Building the Nation

IN AUGUST 1807, a stickball tournament was held at Hiwassee, a Cherokee town in the Valley region of far southeastern Tennessee. This "game," which the Cherokees had "played" for many generations, had been widely employed among southeastern tribes as a manner of conflict resolution. Stickball was a rough and vigorous exercise in which dozens, sometimes hundreds, of men participated on each team. Often lasting for days, players were frequently wounded by blows from the sturdy webbed sticks wielded with ferocity not only to catch and toss the small, hard ball, but also to inflict hits on opposing players. Called "the little brother of war" by the Cherokees, stickball was employed to resolve disputes in instances when large-scale warfare was inadvisable. Cherokees and Creeks, for instance, might field teams and play to reconcile a lesser infraction that did not warrant going into battle. Or rather than go to war against each other, Cherokee towns might play to settle an argument. The actual merits of the dispute were not significant. Recognizing that arguments might go on indefinitely on the basis of differing perceptions that would never find agreement, the southeastern tribes had a more direct way of deciding an issue: whoever won the game won the argument.

Under these conditions, it was sometimes imperative in the view of the citizens of a town that they win the game. In these instances, medicine people worked feverishly on the sidelines, devising the incantations and treatments that would insure success. In these instances, a man might even be willing to give his life toward that end. It was not unknown for players to die in the course of the game. Still, the game continued until one side or the other was spent and the dispute was thus ended.

By 1807, it had been demonstrated to the Cherokees that warfare against European and American colonizers was no longer feasible. Cherokee military confederations and the warrior sides of town governments had

dwindled. Southeastern tribes rarely warred against each other, having determined there was a greater common adversary, the United States. And
internal disputes were increasingly being settled by other means, verbal
and soon-to-be written edicts issued from the body lately referred to as the
National Council. But stickball remained important to the Cherokees as a
display of masculine prowess, tribal tradition, and cultural continuity. By
this time, the tournament at Hiwassee and all such displays were no longer
about conflict resolution, yet the games were still enjoyed by thousands
of Cherokees as they had been throughout the generations. Tribal citizens
traveled from across the Cherokee Nation to wager on the outcomes, feast,
and socialize throughout the days the games went on.

One of the members of the National Council who came to Hiwassee for
the festivities was a long-standing leader named Doublehead. Thirty years
earlier, Doublehead had been among the Chickamaugans—the warrior
confederation emerging out of the Revolutionary War. He and his compatri-
ots on the warrior sides of the town councils had protested fiercely the sale
of tribal hunting grounds in 1775 in the exchange known as Henderson's
Purchase. The warriors had defied the peacetime governments of the Cherokee towns and had continued to skirmish with Tennessee frontiersmen
in the late 1780s and early 1790s. But Doublehead had been among those
who had given up the continuous warfare, signing the Treaty of Holston.
A violent man who had disgusted even other Cherokees by his murdering
of white children during the earlier periods of conflict, Doublehead was
nevertheless a powerful leader among the Lower Towns—those towns that
had relocated to northeastern Alabama and extreme northwestern Georgia
after the land cessions of the late 1700s.

As a spectator at the tournament, Doublehead had been involved in
yet another altercation. In a drunken argument, he had killed a Cherokee
named Bone Polisher. Seemingly unperturbed by the act, Doublehead sat
down for supper that evening at a tavern operated by local Cherokees. As
he took the first bites of his meal, shots were fired in his direction. One
of the blasts hit Doublehead in the lower jaw, shattering it. Thinking they
had killed him, the would-be assassins fled the scene. Later that evening,
after learning that they had not accomplished their mission, they tracked
Doublehead to a nearby farmhouse to which he had fled. Several hours
before daybreak, they burst in on him again and another scuffle took place.
Although shots were fired, none hit, and the attackers could not reload
in the dark. Finally, one of the attackers, Alexander Sanders, wielded his
hatchet and laid it squarely into Doublehead's forehead and skull, killing
him at last.

Of the three attackers, Sanders, The Ridge, and either John Rogers or James Vann (the historical record is unclear on the identity of the third attacker), most were prominent members of the Cherokee National Council (Rogers was an intermarried white trader). They had not killed Doublehead to balance his earlier killing of Bone Polisher. Instead, they considered that Doublehead had committed an even more heinous act. In two treaties in 1805 and 1806, Doublehead had been the apparent ringleader of a minority of councilors who had ceded almost 15,000 square miles of Cherokee land without permission of the entire National Council. For this action, the National Council had assigned these three members to make an example of Doublehead. On this night, they were successful in carrying out the order.

Adapting the Cherokee governmental system and society did not occur without debate and internal conflicts, even violence. The story of Doublehead is perhaps the most dramatic demonstration of the tensions between the older way of governing and the new, younger proponents of national restructuring. Many Peoples around the world, both historically and in the present day, have reacted to colonization by the creation of strong nationalist movements—the devotion to their own national interests, unity, and independence—and in this sense, the Cherokees responded as many others have. But the need to mesh their burgeoning sense of nation with older social principles and values that were decidedly different, even oppositional to those espoused by the United States in its own emerging nationality, resulted in a unique blend of cultural and political traits that often confounded outsiders to the society. The simple directness of stickball, the clear rules of blood law, the networks of obligation and opposites that bound Cherokee society together were increasingly challenged and complicated by the need to defend their very right to continue to exist in their own homelands. Doublehead had just encountered firsthand the passion of the debate.

* * * * * * * * * * * *

Although federal Indian agents to the tribes were established as part of the new policy, the actual implementation of "civilization" in the early 1800s was often secondary to other agendas—placating and subduing warriors and devising ways to coerce additional land cessions from the tribes. Agents soon became active participants in the federal–tribal intrigue. By the first decade of the 1800s, agents were elaborating the long-standing practice of exchanging goods for land by also offering "reserves" to chiefs who would cooperate with the cessions. If regional chiefs would agree to treaties of cession, federal Indian agents promised that 100-square-mile tracts would be carved out of that territory and deeded to individual chiefs. The chief would then move his town onto the reserve and the people would be given all the implements of the civilization project in order to develop little "model villages" on land that would be owned as real estate by a single chief.

While this manner of coercion was offered by agents from the Ohio Valley and Great Lakes areas and throughout the southeastern regions, most Indians realized that this was fundamentally no more than the old barter of land in exchange for goods, and rejected the overtures. But among the Cherokees, some chiefs, including Doublehead, had long-standing relationships with their agent, Return Jonathan Meigs, and indicated their interest in the idea.

A treaty conference was held at Tellico in eastern Tennessee in October 1805 after Doublehead had assured Agent Meigs that he had the votes to approve a cession of a significant portion of the remaining hunting grounds in central and southern Tennessee. Chiefs from the Lower Towns—those towns located in northeastern Alabama and far northwestern Georgia—presented a proposal to the entire council that the additional cessions be made to the United States in exchange for cash, goods, and reserves for Lower Town chiefs. Led by Doublehead, other chiefs who backed the plan included Black Fox (who was the principal chief at the time), Pathkiller, Tahlonteskee, and Duwvli (also known as John Bowles), among others. All were former Chickamaugan warriors.

But Upper Town chiefs—who represented towns in north central and northeastern Georgia, southeastern Tennessee, and western North Carolina, and who comprised about two-thirds of the Council—soundly rejected the idea and declared that there would be no more cessions of Cherokee land. It became apparent that Doublehead did not have a consensus of the Council behind him. Nevertheless, 33 Lower Town chiefs, who comprised only one-third of the body's members, afterward placed their signatures on a treaty that ceded the land anyway, despite the objections of the majority of the council. Four months later, in January 1806, they completed the deal with Agent Meigs by signing a second treaty. In the two treaties combined, over 15,000 square miles in central Tennessee and northern Alabama were ceded. Withheld was an area around present-day Muscle Shoals, Alabama, which became known as "Doublehead's Reserve"—the region where the 100-square-mile tracts were granted to the collaborative chiefs. However, the civilization program was never implemented in this area as "Doublehead found it more remunerative to lease the land to whites rather than to make it a model Cherokee village" (McLoughlin 1986, 105).

In response, the Cherokee National Council issued an edict that anyone participating in such cessions without permission of the entire body would henceforth suffer death. Some of the Lower Town chiefs, including Pathkiller (who later became principal chief in 1817), switched sides and joined the new nationalists promoting a more unified, centralized approach to such dilemmas. But by 1807, with Doublehead clearly identified as the leader of the initiative, the Upper Town chiefs of the Council, lacking any other institution to enact its orders, gave instructions in a secret meeting to three of its members to implement the death penalty on Doublehead.

Doublehead and his associates among the Lower Town chiefs likely believed that they had the right to make the cession of land, since they had merely acted in the manner Cherokee chiefs of towns had always acted—as representatives of independent, autonomous governments. Throughout the 1700s, it had been commonplace for consortiums of regional chiefs to make cessions of land. It had been done in 1775 when Doublehead himself had protested Henderson's Purchase, but nothing had transpired afterward to lessen the status or influence among the Cherokees of any of the chiefs involved, and certainly none had faced a death sentence. It was true that in the 1805–1806 cessions a significant amount of money had been given to the Lower Town chiefs by Agent Meigs, and that the United States probably regarded it as a bribe, but it was less clear that the Lower Town chiefs viewed it as such. After all, hadn't exchanges of land for goods always taken place? How was an exchange of land for money any different?

By insisting that the entire body had to consent to land cessions, the majority comprised of the Upper Town chiefs on the Cherokee Council was seen by some as undermining the authority and autonomy of individual chiefs in favor of the greater body. But the apparent willingness of the nationalist chiefs to do so, by force if necessary, was impressive, and many Lower Town chiefs soon demonstrated a desire to leave the nation, rather than possibly experience acts of violence against them as well. The National Council had "broken" (deposed) Black Fox as principal chief as a result of these events, and after Doublehead's execution, and even though he had later been reinstated as principal chief, Black Fox and others appealed to the United States to relocate them to the Arkansas territory rather than remain with their countrymen in the southeast.

In 1809, about 1,000 Cherokees, primarily from the Lower Towns represented by the offending chiefs and with the support of the United States,
emigrated from the Cherokee Nation and were resettled in north central
and northwestern Arkansas. Led by Tahlonteskee, they thereafter appealed to the United States to provide them with a legally bounded and
protected piece of land, a reservation. The United States was agreeable,
but insisted that the Cherokee Nation had to make additional cessions of
land in exchange for any that might be granted to Cherokees in Arkansas.
The Cherokee Nation refused, but federal pressures to coerce them into
doing so were now bolstered by the demands of those Cherokees in Arkansas Territory.

The critical decade of the 1810s was, therefore, marked by escalating
federal insistence on taking more Cherokee land. As usual, the pressure
was applied to individual chiefs in the hopes of eroding their resolve or
enticing their cooperation through bribes. The Cherokees looked for ways
to strategically counter those pressures, and in 1814, an opportunity presented itself. As part of the American war that had broken out a couple of
years earlier, the War of 1812, some tribes had allied with Great Britain as
the enemy of the United States and Canada in this warfare. They had seen
it as a way to reclaim their own independence from the colonizing Americans, and some were following a prophetic vision of a Shawnee leader,
Tenskwatawa, which had been promoted across the region by his brother
Tecumseh. The vision promised salvation from the Americans if only tribes
would unite militarily. The War of 1812 was seen by some as the opening
by which to do so.

Although the vision had been presented among the southern tribes as
well, all had rejected it as unrealistic. But within the Creek Confederacy,
which was an association of numerous tribal and cultural groups, the prophetic idea appealed to some within its confederation, even as the majority
of the Creeks rebuffed military action against the Americans. Some of the
most culturally conservative among the Creeks, known as "Red Sticks,"
responded to the vision, and in August 1813, they acted by attacking American settlements in Alabama. In their raids, approximately 600 Americans
were killed, including women and children, as well as some Creeks attached to the fort. The majority among the Creeks asked for assistance
from the United States, and the Cherokees were asked for their assistance
as well. Those who volunteered were assigned to the command of three
generals from Tennessee, one of whom was a theretofore unremarkable
fellow named Andrew Jackson.

The Cherokees were allied with the United States by treaty and likely felt it their duty to respond when asked. In addition, they probably did not have any sense that they were opposing the Creek Confederacy. After all, although the Confederacy was divided, its official stance was a rejection of Tecumseh's vision and a continuing acceptance of federal civilization initiatives. But most of all, the Cherokees had a self-serving reason for accompanying Jackson on the campaign. If they could involve themselves in battle and comport themselves with distinction, it would create an obligation to them on the part of the United States and, they hoped, would alleviate the pressure for additional land cessions that was being applied to them by the federal government. In their view, such a serious indebtedness to them would surely bring the United States into the networks of obligations and responsibilities that the Cherokees lived by.

In several battles throughout the fall of 1813 and the spring of 1814, Cherokees, warriors once again, carried out their strategy. In the most famous, the Battle of Horseshoe Bend fought on the Tullapoosa River in Alabama in March 1814, Cherokee warriors salvaged the American victory, which resulted in the deaths of hundreds of Red Stick warriors. "The power of the Creeks was broken," and "[f]rom that day on, [Jackson's] fame began to grow, the ground swell of popularity that would eventually sweep him into the White House. And in his first great military success, as he himself acknowledged, the Cherokees played a decisive role as Jackson would prefer later to forget" (Wilkins 1986, 79).

But the Cherokees' expectation of American gratitude for their service was misplaced. As Cherokees returned home from their service, they discovered that as Jackson's armies had passed through Cherokee territory, they had wreaked destruction to fields and homes on their way. "Indeed, the Cherokees found their homes and families had suffered more at the hands of their white allies than from their enemies, the Creeks" (Wilkins 1986, 80). But upon protest by the Cherokees to the United States, Jackson denied his army's actions. The United States also denied the equal pay and pensions to wounded veterans that had been promised to the Cherokees. But the final and greatest duplicity occurred as the United States punished the Creeks for their "betrayal," despite the fact that only a dissident band among the Confederacy had opposed Americans. As part of the land cession that was demanded of the Creeks, Cherokee lands in northern Alabama were included in the proposed treaty. Only under protest from the Cherokees and the Chickasaws, who also felt they had rights to it, were the lands they claimed removed from the cession forced of the Creeks in 1814.

It was clear thereafter to the Cherokees that neither the United States nor Jackson felt any sense of obligation to them for their contributions as part of Jackson's military campaigns. There would be no reduction of pressure for land cessions on the part of the United States, and instead, those pressures escalated. Although the Cherokees had been successful in having the northern Alabama lands removed from the 1814 Creek cession, within two years, the United States had applied enough pressure to individual chiefs once again to force another major land cession in 1816. And the following year, in 1817, a series of smaller tracts around the periphery of the remaining territory were ceded, again on the signatures of a minority of chiefs of the National Council. The old British and American tactic of advancing a treaty after coercing only a minority to sign on the Cherokee side continued to be effective. From the Cherokee perspective, this continued to be so since the tension between the older governing style, including the autonomy of individual chiefs, as opposed to the new insistence on unified national action was still unresolved.

But the Cherokees also understood that it was not solely their own unresolved nationalism that led to the land cessions of 1816 and 1817. There was another issue as well, a betrayal. Andrew Jackson, the relatively unimportant military man who had asked them to participate in his campaign and whose career the Cherokees had likely saved, was the lead negotiator for the Americans on both of the treaties that took additional Cherokee lands. By the end of the decade, Cherokees had developed a scathing opinion of Jackson.

The cessions of 1817 spurred a major restructuring of Cherokee national government. Throughout the 1810s, the mounting federal pressures had only served to solidify and expand the growing sense of nationalism among Cherokee councilors and the general population. The Council had been formulating written statutes since 1808, and in 1817, an act that dramatically reformed the Cherokee government was passed. As with all the laws, it was written in English, a language the majority of the people neither read nor understood, but that could be held up to federal officials as evidence of the Cherokees' ability to self-govern. The Act of Reform has sometimes been called "the first Cherokee constitution." Although technically not of that stature, the act nevertheless established a government that later solidified in just such a document. It signaled that "they were ready now to institutionalize their sense of nationhood" (McLoughlin 1986, 226).

In 1820, additional legislation was passed by the National Council that eliminated the selection of headmen by "towns," a system that had become archaic by that time, in favor of election by popular vote of members of the National Council. The nation's territory was divided into 8 electoral districts, with 4 representatives to be selected from each of the districts, for a total of 32. In addition, a body known as the National Committee, which had been established in 1809 "to act as an administrative aid to the principal chief," was codified in 1817 and expanded to 13 members who "administered the day-to-day activities of Cherokee government between annual sessions of the national council," thus functioning more as a cabinet than a second legislative house as it has sometimes been described (Champagne 1983, 91). The 1820 legislation also established, for the first time in Cherokee history, judicial districts from the eight electoral districts. The Cherokees finally had a replacement for their system of blood law, which they had given up in 1810 by statute and an agreement among the clans. Within only a few years, the court system had been elaborated to a three-tiered system comprised of district courts, circuit courts, and a Supreme Court.

The dramatic governmental restructuring had, in fact, been underway for years, and by the time it was legislated in 1817–1820, it was already becoming familiar to most Cherokee citizens. There was little or no protest about the codification of the system. The electoral process was perhaps the newest element to the Cherokees, and in their usual fashion, they adapted it to their own understandings of principles for selecting leadership. Although under the law only men could vote, the initial elections consisted of men of the household who attended large meetings at which hands were publicly raised in favor of particular candidates. This probably did not seem unfamiliar to either Cherokee men or women. After all, Cherokee men had long acted as the public interface between the families and clans at home and the larger world. Women understood this as an appropriate role for men, rather than that women were disallowed from voting. When Cherokee men cast a vote, they were almost certainly voting the consensus of their household, a consensus that had been arrived at after discussions with the women of that household and that strongly reflected the women's wishes as well. Americans, on the other hand, seeing only the superficial appearance of exclusively men who voted, also approved the new Cherokee practices as they seemed to support American notions of "civilization" as a system where women remained at home, neither seen nor heard in the political realm.

Cherokees hoped that the governmental restructuring would end the practice of minorities of chiefs signing treaties of land cession. But amendments in 1819 to the previous treaty ceded still more small tracts on the periphery of the nation's territory. Between the two years of cessions,

particularly those of 1817, several thousand Cherokees were suddenly dis-
placed from their homes that were situated on ceded lands. With their only
choices being to move within the remaining boundaries of the Cherokee
Nation or to remove to the Arkansas reserve, about 3,000 elected to leave
the majority of their people and immigrate to Arkansas to join those
who were already there. Their main impetus being to get away from the
Americans encroaching onto their lands and pressuring them to change
their way of life, this group became known as the "Old Settlers" among
the Cherokees. Although the 3,000 Cherokees who left in 1817–1819 inspired the designation, in later years, "Old Settler" was used to refer to
the steady trickle of Cherokees who moved west throughout the 1820s
and the early 1830s. In exchange for the coerced cessions of eastern land
between 1816 and 1819, the United States created a legally bounded "reservation" for the Cherokees in Arkansas. The diamond-shaped tract of
land was in northwestern and north central Arkansas, bounded on two
sides by the White River and the Arkansas River. Although occupied by
those who became known as "western" Cherokees—former Chickamaugans and the 1809 emigrants, as well as Old Settlers—the government
that received the cession of land was named in the treaty as "the Cherokee Nation," the government that was still located in the southeast.

Also as a result of the 1819 cessions, towns in western North Carolina
that had been known in the 1700s as the Middle Towns were suddenly outside the remaining boundaries of the Cherokee Nation. This area was still
relatively heavily populated by Cherokees, and they tended to be among
the most conservative in the nation. The 1817–1819 treaty gave Cherokees
on ceded lands a choice to remain and accept a 640-acre reserve as well
as U.S. citizenship. While many Cherokees opted to leave instead, in the
region of western North Carolina, at least 49 families accepted the tracts of
land and chose to remain in their ancient communities. In a region of the
Smoky Mountains that many Cherokees regarded as the nucleus of Cherokee existence, these families coalesced around beliefs, practices, and sites
that were critical to the Cherokee patrimony. Although they lost much of
the land anyway and were trapped in a tenuous legal position for over a
century, the Cherokees of western North Carolina ultimately found the way
to remain in the homelands. And "since the boundary of the diminished
tribal domain was nearby, they could enjoy frequent contact with their relatives who were still part of the Cherokee Nation" (Finger 1984, 10).

But provisions of the Act of Reform of 1817 also established a residency requirement as part of the criteria for Cherokee Nation citizenship.
A Cherokee had to reside within the boundaries of the nation in order to

retain that citizenship. Therefore, by the Cherokees' own law, those who immigrated to Arkansas lost their citizenship in the Cherokee government as a result, and those Cherokees who accepted reserves and remained on ceded land also relinquished their citizenship by that action. For those in western North Carolina who were thereafter called the Oconoluftee Cherokees (named after a local river), the 1800s was a long century of evading removal, protecting ancient lands and sites, and ultimately emerging as a separate government from the Cherokee Nation that today is known as the Eastern Band of Cherokee Indians.

By the late 1810s, the dispersion of Cherokees was becoming alarming. For those who continued to reside and fight for the remaining territory in the southeast, the dawn of the 1820s was grim. Fortunately, the Cherokees had strategic leadership that was preparing for the struggle ahead. Among those nationalist chiefs was a rather unusual individual called The Ridge. He was typical of the majority of Cherokees in that he spoke only Cherokee and had been raised deeply in the hunter–warrior traditions of the 1700s. But unlike many Cherokees of his background, The Ridge had joined from the start in the cause of developing a more unified, centralized national government. He had been among those who had been revolted by Doublehead's murdering of children and had opposed Doublehead and the Lower Town chiefs in the land cessions of 1805 and 1806. The Council had sent him as one of the executioners of Doublehead, and in those years, he had gained his name as he proclaimed to the Council that the Americans would return again and again for further cessions of land. His colleagues later stated that he had seen the future as if standing on a high ridge, and thus he became "The Ridge." He had fought at Horseshoe Bend with the Cherokees who had been with Andrew Jackson and had gained the rank of major as a result. He afterward used the title as a first name, and Cherokees knew him ever after as "Major Ridge." As his career progressed, "the impact of The Ridge's example upon his tribesmen would be hard to overrate" (Wilkins 1986, 6).

Also at Horseshoe Bend was a younger aide whom Major Ridge had treated as a protégé. Born into very different circumstances, John Ross was the descendant of Scotsmen who had married into the Cherokees in the early and middle 1700s. Subsequent generations of the Shorey, McDonald, and Ross families from which he was descended had continued to marry and remain among the Cherokees, although also entirely acculturated to Euroamerican ways. They spoke English, had American-style educations, and were occupied in business and agricultural professions. In many respects, Ridge and Ross could not have been more different, but just as

Major Ridge, color lithograph by I.T. Bowen.
(Courtesy of the Research Division, Oklahoma
Historical Society)

Ridge had come from a traditional background yet found value in acculturation, Ross had come from an acculturated background and found value
in Cherokee tradition, and "as a youth Ross favored the ancient dress and
customs of his people" (Moulton 1978, 6). Still, it seemed an unlikely alliance, and might have been if not for the times and the vision of nation that
the two shared. Together, they inspired and allied the older traditionalist
and younger nationalist generations on the Council throughout the dangerous years of the 1820s.

That decade saw the rapid development of many social and economic
institutions among the Cherokees. But "Cherokee support for these pro-
gressive governmental developments was not unanimous" (Malone 1956,
87). From 1824 to 1827, a traditionalist movement demonstrated strong
resistance to another proposal emerging from the National Council—a
Cherokee constitution. While most members of the Council were debat-
ing the establishment of a document of overarching governing principles
that would politically unify the communities of their nation permanently, a

few were suspicious of what they perceived as further emulation of American governing systems that often seemed so unfamiliar to many Cherokee people, and sometimes at odds with tribal values, despite efforts to reconcile the two ways. This sentiment was most strongly represented on the Council by an elder named White Path. Deposed from the Council by other councilors in 1826 due to his continuing objections to constitutional government, White Path consolidated his influence among conservative Cherokee people by fomenting what became known as "White Path's Rebellion." Its targets were primarily the missionaries and their activities, as they were probably the most accessible representatives of acculturation, and it was their services, missions, and revivals that were disrupted by resistant Cherokees.

But White Path's movement was not a prophetic desire to return to old ways. It differed from earlier movements that had emerged in critical times in that it was focused entirely on immediate, contemporary issues, particularly the development of a constitution. It did not seek to eradicate the governmental changes made in the 1817 Act of Reform. It did not seek to roll back statutory law in favor of a return to blood law. It did not challenge the authority of Cherokee courts or law enforcement. Its primary message to its governmental leaders seems to have been to slow down. "At its base, the rebellion was a reaction against the pace and pervasiveness of acculturation rather than against acculturation itself" (McLoughlin 1986, 366). In these years, when Cherokee leadership was making swift and strategic moves to counter strong federal coercion to cede lands and remove, many Cherokee people were having a difficult time grasping the changes or comprehending the reasons for them. The movement implored for more time for Cherokee citizens to become accustomed to the existing changes before still others were made. The movement "seemed to threaten opposition, but when the situation was explained, White Path's fears were allayed and the trouble subsided" (Wilkins 1986, 203).

In 1827, there was a momentous occurrence in the Cherokee Nation. After decades of struggle and debate, the Cherokee Nation was solidified as a national government when its legislative body, the National Council, ratified its first constitution. This represented the pinnacle of the nationalist movement's efforts that had begun 36 years earlier with the declarations of nationhood framed in the 1791 Treaty of Holston. There had been crises, violence, and continuing losses of land as the tension between the old ways and the new vision had erupted. But the passage of the 1827 Cherokee Constitution was discussed and debated in passionate, yet civil missives and oratory. In the end, the efforts of the conservative Cherokees involved in White Path's Rebellion had been successful. Although the Council had wanted to make still more significant changes, the constitution primarily mirrored the governmental changes made between 1817 and 1820—changes the Cherokee people had been living under for 10 years already and with which they were becoming quite accustomed.

There was at least one major change, however. Although Cherokees had been electing their legislators since 1817, the principal chief had still been selected by the National Council from one of their own and he had generally served from the time of his selection until his death. The new constitution provided that the principal chief would thereafter be elected by the General Council (the combination of the National Council and Committee) to serve a term or terms of four years each with no term limits. The first election was slated for 1828. But in 1827, before the constitutional structure was in place, the Principal Chief Pathkiller passed away. He was succeeded by the second chief, Charles Hicks, but two weeks later, Hicks also passed away. Because the election would not take place until the following year, the Council continued for the time being with the tradition of selecting someone from within their ranks to be the principal chief.

Major Ridge was the obvious choice. He was the most senior member of the Council and an individual who straddled both the world of the traditionalists within which he had been raised and which had formed his worldview, and the world of the more acculturated Cherokees with which he had also become comfortable as he became more economically and politically prominent within the nation. He was the logical selection, but instead, feeling that the Cherokee Nation needed a different kind of leader in the critical times it was facing, Ridge "seems not even to have made himself available" (Wilkins 1986, 204) for the office. He encouraged the selection of a younger chief, educated and English-speaking, as he felt would best serve the nation's interests at this point. "I have no fears respecting the conduct of you young men," he stated. "I know you are decided friends of this our native country" (quoted in Wilkins 1986, 204). Two of the younger chiefs, William Hicks and John Ross, stood for the office, and Hicks was elected, which may have represented a last acquiescence to tradition by the Council, as he was the brother and therefore clan relative of the last and late principal chief, Charles Hicks.

But the following year, in 1828, and under the terms of the recently implemented constitution, another election by the General Council was slated, and at that time, Ridge's acolyte, John Ross, was elected overwhelmingly by the body. Ross was 38 years old, barely old enough under the new document to hold the office, when he assumed the helm of the nation, and it was the beginning of 38 years as principal chief. He held a title that had been established by the 1827 Constitution as a far more powerful position than it had previously been. No longer simply a representative spokesperson of the consensus of the Council, the principal chief became an office with a great deal of power in its own right—the executive branch of the Cherokee national government.

The development of the Cherokee constitution spurred consternation within the state of Georgia, in particular. Since the 1802 Georgia Compact, the state and its citizens had existed under the expectation that at some point, the United States would fulfill its end of the bargain by extinguishing Indian titles within the state's limits and removing Indians from the state boundaries. Having exercised patience for 25 years as the United States

Principal Chief John Ross lithograph. (Courtesy of the Research Division, Oklahoma Historical Society)

failed to achieve the objective, Georgia was particularly alarmed by the declaration on the part of an Indian nation within its boundaries of its own national sovereignty and territory. The Cherokee constitution signaled its territorial permanence to the southern states within which the Cherokee Nation remained—Georgia, Tennessee, Alabama, and North Carolina—and for Georgia, within which about half the Cherokee territory was located, this was a particular affront as the United States had made specific promises otherwise to the state.

With the election of Andrew Jackson as president of the United States in 1828, Georgia had reason to hope that the guarantees made in the 1802 Georgia Compact might finally be realized. Jackson had campaigned on promises that Indian Removal would at last be implemented in the south as it had been in the northern areas in the 1810s and 1820s, and he had demonstrated his ability to be forceful with the tribes in his treaty dealings with the Creeks and Cherokees throughout those same decades. He was a southerner from Tennessee, a frontiersman like many, but who also had a personal interest in the removal of the Cherokees as he speculated in land within the state limits. But for the Cherokees and other tribes in the south, the election of Jackson led to foreboding as the pressures for cessions and removal, which had already been heavy, were certain to escalate.

In the same year, the Cherokees who had immigrated to Arkansas and had lost their citizenship in the Cherokee Nation under the Cherokees' own laws were facing a second relocation. Arkansas territory, which included the present states of Arkansas and Oklahoma, was being divided, as Arkansas desired to become a state within the union. Only the eastern portion of the territory was included within the state, and the western portion was to be reserved for tribes to be removed from the south and other parts of the country. The Cherokee reserve in northern Arkansas reminded Arkansans of what would be a fractured state sovereignty in the same way the Cherokee lands in Georgia reminded that state of the same. The clamor for Cherokee removal was thus occurring in two locations as Arkansans wanted Indians out of their burgeoning state as well.

In 1828, again by a process of wearing down the resolve of western Cherokee leadership as federal "government officials cajoled, whiskeyed, and bribed them into signing an agreement" (Hoig 1998, 139), the Cherokees in Arkansas traded their reserve for 15 million square acres of land slightly to the west, in an area that was emerging as "Indian Territory"—later to become the state of Oklahoma. These events were watched closely by the Cherokee Nation's leadership in the east as well. Once more, although the eastern leadership was not a part of negotiating the exchange of Arkansas

lands for those in the Indian Territory, the government the land was ceded
to by the United States was nevertheless the Cherokee Nation. The location
of their own proposed removal was now well defined. About 4,500 Cherokees from Arkansas moved into the new area and began to establish their
farms and plantations. But those in the east remained entrenched there as
the fight to save their southeastern homelands escalated.

As Georgia began to formulate its next moves, it was spurred by yet another significant event. In 1828 or 1829, gold was discovered near present-
day Dahlonega (meaning "yellow" in Cherokee), Georgia. According to
historian David Williams, although many anecdotal accounts exist suggesting an earlier date of discovery, "there is no documentary evidence
of the discovery of gold in Georgia until August 1, 1829" (1993, 24) when
a notice appeared in a Milledgeville (then the capital of Georgia) newspaper. Although it is probable the Cherokees had known of the existence of gold in their territory for many centuries (there are stories of a
Cherokee taking gold with him when visiting London in the 1700s), the
"discovery" of this precious metal by whites in the area was the impetus
for a gold rush into the region. The discovery only hastened action Georgia had been contemplating since the development of the 1827 Cherokee
Constitution. In 1829, Georgia passed the first of two laws that denied
Cherokee claims of territorial and governmental jurisdiction within its
northern lands of the state, and began to assert Georgia's claims of dominance over the Cherokees.

The first law ignored all Cherokee claims to territorial possession within
the state, declaring that Cherokee lands were now divided into five counties of the state of Georgia—Carroll, DeKalb, Gwinnett, Hall, and Habersham. It further asserted that Georgia law was now extended over the
Cherokees and Cherokee law was nullified in the same area, thus asserting
state jurisdiction over the Indian nation within its boundary. In sections
clearly aimed at Cherokees, it established harsh penalties—four years at
hard labor—for anyone discouraging Indians from meeting with federal
officials for the purpose of treaty making or for anyone discouraging
Cherokees from enrolling to emigrate west. Branch by branch, executive,
legislative, and judicial, it outlawed the functions of Cherokee government
within the limits of Georgia. In a particularly interesting section, it declared
that "no Indian or descendant of any Indian residing within the Creek or
Cherokee nations of Indians, shall be deemed a competent witness in any
court of this state to which a white person may be a party."[1] This prevented
Cherokees from testifying against not only those who were in the process
of stealing their resources, but also those who would soon be paid by the
state to harass and terrorize them from their own homes. These laws,

Recreation of the Cherokee National Council meeting house, New Echota Historic Site, Calhoun, Georgia. (Courtesy of the Georgia Department of Natural Resources—State Parks and Historic Sites Division)

including the section deeming the testimony of Indians as "incompetent" when presented against whites, were on the books in the state of Georgia until the late 20th century!

While the 1829 law focused on Georgia's priority in asserting state jurisdiction over the tribes within its borders, the law passed the following year focused on internal matters within Cherokee society. The 1830 law concentrated on the Cherokee courts, elaborating the previous law by prohibiting Cherokee court orders that might be issued in any of the other states from being enacted within Georgia. It also criminalized anyone attending or participating in a Cherokee court proceeding. It asserted Georgia's jurisdiction over labor within the Cherokee Nation by declaring that all white persons who were not citizens of that nation had first to apply to Georgia for a license and swear an oath of allegiance to Georgia before taking employment in the Cherokee Nation. Although the law impacted mechanics, businessmen, and teachers who worked in the Cherokee Nation, its primary targets were missionaries, whom Georgia feared would foment resistance among the Cherokees.

Of most immediate importance to the everyday Cherokee, the law established a state militia called the "Georgia Guard." Raised "for the protection of the mines," the sections also allowed the Guard to "[enforce] the laws of force within the Cherokee nation, ... to be employed on foot, or mounted, as the occasion may require, which shall not consist of more than sixty persons."[2] Subsequent sections elaborated the pay these 60 individuals would receive to act as a state-supported vigilante force against the Cherokees.

Together, the two laws, commonly called the Georgia Harassment Laws, signaled to both the United States and the Cherokee Nation that Georgia's patience had run out. If the United States, in almost 30 years, would not or could not persuade the Cherokees to cede their land by treaty in legal fashion according to the requirements of the U.S. Constitution and federal laws, then Georgia would take matters into its own hands.

The Georgia Harassment Laws cast federal lawmakers into a quandary. While they may have understood Georgia's frustration with the situation that had lingered since 1802, Georgia nevertheless appeared to be rejecting the exclusive privilege of the United States to make treaties with tribes. For federal lawmakers who may have agreed with the overall policy, Georgia's actions nevertheless violated the supremacy of federal levels of jurisdiction they also understood had been created in the Commerce Clause of the Constitution, which stated that only Congress could pass regulatory laws pertaining to the tribes within the country. The tension between federalist and states' rights positions in the American political arena was beginning to heat up in several ways, and the issue of Indian removal became an indicator of the fissure that would later fracture the country in the American Civil War.

Cherokees also realized the import of Georgia's actions. But while leadership searched for ways to test the validity of Georgia's actions, they were also faced with the persistent threats that Georgia's vigilante force was posing to everyday Cherokee citizens. As the Georgia Guard roamed the Cherokee countryside looting, beating, and terrorizing residents, sometimes evicting them forcibly from their homes, the natural human inclination was to strike back. But as the violence escalated, Principal Chief Ross and his political lieutenants urged all Cherokees to keep strong check on their impulses in order not to give the state or the federal government justification to further occupy the Cherokee Nation. "Ross never deviated from his strategy of peaceable, passive resistance. That it proved insufficient should not detract from the imaginative, daring, and increasingly desperate path down which he led his people" (Perdue and Green 2007, 70). Remarkably, the Cherokees on the whole endured the harassment, giving their leadership time to seek a measured, strategic path through the crisis.

But in 1830, the federal government found its own way out of the quandary. With the passage in that year of the Indian Removal Act, the federal Congress now mandated by law the removals of the southeastern tribes as well, aligning it with Georgia's overall objective. As yet another new decade dawned, the Cherokees wondered, would the stunning achievements they had made during the 1820s—the development of the syllabary, their newspaper, the schools, the increasing complexity of their economy, the nationalist centralization of their government, and their statutory laws and constitution—be strong enough to hold off the rising political tide that had now turned sharply against them?

Notes
1. See Primary Documents, The Georgia Harassment Laws.
2. See Primary Documents, The Georgia Harassment Laws.

References

Brown, John P. *Old Frontiers, the Story of the Cherokee Indians from Earliest Times to the Date of Their Removal to the West, 1838.* Kingsport, TN: Southern Publishers, Inc., 1938.

Champagne, Duane. "Symbolic Structure and Political Change in Cherokee Society." *The Journal of Cherokee Studies* 8, no. 2 (Fall 1983): 87–101.

Conley, Robert J. *The Cherokee Nation, a History.* Albuquerque: University of New Mexico Press, 2005.

Cotterill, R. S. *The Southern Indians, the Story of the Civilized Tribes before Removal.* Norman: University of Oklahoma Press, 1954.

Finger, John R. *The Eastern Band of Cherokees, 1819–1900.* Knoxville: University of Tennessee Press, 1984.

Hoig, Stanley W. *The Cherokee and Their Chiefs, in the Wake of Empire.* Fayetteville: University of Arkansas Press, 1998.

Malone, Henry T. *Cherokees of the Old South, a People in Transition.* Athens: University of Georgia Press, 1956.

McLoughlin, William G. *Cherokee Renascence in the New Republic.* Princeton, NJ: Princeton University Press, 1986.

Moulton, Gary E. *John Ross, Cherokee Chief.* Athens: University of Georgia Press, 1978.

Perdue, Theda. "The Conflict Within: Cherokees and Removal." In *Cherokee Removal, before and after,* edited by William L. Anderson. Athens: University of Georgia Press, 1991.

Perdue, Theda and Michael D. Green. *The Cherokee Nation and the Trail of Tears.* New York: Viking Penguin, 2007.

Royce, Charles C. *The Cherokee Nation of Indians* (Fifth Annual Report of the Bureau of Ethnology, Smithsonian Institution, 1883–1884). Whitefish, MT: Kessinger Publishing, 2006 (reprinted).

Rozema, Vicki. *Cherokee Voices, Early Accounts of Cherokee Life in the East.* Winston-Salem, NC: John F. Blair, 2002.

Starr, Emmett. *History of the Cherokee Indian, and Their Legend and Folklores.* Baltimore, MD: Genealogical Publishing Company, 1921 (reprinted).

Thornton, Russell. *The Cherokees: A Population History.* Lincoln: University of Nebraska Press, 1990.

Walker, Charles O. *Cherokee Footprints*, Vol. I. Jasper, GA: Charles Walker, 1988.

Wilkins, Thurman. *Cherokee Tragedy, the Ridge Family and the Decimation of a People.* Norman: University of Oklahoma Press, 1986.

Williams, David. *The Georgia Gold Rush, Twenty-Niners, Cherokees, and Gold Fever.* Columbia: University of South Carolina Press, 1993.

Woodward, Grace Steele. *The Cherokees.* Norman: University of Oklahoma Press, 1963.

FOUR

Rhetoric and Strategies of Resistance

IN 1824, Georgia legislators insulted the Cherokees' intelligence. In a letter directed to President James Monroe, the congressional delegation of the state of Georgia accused the Cherokees of employing ghostwriters in their recent communications with the secretary of war protesting the pressure the Cherokee Nation endured to cede additional lands and remove west. The Cherokee response to the Georgians, written by its own lobbying delegation while in Washington, appeared in the *Essex Register* of Salem, Massachusetts, on May 20 of that year. Composed and signed by Cherokee National Council members John Ross, George Lowry, Elijah Hicks, and Major Ridge, the Cherokees employed sharp rhetorical arguments to defend not only the sanctity of their relationship with the federal government, but also the intellectual acumen of their leadership:

> Not satisfied with wishing the Executive of the United States violently to rupture the solemn bond of our rights to our land and to put at defiance the pledges which existing treaties contain guarantying to us our lands, it is attempted to take from us the intellect which has directed us in conducting the several negotiations with commissioners appointed to treat with us for our lands, and with the Executive government, by the unfounded charge, that "*the last letter of the Cherokees to the Secretary of War, contains internal evidence that it was never written or dictated by an Indian.*" Whilst we expect to be complimented on the one hand, by this blow at our intelligence, we cannot, in justice, allow it to pass, upon the other, *without a flat contradiction*. That letter, and every other letter, was not only *written*, but dictated by an Indian. We are not so fortunate as to have such help.—The white man seldom comes forward in our defense. Our rights are in our own keeping . . . Our letters are our own; and if

they are thought too refined for "Savages," let the white man take it
for proof that, with proper assistance, Indians can think and write for
themselves [emphasis in the original].[1]

By the early 1820s, the Cherokees boasted some young adults in a generation that had achieved what their nationalist parents had hoped for:
fluency and literacy in English as well as Cherokee. Younger Cherokee
leadership consulted in the Cherokee language with their elders on the
Council and then translated not only words, but Cherokee notions of
rights and obligations into English. In doing so, they frequently used the
rhetorical ideals and principles of the United States itself to expose the
dubious justifications of its policies and to remind its citizens of their
own national values. "In this context of state coercion and federal neglect,
Cherokee leaders adopted a style of address and language that would provide the foundation for their political writings for the rest of the century"
(Denson 2004, 27).

Two young leaders in particular, John Ridge and Buck Oo-watie (Major
Ridge's son and nephew, respectively), had been educated in a New
England prep school and had personal experience with the contradictions between rhetoric and actions. Located in Cornwall, Connecticut, the
school, established in 1817 by the American Board of Commissioners for
Foreign Missions (ABCFM), was designated predominantly for students
from regions of American and European colonialist enterprises: Hawai-
ians, Polynesians, East Indians, Malaysians, Chinese, and Marquesans,
as well as American Indians. Oo-watie, who had previously attended the
Moravian mission school at Spring Place, Georgia, was one of its first Cherokee students, arriving in 1818. He was soon introduced to an American
philanthropist and author named Dr. Elias Boudinot, who pledged annual
support to the young man and also bestowed to him the use of his name.
Buck Oo-watie, thus known afterward as Elias Boudinot, was joined at
the school in 1819 by his cousin John Ridge. Although both were noted as
remarkably intelligent and refined young men, Boudinot was regarded as
a particular success by the missionaries, evidenced by his piety and devotion to their Christian teachings.

But the two young men ultimately caused the greatest imaginable offense to the good people of Connecticut. In 1824, John Ridge married one
of the white daughters of the community, Sarah Northrup. And two years
later, Elias Boudinot followed suit when he wed Harriett Gold. Although
the families of the Cherokee men were among the more acculturated of
the tribe, Christian, and clearly wealthy even by American standards, both

marriages had initially been opposed by the parents of the brides. And although they had relented in the faces of their daughters' insistence, the citizens of Cornwall did not approve. The unrest in the town was palpable when the Ridge–Northrup nuptials occurred, but when Boudinot became engaged to Miss Gold in 1826, Cornwall erupted in violence, burning the two in effigy, the flames lit by her brother. The "incident had taught them that the idealistic North was not so fair-minded and friendly towards the Indians as it pretended to be" (Starkey 1946, 71). Not surprisingly, both couples chose to live in the Cherokee Nation and raise their children as Cherokee citizens.

Ridge and Boudinot had been shaken by what they surely perceived as the insincerity of the Connecticut townspeople, who had professed their admiration and regard for the accomplishments of the two and the virtue of Boudinot in particular. Their mistake had been in assuming they were thus taken as equals to the whites in the town, a mistake their courting of the townswomen brought into sharp focus. In the end, despite their achievements and their piety, they were still Indians, and as their councilors had noted in their protest to the Georgia delegation in the same year, "The white man seldom comes forward in our defense. Our rights are in our own keeping." The year after the Boudinot–Gold marriage, the school closed, ending any looming threats of additional marriages between white women and men of color, but also eliminating educational possibilities for aboriginals who might use their training to defend their rights.

But the townspeople's rage had given Ridge and Boudinot additional incentive to expose the contradictions between American ideals and federal actions. As the 1820s progressed and turned into the critical decade of the 1830s, Ridge acquired the skills of an attorney and Boudinot the skills of an editor. They worked with their elders, both traditionalists and nationalists, to build strategies and create alliances. The Cherokees both inspired and contributed to some of the loftiest rhetoric ever produced in the American nation or their own nation on the subject of rights and moral imperatives. They left no doubt in the minds of many Americans of their time that, "Our letters are our own. . . . Indians can think and write for themselves."

* * * * * * * * * * * *

By the late 1820s, only 12,316 square miles of land remained to the Cherokees after their last cession in 1819. Half of that territory was in northern Georgia and the remainder was in Alabama, Tennessee, and North Carolina.

About 18,000 people, predominantly Cherokees but also about 200 intermarried whites and 1,600 black slaves owned by some Cherokees, occupied that territory. About half were in Georgia and the remainder in the
other states.[2] In addition, over 50,000 non-Indians, predominantly whites
but also some free blacks, had intruded into the Cherokee Nation's territory in Georgia and were squatting on its land.

Most Cherokees lived in a manner similar to that of frontier whites.
They had small cabins and farmed a few acres of land. They raised a
few head of livestock and made their own clothes and other household
possessions. They supplemented their crops by hunting game and small
animals, and they gathered fruits, nuts, and greens. They made their own
medicines and had recently begun to import others from Americans as
well. Within their people were blacksmiths and gunsmiths, millers and
miners, tavern owners and ferrymen, merchants, and plantation operators. As a society, the Cherokees were meeting most of their own basic
needs.

But the passage of the Georgia Harassment Laws led to a systematic
impoverishment of the Cherokees throughout the early years of the 1830s,
as state forces began to strip them of their property and their homes. As
the laws went into effect, President Jackson's supporters in Congress introduced the Indian Removal Act in 1830, as southern politicians had long
wanted. It also sent a strong message to Cherokees who "had been led
by friendly Congressmen to believe that Congress would support them
against Georgia. Until Congress had given unmistakable proof that it had
no such intention, it was useless, said [Tennessee Governor William] Carroll, to talk to the Cherokees of removal" (Starkey 1946, 122). The act was
intended to dispel Cherokee illusions.

The Indian Removal Act was directed at the Five "Civilized" Tribes
still located in the southeastern part of the United States—the Cherokees, Creeks, Choctaws, Chickasaws, and Seminoles (a group that had
split from the Creek Confederacy in the late 1700s and had moved into the
Florida swamps, evolving through the years to be regarded as a separate
tribe)—since this was one of the last regions of the eastern United States
where tribes had not yet been removed to the west. In 1827, one of the
Five Tribes, the Creek Confederacy, had already been forcibly ousted from
Georgia (although still present in Alabama), largely as a result of what
many Creeks regarded as a treasonous betrayal by some of their leaders
in signing a removal treaty with the United States against the will of the
majority of the Creek Council and people. And in 1830, as the Congress

contemplated the Indian Removal Act, the Choctaws—amidst much internal controversy—had also signed the Treaty of Dancing Rabbit Creek, acquiescing to their removal to the same territory in the west, which was undertaken in 1831–1832.

But even in this legislation, Indian removal was not forced. The act made it clear that a legal *exchange* of lands would take place by treaty—in short, with agreement from the tribes. If the tribes would agree to relinquish their southeastern lands, they would receive lands to the west of the Mississippi River in an exchange. The act required that the titles of other more western tribes must have been legally extinguished before the easterners were moved in, and that the lands not be claimed by an existing territory or state. From the tribal perspective, Section Three of the act was the most important article. It stated

> that in the making of any such exchange or exchanges . . . the United States shall secure and guaranty to [the tribe or nation], and to their heirs or successors, the country so exchanged with them; and if they prefer it, that the United States will cause a patent or grant to be made and executed to them for the same.[3]

This section gave to any tribe making an exchange a "fee simple" patent or private property ownership of their new lands in the Indian Territory, rather than the land being held in a legal trust for them by the United States, as was the "reservation" landholding status of most other tribes throughout the 1800s. Section Four promised compensation to individual tribal members for improvements and possessions left behind, and Section Five promised to pay for the expenses of removal and to provide support for the tribe for one year after its arrival in the west. Section Six promised protection from intrusion into their new lands by outsiders, and Section Seven continued the federal superintendency of tribes through Indian agents, but also validated the continuing existence of tribal treaty rights that had not been annulled.

Many legislators thought it more than a fair offer to the tribes. But tribal response, predictably, was cold. By what right, they demanded, did the United States move a people from their homelands—lands that had been occupied for centuries, if not millennia, before the United States had even come into existence? Although the Creeks and Choctaws had already succumbed to the removal policy, largely due to what many regarded as treacherous betrayals by some of their own leaders, the Cherokees were determined to fight with all their skills any efforts by the United States to take their remaining lands and remove them to the west.

Regarding the proposed legislation as consenting to aggressive states' rights assertions on the part of Georgia, whose state harassment laws appeared to violate the federal constitution and laws, some legislators rejected the Indian Removal Act on the grounds of defending a strongly federalist position. Although Indian rights were not the primary concern of these Congressmen, the Cherokees nevertheless cultivated alliances with them out of a common goal—the defeat of the legislation—even though the rationales for wanting that defeat differed. Most representatives from the more northern states, particularly in New England, were strong federalists, accurately reflecting the sentiments of their constituents. The Cherokees made alliances with these representatives and lobbied alongside them to persuade the votes of still others.

Although the defense of federalism may have been the primary motivation for many of the Congressmen, some others held genuine concern for justice and the rights of the Indians. In eloquent speeches made during the congressional debates, prominent senators and representatives—such as Peleg Sprague of Maine, who quoted Shakespeare; Theodore Frelinghuysen of New Jersey, who opined for three days; and David Crockett—defended Cherokee interests. Crockett, in particular, as a Tennessean, based his stance in opposition to the bill as a defense of human rights, regarding the act as a cruel and unjust measure. Vocal and sincere in his messages to his colleagues in the Congress, Crockett's call to morality undoubtedly caused discomfort and irritation in those who promoted Indian removal as a benevolent policy. His constituents in Tennessee were especially unforgiving of his integrity and voted him out of office at the next election. Even though they returned him to Congress a few years later, Crockett continued to challenge them to a higher standard, and they removed him again for the last time in 1836, precipitating Crockett's departure to Texas and, ultimately, his demise at the Alamo by the end of that year.

The Cherokee cause was supported on humanitarian grounds by still others. In general, the greater numbers of more politically liberal and reform-minded people in the North opposed the act and directed their representatives to shun it. Additionally, many of the governing boards of the missionaries and their societies who worked among the Cherokees were located in New England. Most prominently, the ABCFM and one of their leaders, Jeremiah Evarts, were strong opponents of the policy and the Indian Removal Act that represented it. Evarts, who wrote a series of anti-Jacksonian essays under the pseudonym of "William Penn," was particularly vocal in his condemnation of removal policy. He uncompromisingly defined the issue as an abrogation of national morality, stating

> Foreign nations should be well aware, that the People of the United States are ready to take the ground of fulfilling their contracts so long only, as they can be overawed by physical force; that we as a nation, are ready to avow, that we can be restrained from justice by fear alone; not the fear of God, which is a most ennobling and purifying principle; not the fear of sacrificing national character, in the estimation of good and wise men in every country, and through all future time; not the fear of present shame and public scorn; but simply, and only, the fear of bayonets and cannon.[4]

But some of the most eloquent opposition came from the Cherokees themselves, especially the editor of the *Cherokee Phoenix*, the newspaper they had established in 1828, and which was becoming one of the Cherokees' most effective tools for lobbying their cause. As editor, Elias Boudinot was powerful and persuasive in articulating the Cherokees' position. In regard to the Indian Removal Act, Boudinot, like Evarts, equated its passage with the violation of national morality, as well as the law itself. Upon its passage by the Senate, he wrote

> It has been a matter of doubt with us for some time, whether there would be sufficient virtue and independence in the two houses of Congress, to sustain the plighted fate of the Republic, which has been most palpably sacrificed by the convenience of the Executive. Our doubts are now at an end—the August Senate of the United States of America (tell it not in Gath, publish it not in the streets of Askelon) has followed the heels of the President, and deliberately laid aside their treaties. They have declared they will not be governed by these solemn instruments, made and ratified by their advice and consent.[5]

Some analysts have recognized the Indian Removal Act as one of the most controversial pieces of legislation in the first half of the 1800s, and its debate was punctuated in defense of the Indians by some of the most soaring rhetoric yet known in American politics. Ultimately, it was for naught, but not without a very close call for Jackson and his supporters in Congress. As the commitments were being assessed in the days before the vote, the House of Representatives was evenly split and it appeared the vote was a 99–99 tie, resulting in the overall defeat of the bill. President Jackson, in

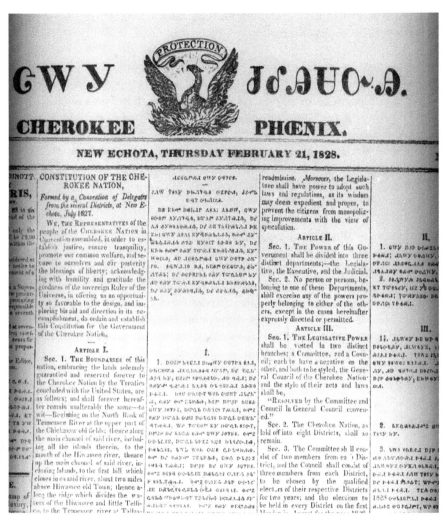

Front page of the first edition of the *Cherokee Phoenix*, published in 1828, New Echota Historic Site, Calhoun, Georgia. (Courtesy of the Georgia Department of Natural Resources—State Parks and Historic Sites Division)

the last moments, struck some deals with a few of the recalcitrant legislators. In the end, the bill passed in the Senate by a 28–19 margin, split along straight party lines, with Jacksonian Democrats voting for it and Whigs (the opposing party) against it. In the House of Representatives, the previous 99–99 tie (and a few undecided) had shifted however, and ultimately, the bill was passed by a 102–97 vote. Jackson had been successful in pressuring several representatives to change their votes. The Indian Removal Act had passed and federal policy was now federal law. But the vote had also revealed deep divisions within the American society on the questions of not only federal Indian policy, but in particular the tensions between federalism and states' rights. The vote reflected a split that erupted 30 years later into the American Civil War.

Although the bill had passed, the Cherokees and other impacted tribes were not inclined to simply acquiesce to the bill's provisions and its assumptions of the inevitability of their removal. Boudinot's rhetoric was now inspirational to his countrypeople as well.

> Let then the Cherokees be *firm* and *united*—Fellow citizens, we have asserted our rights, we have defended them thus far, and we will defend them yet by all lawful and peaceable means.—We will no more beg, pray and implore; but we will *demand* justice, and before we give up and allow ourselves to despondency we will, if we can, have the solemn adjudication of a tribunal, whose province is to interpret the treaties, *the supreme law of the land*. Let us then be *firm* and *united*.[6]

The Cherokees and their allies had conducted a tremendous lobbying campaign to defeat the bill, and despite its passage, the campaigns against the policy continued. Although the lobbying of Congress was pointless for the moment, the maintenance and strengthening of relationships with American supporters was critical to an ongoing resistance. The Cherokees continued to cultivate the support networks and combined that effort with a public opinion campaign. Believing it was vital that the American public be educated to the policy of Indian removal, the Cherokees had for some time employed their resources, both material and human, to that educational process.

The Cherokee approach was two-pronged. First, the young nationalist advocates of the Cherokee Nation, John Ridge and Elias Boudinot, were employed strategically by the National Council and the mission societies. Sent on speaking tours in regions of the country where the Cherokees could expect to receive and build support, Ridge and Boudinot were the featured orators at lectures and town hall meetings throughout New England. They likewise deepened, along with other representatives of the Cherokee government, their relationships with supportive politicians in Washington, D.C. These efforts were extremely productive for the

Cherokees in a number of ways. Not only was their case made in a rhetorical manner that appealed to the politically influential urban middle classes of Americans, the fact that it was delivered by Cherokees who were entirely Indian in their physical appearance while obviously very educated and refined in their dress, vocabulary, and mannerisms served to convince many whites that Indians could not only think and write, but also speak for themselves.

The tactical use of the *Cherokee Phoenix* was also of importance. As a bilingual newspaper, it could reach even wider audiences than the young Cherokee men, and the Cherokees began to produce the paper in increasing quantity. Just as American audiences had been impressed with not only the Cherokees' message, but also the eloquence of its messengers, Ridge and Boudinot, the *Cherokee Phoenix*, the first newspaper ever to be printed by an Indian nation, delivered additional messages about the nature of the Cherokee language and literacy. At a time when Indian languages were believed to be primitive and incapable of complex expressions, the articles and essays in the *Cherokee Phoenix* served to dispel such attitudes. By distributing it in Washington, D.C. and the major population centers of the north, as well as to foreign governments, the Cherokees hoped that others would apply pressure on the United States as well. The strategy worked on many levels. Great Britain, somewhat ironically, protested the policy of the United States in removing Indians from their homelands. And it was a great triumph for editor Boudinot when his editorials began to be reprinted by major newspapers in Boston, Philadelphia, and New York, providing an even greater audience for the critical arguments in support of Indian national sovereignty, who also lobbied their congressional representatives.

But the *Cherokee Phoenix* was primarily distributed, of course, among the Cherokees themselves, since as much as 90 percent of the Cherokee population was by then able to read its articles printed in the Cherokee syllabary. Although "it did not present all of its reading matter in parallel English and Cherokee texts, but only a relatively small percentage of it" (Kilpatrick and Kilpatrick 1968, 3), the *Phoenix* was nevertheless instrumental in keeping the Cherokee citizenry well-informed about the actions of their leadership in Washington, D.C., resulting in a very educated and unified population in resistance to removal and holding full faith and confidence in their leaders to oppose the policy.

The Cherokees conceived still other responses to federal and state actions. Throughout most of the 1820s, they had been considering a possible action in federal court to define their rights. A Supreme Court decision in

Recreation of the interior of the *Cherokee Phoenix* printing office, New Echota Historic Site, Calhoun, Georgia. (Courtesy of the Georgia Department of Natural Resources—State Parks and Historic Sites Division)

1823 in a case called *Johnson v. McIntosh* had been of particular concern. In that decision, Chief Justice John Marshall had upheld the European Doctrine of Discovery, which gave a supremacy of claim to purchase Indian lands to the "discovering" European nation and "had been a convention of intra-European diplomacy that was intended to keep colonial powers from making overlapping land claims" (Norgren 2004, 56), as also applicable to American titles to Indian lands. Ultimately, the court had ruled that, although Indians clearly had long-standing usufruct rights to their lands, which it characterized as "occupancy" rights, since they could not actually produce a deed or document of title, full title or "fee simple" ownership rested with the United States as the only entity who could take possession of Indian lands upon their relinquishment. Although the specifics of the case concerned the transfer of Indian lands to an individual (as was also denied under federal law in the Trade and Intercourse Acts of the 1790s), the decision strongly implied that no tribe within U.S. boundaries would be regarded as having true land titles.

But as Georgia passed and began to implement its harassment laws, apparently in violation of the Commerce Clause of the Constitution which stated that only Congress could pass regulatory laws regarding affairs with the Indian nations, the Cherokees began to wonder if even their jurisdiction within territory over which they clearly held at least occupancy rights, according to the court's 1823 decision, would be upheld. Yet, the process of entering federal court to test and establish the fullness of their jurisdiction was difficult. First, it would require an action that implied the Cherokees' larger grievance, and that the action and its implication were strong enough to carry through a lengthy court battle. Second, it was expensive, and finding attorneys who were skilled enough and willing to take a case if the plaintiff was unable to pay them accordingly would be difficult. To that date, the Cherokees had found neither the circumstances nor the resources to carry into court.

But in 1829, shortly after Georgia enacted its new laws, a murder occurred in the Cherokee Nation. A Cherokee man named George Tassels, sometimes known also as Corn Tassels or George Corn Tassels, was accused of murdering another Cherokee. The killing had taken place within the boundaries of the Cherokee Nation and the Cherokee Lighthorse, the nation's law enforcement unit, had arrested Corn Tassels. But as they were holding him for trial, the Georgia Guard, the vigilante force recently established under Georgia's Harassment Laws, forcibly kidnapped Corn Tassels from the Cherokees, removed him from Cherokee Nation boundaries, and ultimately placed him on trial in a state court. In 1829, the case was entitled *Georgia v. Corn Tassels*.

As expected, Georgia found Corn Tassels guilty and sentenced him to be hanged. But the Cherokees had managed to engage an attorney, not to defend Corn Tassels, but in anticipation that Georgia would act in a fashion that might give the Cherokees just what they needed to approach the federal court with a strong case. Although funds were a problem, they convinced two attorneys who were sympathetic and interested in the issue to take up the Cherokees' cause. The lead attorney was William Wirt, the former attorney general of the United States under Presidents James Monroe and John Quincy Adams. He was assisted by John Sergeant, a former member of the House of Representatives. Both were strong federalists and anti-Jacksonians.

Upon Corn Tassels's sentencing by the Georgia state court, one of Wirt's first actions was to file a writ of error with the federal court. Contending that Georgia's prosecution of Corn Tassels was in error as the state had no jurisdiction under federal law, the writ included a request for a stay of execution of Corn Tassels by the federal court. In December 1830, the Supreme Court granted the writ. "But Georgia, to show her contempt for federal interference, in state affairs, ignored the summons and expedited Tassel's execution" (Woodward 1963, 164). Georgia had hoped to render Wirt's effort irrelevant, but the implications of the case were not about Corn Tassels's crime, but about Georgia's lack of jurisdiction within Cherokee territory, and Wirt continued his preparation of the case. In March 1831, it was accepted by the U.S. Supreme Court and is known as *Cherokee Nation v. Georgia*.

Wirt's first challenge was to establish to the court that they had "original jurisdiction," meaning that they were properly the first level of federal court to hear the case. This was difficult as most cases in federal courts work through lower levels of district and appellate courts before ever reaching the Supreme Court. Wirt sought a way to take the case directly to the Supreme Court where there were indications that some justices were sympathetic to hearing the Cherokees' cause. Out of this necessity, Wirt conceived an innovative, but risky, legal strategy. Under the Constitution, certain kinds of cases will bypass lower levels of courts and be heard directly by the Supreme Court, and Wirt sought to establish that the Cherokees' case was one such instance. Focusing on the fact that original jurisdiction to the Supreme Court exists in cases in which a foreign government is suing a state, Wirt's foundational argument was that the Cherokee Nation was a foreign government. Following this argument, Wirt's argument—should the premise that the Cherokee Nation was a foreign government be accepted by the court—went on to detail the actual merits of his case, essentially stating that Georgia's attempts to extend state law over the Cherokee Nation violated the federal Trade and Intercourse Acts, federal treaties between the United States and the Cherokee Nation, and most importantly, the Commerce Clause of the United States Constitution by usurping Congress's exclusive plenary authority when it passed regulatory laws over the tribes within its borders. Wirt's rationale was thus a strong federalist argument.

On the day of opening arguments, Wirt and Sergeant stood alone in front of the Supreme Court of the United States. Not only had Georgia not bothered to seek an attorney of equal caliber to argue their case, they had not deemed it important to appear at all. Taking a strong states' rights position, Georgia refused to dignify by appearing in federal court what would not be allowed in its own state courts under its harassment laws, since Indians were deemed "incompetent" to testify under Georgia state law. Just as its states' rights assertions had challenged the Congress to find the way to avoid open confrontation between federalist and states' rights advocates, Georgia now posed the same challenge to the federal judiciary.

Congress had avoided the confrontation by passing the Indian Removal Act. The Supreme Court found another method of sidestepping the issue. Although the court could have determined that Georgia was in default by not appearing, Wirt's basic premise—the necessity of first convincing the court that they held original jurisdiction in the case— provided the court with the way to mitigate the potential confrontation over states' rights. In its decision, rendered in January 1831, the Supreme Court determined that

> Though the Indians are acknowledged to have an unquestionable, and, heretofore, unquestioned right to the lands they occupy, until that right is extinguished by a voluntary cession to our government; yet it may well be doubted whether those tribes which reside within the acknowledged boundaries of the United States can, with strict accuracy, be denominated foreign nations. They may, more correctly, be denominated domestic dependent nations. They occupy a territory to which we assert a title independent of their will, which must take effect in point of possession when their right of possession ceases. Meanwhile they are in a state of pupilage. Their relation to the United State resembles that of a ward to his guardian.[7]

In this simple paragraph from the majority opinion, authored by Supreme Court Chief Justice John Marshall, the high court struck down Wirt's basic premise that the Cherokee Nation, and by implication all Indian nations, were "foreign" governments. The mainstay of Marshall's argument was that the treaties, by which many tribes had placed themselves as protectorates of the United States, as well as their physical presence within U.S. borders, nullified any claims to being foreign governments. By denying Wirt's assertion of its own original jurisdiction, the court was thus relieved of considering the actual merits of the case, neatly sidestepping the conflicts between federalist and states' rights arguments. Of the six justices who heard the case, "two concluded that the Cherokee Nation was neither a foreign state nor a sovereign nation and that Cherokee individuals were subjects of the state of Georgia. Two argued that that the Cherokee Nation was sovereign, had standing before the Court as a foreign state, and was entitled to protection against the unconstitutional laws of Georgia. And two, including Chief

Justice John Marshall, decided between the two extremes. The Cherokee Nation lacked standing because it was not a foreign state, but it deserved to be recognized and respected, although as what was not altogether clear, despite Marshall's efforts to describe it" (Perdue and Green 2007, 81). In the end, the Cherokees had lost since four justices had voted to deny the Cherokees' claims to being a "foreign" government.

The dissenting opinion—written by one of the judges in the minority, Justice Smith Thompson, with concurrence by Justice Joseph Story—countered the claims of the majority that treaties and its presence within U.S. borders had invalidated to any extent the Cherokees' inherent sovereignty.

> It is manifest from these cases, that a foreign state, judicially considered, consists of its being under a different jurisdiction or government, without any reference to its territorial position. . . . So far as these states are subject to the laws of the union, they are not foreign to each other. But so far as they are subject to their own respective state laws and government, they are foreign to each other. And if, as here decided, a separate and distinct jurisdiction or government is the test by which to decide whether a nation be foreign or not; I am unable to perceive any sound and substantial reason why the Cherokee Nation should not be so considered. It is governed by its own laws, usages, and customs: it has no connexion [*sic*] with any other government or jurisdiction, except by way of treaties entered into with like form and ceremony as with other foreign nations.[8]

The argument held that Cherokee sovereignty was "inherent," established as an essential aspect of the Cherokee Nation's existence, and that the fact it had entered into treaties with the United States, as had many other "foreign" governments, did not invalidate its original status as a separate governing entity. But the argument in support of Cherokee, and Indian sovereignty generally, was not accepted by the majority on the court.

However, in the language from Justice Marshall's majority opinion, two important concepts were established that formed the cornerstones of federal Indian law ever after. First, in denominating Indian nations as "domestic dependent nations," Marshall and the court had created a new level of law and jurisdiction in the United States. To that date, the descending levels of jurisdiction had been from federal to state (although still challenged by many southern states in particular) to county to municipality. The court's decision made it clear that there was another level of law and jurisdiction in within the country—that held by the Indian tribes. The case had essentially asked the court to determine whether state law applied over tribes, and although the court acknowledged tribal jurisdiction as existing in the creation of a new category called "domestic dependent nations," it did not make a judgment as to where the level of tribal jurisdiction was located, either above or below *any* other level of jurisdiction in the country. Thus, the category was created but its parameters were left completely undefined, at least in this case. Federal courts continue to refine the meaning of "domestic dependent nations" to the present day.

Additionally, the *Cherokee Nation v. Georgia* case established the federal trusteeship over the Indian nations within its borders. When Chief Justice Marshall stated that the relationship between the tribes and the United States was that of a ward to its guardian, another cornerstone of federal Indian law was created. Defined by federal courts as a "trust responsibility" that the United States holds to the tribes, the guardianship has included special federal assistance to tribes and their citizens in health, education, housing, and many other programs. The trust responsibility exists as an exchange for the taking of their lands and the losses of the means of subsistence and independence that resulted.[9]

The Cherokees had lost their case on a legal technicality, but the central question of the case—whether state laws applied over the tribes within them—had not been considered. There was still a possibility to bring a case to federal court, but it would require a different legal strategy. As the Cherokees and their attorneys began to contemplate a new approach, Georgia again acted on its harassment laws. In sections of the 1830 law, Georgia had required all white citizens of the United States who were working within the Cherokee Nation to swear allegiance to Georgia and to be licensed by the state before beginning their employment among the Cherokees. These sections of the law had been aimed at missionaries in particular, as the state believed some of them were encouraging Cherokee resistance, as indeed they were. Upon the passage of the laws, many missionaries simply moved out of Georgia and into the other three states within which the Cherokee Nation was also located—Alabama, Tennessee, and North Carolina. But the ABCFM and its dozen missionaries who worked within the limits of Georgia instead wrote to their governing board in New England for guidance. Was it the board's desire that the missionaries move their missions out of state, or that they swear the allegiance to Georgia and procure licenses, or that they continue to missionize within Georgia without seeking the licenses now required by the state? The board had little to offer in the way of guidance. Do what you think is best, they replied.

In this moment of delay, as the missionaries sought guidance, Georgia acted. In the spring and summer of 1831, Georgia arrested 11 ABCFM missionaries and by September, had tried and sentenced them to 4 years at hard labor. At this point, "there was no want of support from the American Board as to the stand its missionaries had taken. Indeed, letters from the Board reveal something of a rejoicing in the fact that events had reached the point of imprisonment. The time was ripe for a martyr to appear" (Bass 1936, 139). Jeremiah Evarts seemed particularly gratified by the missionaries' apparent martyrdom, as he had virtually sought it from one of them in an earlier letter. But much to Georgia's relief, as it now found itself in a national public relations quandary by having arrested and imprisoned men of God, nine of the missionaries also lost their will, sought the licenses, and accepted pardons from the state. But unfortunately for Georgia, two of the missionaries, Reverend Samuel Worcester and Dr. Elizur Butler (who was a physician as well), refused the pardons and forced the state to imprison them, hoping to further the Cherokees' cause by doing so. "The loyal support given by the American Board to the [Cherokee] nation's interests had transformed the previous coolness toward it into warm admiration. Cherokees sent letters to Worcester and [Butler] at the prison, donated money to provide them with comforts, and . . . feelings toward the American Board . . . were now extremely positive. The audacity of the Georgians seemed at last to have played into the hands of their most determined opponents" (McLoughlin 1995, 264).

The Cherokees now had a new case to advance into federal court. Although they would not be a named party to it, since the missionaries would stand as the plaintiffs, the questions were nevertheless the same. Could the state of Georgia assert its own sovereignty and jurisdiction into a tribal nation's territory? Could a state pass regulatory laws over a tribe within its borders? Could a state take territory from a tribe without the intercedence of the United States? The missionaries retained William Wirt and John Sergeant again, who were delighted with their plaintiffs, men with whom Americans would have a great deal of sympathy. In February 1832, *Worcester v. Georgia*, the second of what came to be known as The Cherokee Cases (along with *Cherokee Nation v. Georgia*), was entered with the U.S. Supreme Court.

"The Georgia action against the Cherokees was Wirt's great opportunity to return the Cherokees' case to the Marshall court. Although it was not clearly a property rights question, Marshall used the case of *Worcester v. Georgia* as a pretext to examine all Cherokee treaties, and in a wide-ranging interpretation observed that the Cherokees never had yielded their sovereignty" (Moulton 1978, 46). The court's decision was rendered remarkably quickly, only a few weeks later. In language that provided yet another cornerstone defining the relationships between the tribes, the federal

The Reverend Samuel A. Worcester, American Board of Commissioners for Foreign Missions, and plaintiff in the *Worcester v. Georgia* case. (Courtesy of Houghton Library, Harvard University)

government, and the states, Chief Justice John Marshall, who also voted in the majority in this case, declared in his written opinion:

> The very fact of repeated treaties with [the Cherokees] recognises [*sic*] [their title to self-government]; and the settled doctrine of the law of nations is, that a weaker power does not surrender its independence— its right to self-government, by associating with a stronger, and taking its protection. A weak state, in order to provide or its safety, may place itself under the protection of one more powerful, without

stripping itself of the right of government and ceasing to be a state. Examples of this kind are not wanting in Europe.[10]

In language that was almost identical to that in a section of Justice Thompson's dissenting opinion from the *Cherokee Nation v. Georgia* case, Marshall had seemingly made much the same argument that had been made by Thompson only a year earlier. Without going so far as to state that the Cherokees were a "foreign" government, Marshall and the majority nevertheless agreed that the Cherokees' rights of territorial sovereignty had not been extinguished simply because they had entered into treaties with the United States and placed themselves as protectorates of that government. In fact, Marshall noted, the existence of treaties actually confirmed the tribe's governmental status, and the historic existence of protectorates in Europe provided a model for the relationship of all Indian nations with the United States.

Marshall's opinion continued:

The Cherokee nation, then, is a distinct community, occupying its own territory, with boundaries accurately described, in which the laws of Georgia can have no force, and which the citizens of Georgia have no right to enter, but with the assent of the Cherokee themselves, or in conformity with treaties, and with the acts of congress. The whole intercourse between the United States and this nation, is, by our constitution and laws, vested in the government of the United States.

The act of the state of Georgia, under which the plaintiff in error was prosecuted, is consequently void and the judgment a nullity.[11]

The missionaries, and by extension the Cherokee Nation, had won! Although legal scholars have argued ever since about Marshall's intentions and the reasons for the apparent shift in his, and the majority's, sentiments, the decision established another seminal concept in federal Indian law. Although the *Cherokee Nation v. Georgia* case had created the jurisdictional category of "domestic dependent nations" that included the tribal governments within the United States, it had left the parameters undefined. Were the tribes jurisdictionally above the state or below it? Above the federal government or below it? Above or below any other level of law and jurisdiction? The *Worcester* case had defined one important parameter in unequivocally stating that, within their own territories, the tribes were (and are) above the state and, at that time by the reasoning of the decision, on a par with the federal government.[12] The tenet that

the tribes hold a status higher than that of states has been another fundamental, but widely misunderstood aspect of tribal sovereignty within the
context of the United States.

For the Cherokee Nation, the import of the decision was immediately
clear. The Georgia Harassment Laws had been struck down by the highest federal court. It perhaps remained unclear as to whether they would
still be required to remove, but if they were, it would be under the terms
of the federal Indian Removal Act, which required a treaty, rather than by
pressure and force resulting from the terrorism of the state of Georgia. Certainly many Cherokees believed that if a treaty was required, there would
be no initiative for it forthcoming from their own leadership. The Cherokee citizenry was entirely united in their opposition to relinquishing their
homelands. Their position appeared to be settled, and their rights to their
remaining territory as secure as they had been for some time.

Certainly the editor of the *Cherokee Phoenix* believed this to be the
case. Writing for his countrypeople in effusive language, Elias Boudinot
called the decision "a great triumph on the part of the Cherokees so far
as the question of their rights were concerned. The question is forever
settled as to who is right and who is wrong. . . . It is not now before
the great state of Georgia and the poor Cherokees, but between the U.S.
and the state of Georgia" (quoted in Wilkins 1986, 235). As word spread
throughout the Cherokee Nation in the weeks after the decision, the eu-
phoria was palpable. "In every community, it seemed, the people celebrated with 'Rejoicings Dances and meetings.' As William Williamson, an
officer in the Georgia Guard stationed in the Cherokee country, reported
to [Georgia] Governor Lumpkin, 'They not only believed that the right of
Jurisdiction was restored but that they were Sovereign independent nation & the U.S. bound by Treaty to afford them protection'" (Perdue and
Green 2007, 88).

There was a sense of vindication on the part of the Cherokees. Over the
past 40 years, their efforts to build a nation, to educate themselves, and to
shift their system of law and government to more closely resemble that
of the United States while still keeping a sense of cultural tradition and
values had not been as much because they desired to be like Americans as
because they desired a way to defend one of their strongest cultural values—their relationships with the land that had been theirs for centuries—
in ways that Americans would understand and respect. As stated by legal
scholar Jill Norgren, "It is the ultimate irony that the Cherokee, only recently described by the *Tassels* court as a people 'incapable of complying
with the obligations which the laws of civilized society imposed,' maintained

their faith in the rule of law—even an enemy's law—and it's promise of justice" (2004, 98). At this moment, with a great victory in the highest court of the United States, it appeared that faith had at last been rewarded.

Notes

1. *Essex Register*, Salem, MA, XXIV, no. 41, Thursday, May 20, 1824.

2. These figures can be approximated from the 1835 Cherokee Census, available from the Oklahoma Chapter of the Trail of Tears Association.

3. See Primary Documents, The Indian Removal Act (1830).

4. William Penn [Jeremiah Evarts], *Essays on the Present Crisis in the Condition of the American Indians* (Boston: Perkins & Marvin, 1829), reprinted by Francis Paul Prucha, ed., *Cherokee Removal: The "William Penn" Essays and Other Writings by Jeremiah Evarts* (Knoxville: University of Tennessee Press, 1981), 49–51, and quoted in John A. Andrew III's *From Revivals to Removal, Jeremiah Evarts, the Cherokee Nation, and the Search for the Soul of America* (Athens: University of Georgia Press, 1992), 187.

5. Elias Boudinot, in the *Cherokee Phoenix*, May 15, 1830. Reprinted in Theda Perdue, ed., *Cherokee Editor, the Writings of Elias Boudinot* (Athens: University of Georgia Press, 1996), 117, 118.

6. Ibid., 118.

7. See Primary Documents, *Cherokee Nation v. Georgia*, majority opinion.

8. Ibid., dissenting opinion.

9. However, the trust responsibility also continues federal oversight of tribes, particularly in the economic realm, for it also requires federal permission for the leasing and sale of tribal lands and allotments, as well as federal management of accounts containing the revenues derived from the lease and sale of lands and resources, including permission of Indian lessors to draw on their own accounts. By the late 20th century, it was discovered that billions of dollars of individual tribal monies were unaccounted for, resulting in a major class action lawsuit against the United States and a multimillion dollar settlement with individual Indian claimants.

10. See Primary Documents, *Worcester v. Georgia*.

11. Ibid.

12. Subsequent federal court decisions have reduced the tribal level of jurisdiction below that of the federal, but still above the state in all but specific instances.

References

Andrew, John A. III. *From Revivals to Removal, Jeremiah Evarts, the Cherokee Nation, and the Search for the Soul of America*. Athens: University of Georgia Press, 1992.

Bass, Althea. *Cherokee Messenger*. Norman: University of Oklahoma Press, 1936.

Carter, Samuel III. *Cherokee Sunset, a Nation Betrayed, a Narrative of Travail and Triumph, Persecution and Exile.* New York: Doubleday, 1976.

Denson, Andrew. *Demanding the Cherokee Nation, Indian Autonomy and American Culture 1830–1900.* Lincoln: University of Nebraska Press, 2004.

Foreman, Grant. *Indian Removal.* Norman: University of Oklahoma Press, 1974.

Gaul, Theresa Strouth. *To Marry and Indian, the Marriage of Harriett Gold & Elias Boudinot in Letters, 1823–1839.* Chapel Hill: University of North Carolina Press, 2005.

Hicks, Brian. *Toward the Setting Sun, John Ross, the Cherokees, and the Trail of Tears.* New York: Atlantic Monthly Press, 2011.

Kilpatrick, Jack Frederick and Anna Gritts Kilpatrick, eds. *New Echota Letters, Contributions of Samuel A. Worcester to the Cherokee Phoenix.* Dallas: Southern Methodist University Press, 1968.

McLoughlin, William G. *Cherokees & Missionaries, 1789–1839.* Norman: University of Oklahoma Press, 1995.

Moulton, Gary. *John Ross, Cherokee Chief.* Athens: University of Georgia Press, 1978.

Norgren, Jill. *The Cherokee Cases, Two Landmark Federal Decisions in the Fight for Sovereignty.* Norman: University of Oklahoma Press, 2004.

Perdue, Theda, ed. *Cherokee Editor, the Writings of Elias Boudinot.* Athens: University of Georgia Press, 1996.

Perdue, Theda and Michael D. Green. *The Cherokee Nation and the Trail of Tears.* New York: Viking Penguin, 2007.

Prucha, Francis Paul. *Cherokee Removal: The "William Penn" Essays and Other Writings by Jeremiah Evarts.* Knoxville: University of Tennessee Press, 1981.

Smith, Daniel Blake. *An American Betrayal, Cherokee Patriots and the Trail of Tears.* New York: Henry Holt and Company, LLC, 2011.

Starkey, Marion. *The Cherokee Nation.* New York: Alfred A. Knopf, 1946.

Strickland, William. "Cherokee Rhetoric: A Forceful Weapon." *The Journal of Cherokee Studies* 2, no. 4 (Fall 1977): 375–84.

Wilkins, Thurman. *Cherokee Tragedy, the Ridge Family and the Decimation of a People.* Norman: University of Oklahoma Press, 1986.

Woodward, Grace Steele. *The Cherokees.* Norman: University of Oklahoma Press, 1963.

FIVE

Betrayal and Division

LEGENDS ARE AN IMPORTANT PART of developing a national character through the telling of story and history. Like all peoples, the Cherokees have notable legends—tales of events that may or may not have actually occurred but that are nevertheless widely believed and retold. Whether or not they are true is perhaps not as important as whether people believe them, or whether they imply a more general truth or reality. In the United States, President Andrew Jackson has inspired many heroic national legends, but there are southeastern Indian nations who also have their legends. Among the Cherokees, the legends about Jackson are significant, reflecting not a hero, but a devil.

As a language that easily lends itself to punning, an ability used widely by fluent Cherokee speakers as a source of amusement, the phonetic pronunciation of the name "Jackson" is adapted in Cherokee as "Tseg'sin." However, the last syllable is too close to a Cherokee word for "devil" (perhaps Satan)—"sgin'"—and the Cherokees could not resist a mutation of Jackson's name into "Tseg'sgin'." Thus, Andrew Jackson became "Jack the Devil" in Cherokee stories. Although retold orally among elder Cherokee traditionalists, the farcical stories about Andrew Jackson have been recorded in writing in only one text thus far. The Tseg'sgin' stories display nothing "of the folk-hero who wins from a position of weakness. Essentially he is unlovable, reprehensible, basically dull. He lucks into some of his greatest victories" (Kilpatrick and Kilpatrick 1995, 99). The Cherokees felt that *they* had been responsible for saving two of Jackson's earlier victories during the War of 1812, and that without those salvations, Jackson would never have had his great victory at New Orleans, would never have been a great American military hero, and would never have been able to launch a political career based on his renown. And yet, their contributions had been denied and even betrayed by Jackson. In these Cherokee

legends told "among the conservatives where one finds Tseg'sgin' stories being exchanged, the name of Andrew Jackson, the man who repaid
Cherokee friendship and valor at Horseshoe Bend with the horrors of the
Trail of Tears, is the symbol of trickery and deceit and of opportunism at
the expense of others" (Kilpatrick and Kilpatrick 1995, 99).

Many American Indian peoples have trickster stories. In these stories, the
central animal character—usually a rabbit, coyote, or raven, depending on
the part of the continent where that particular people is located—undertakes
to win or better himself by deceiving another more simple, honest animal. In
nearly all of the stories, the trickster is himself ultimately undermined, often
by his own cleverness getting the best of him, but sometimes by the persistent integrity of the other animal. These stories teach children and remind
the adult listener of tribal values, reinforcing the beliefs that if the group
holds to their values, their righteousness will prevail in the end. But how do
a people cope with concrete evidence that their rectitude will be ignored
and their victories rendered meaningless? How do a people retain a sense
of power over themselves when all appearances suggest that they are completely without power to impact their situation?

The great victory in the U.S. Supreme Court was the pinnacle of the
efforts of the Cherokees to defend their territory and their political and
cultural sovereignty. Cherokee emotions ran high as word of the victory
spread among the communities. But in Washington, D.C., as John Ridge
and Elias Boudinot sought enforcement of the court's ruling, their senses of
elation quickly evolved to consternation and then doubt that any response
would be forthcoming from the Congress or the executive branch. Upon
finally securing a meeting with President Andrew Jackson, legend states
that Jackson told John Ridge, "Chief Justice Marshall has made his decision, now let *him* enforce it." Although little evidence exists to support that
Jackson ever made the statement, the legend is widely repeated and generally believed to be true. Its truism is in the apparently accurate description of Jackson's sentiment. He would do nothing to enforce the court's
ruling.

Still another legend expresses the sentiment of other Cherokees of the
time. One of the Cherokees who had fought with Jackson at the Battle
of Horseshoe Bend, a man named Junaluska, was reputed to have saved
Jackson's life during the battle. Although there is no evidence that this
actually occurred, certainly many Cherokees believed they had meta-
phorically saved Jackson's "life"—his reputation and aspirations—by
their brave actions that had turned the tide toward an American victory.
Evidence does exist that Junaluska later stated that had he known what
Jackson would turn out to be, he would have killed the man himself at the

fated battle. The sense that Cherokees had once held the power to impact their destiny was still displayed in this reaction, but the statement also evidences regret and a sense that their own empowerment was slipping from them.

But President Andrew Jackson's greatest betrayal of the Cherokees was yet to come, and when it did, the everyday Cherokee person was left without any ability to understand it within their own moral code. In their world, a victory—whether in stickball or in the Supreme Court— was the final decision. A debt, even if incurred decades ago at Horseshoe Bend, was still to be honored. For many Cherokees, there was no understanding of this man. The Tseg'sgin' stories emerged perhaps as a coping mechanism for the everyday Cherokee person. The stories are notable in that the crafty Tseg'sgin' always wins. Unlike other trickster stories, he is never undone by his own wiliness, and he is never defeated by the persistent integrity of honest creatures. While most of the stories are longer and more complex, one of the simplest is ultimately flat, as is the feeling of resignation in the face of injustice. In this version, the Cherokees may be regarded as a metaphorical "rich man." Recorded by Jack and Anna Gritts Kilpatrick as told by a Cherokee individual in North Carolina named Dalala,

> Tseg'sgin' has a racehorse. There was a rich man who also had a racehorse. They agreed to have a race and bet on it.
>
> When the day for the race came, Tseg'sgin' dug a hole in the road over which they were going to race. He dug the hole very deep.
>
> When they raced, the rich man fell into the hole, and Tseg'sgin' ran on and won the race.
>
> That's all. (1995, 100)

＊＊＊＊＊＊＊＊＊＊＊＊＊

John Ridge and Elias Boudinot were engaged in their continuing campaign to raise funds and awareness in New England when they received news of the missionaries' victory in the Supreme Court. Traveling immediately to Washington, they were well-received by those senators who had supported the Cherokees' cause. Meeting up in the capital with two other Cherokee leaders, William Shorey Coody (Chief Ross's nephew) and National Treasurer John Martin, Ridge and Boudinot, who may have been encouraged at first by the reactions of their friends in Congress, became increasingly concerned as days and then weeks passed without any action on the part of the federal government. It appeared that despite the great victory, there was, in fact, nothing in American law at that time to actually compel any branch of government to adhere to a Supreme Court decision, certainly nothing compelling the use of force if necessary.

Upon arriving in Washington, Ridge had sought a meeting with President Jackson, which was granted. Armed with questions and suggestions regarding enforcement of the decision and release of the missionaries, as well as requests for federal troops to protect the Cherokees from the harassment of state militias in Georgia and Alabama, Ridge may have been encouraged when President Jackson greeted him with a warm handshake and congratulations on the great victory. But he was undoubtedly badly taken aback when, in the next breath, the president urged him to return home and prepare his people to move to the west. Protesting that their victory in the Supreme Court precluded them from having to make any such plans, Ridge was becoming increasingly aware that the president did not intend to change anything about his policies or actions in regard to Indian removals. Although there is little evidence to support that Jackson ever stated (as legend has it), "John Marshall has made his opinion, now let *him* enforce it," it was becoming quite clear that Jackson indeed held this attitude, which many interpreted as contempt for the highest court. In fact, in private, he had already conveyed to Georgia officials that he would do nothing, thus encouraging Georgia's continuing defiance of federal law and jurisdiction.

The Cherokees were able to secure another significant meeting, this time with Justice John McLean of the Supreme Court. McLean had voted in their favor, but had not signed on to the arguments in Chief Justice Marshall's majority opinion, which strongly supported Indian sovereignty, albeit a "dependent" sovereignty. Instead, in an opinion of concurrence, McLean had stated a more strictly federalist rationale for his opinion that the missionaries had been improperly prosecuted. Limiting his arguments only to the Georgia laws and the missionaries' imprisonment, McLean reasoned that indeed federal laws and the U.S. Constitution had been violated. But he did not go so far as to make broader statements upholding Indian sovereignty, as the other justices in the majority had. McLean, in fact, felt that Indian sovereignty was doomed, and in the meeting with the Cherokee delegation, he said as much to them, urging them to negotiate a strong treaty, accept land in fee simple as offered by the Indian Removal Act, and establish a delegate to Congress as a means of furthering their future interests—interests he saw as now lying in the west.

Even more devastating to the Cherokees, however, than McLean's admonitions were those of Senator Theodore Frelinghuysen of New Jersey.

A long supporter of the Cherokees' resistance, Frelinghuysen wrote to the missionaries' board of directors and also expressed his encouragement of Cherokee removal. Although still considering that Indian removal was a tragedy, Frelinghuysen regarded it as "naïve" on the part of the Cherokees to believe that they might prevail through further resistance.

As legislators in Washington who had worked adamantly alongside the Cherokees for several years began to desert the struggle in the face of non-enforcement of the Supreme Court decision, even Worcester and Butler's attorney in their original case in the state court, Elisha Chester, relinquished the fight and urged his clients to do so as well. With support dissipating in all quarters, Ridge and Boudinot seemed to be confronting doubts of their own. Had they indeed been naïve to believe that Cherokee rights might be upheld in the American courts? That a president would follow his own constitutional requirements? That their people and their governmental sovereignty could find respect and exist alongside those who seemed determined to take their homes and their land, through acts of terror if necessary? Several months after the court's decision, with no movement on the part of federal or state entities to release the missionaries, nor deploy federal troops to protect Cherokee rights and lands, not to mention protect their personal physical well-being, the Cherokee delegation at last left Washington, disillusioned in their belief that an Indian nation and people could find justice in American political systems. None had given up on the hope of an intact Cherokee Nation, culture, and society. However, Ridge and Boudinot had come to believe that it would not be possible to preserve their people in their homelands in the American south.

John Ridge and Elias Boudinot, young men who from their childhood had developed identities as strong Cherokee nationalists as well as the training and resources to believe that they would be among those who would bring the Cherokee Nation into full fruition, now found themselves in the extremely unsettling position of advocating a final cession of land and the removal of their people to the west. In an earlier generation, actions such as these had caused Major Ridge (their father and uncle, respectively) to kill Doublehead, as they well knew. But as the most prominent member of the National Council, the senior Ridge's support for the change in position would be critical to convincing Cherokees to turn in a different direction. It would also place him at odds with his protégé, John Ross, now the principal chief of their nation. As they returned home, the younger Ridge and Boudinot surely contemplated the daunting task ahead of persuading John's father to change his opposition to land cession—opposition he had maintained for decades.

Elias Boudinot, editor of the *Cherokee Phoenix*. (Courtesy of the Research Division, Oklahoma Historical Society)

However, the elder Ridge also had great regard for his son's education and experience in dealing with federal officials. Ridge also knew that he had "dedicated [his son] to the service of the people, an understanding [John] had never evaded, no matter how strong his personal ambition. . . . What mattered the most was the Cherokee people, a consideration always at the back of his mind; they could not be allowed to perish" (Wilkins 1986, 237). Although it was not easy, and John Ridge and Boudinot were questioned extensively by Major Ridge, the senior Ridge was ultimately convinced of the futility of the cause. He and his son now began to advocate a new policy among their colleagues on the National Council. Seeing no future in their southeastern homelands for either their nation or their people, the Ridges argued that the Cherokee Nation must now envision its existence in another place and that the Cherokee people must leave behind the lands they had known for a millennium, the small farms and communities that had sustained their lives, and even the graves of their ancestors in order to begin again in an unknown land far to the west—a direction that was symbolically associated with death in Cherokee cosmology.

Elias Boudinot, as editor of the *Cherokee Phoenix*, knew that their change of heart would not be understood or welcomed, and that the majority of the Cherokee people would have great difficulty entertaining the idea of leaving the homelands behind. He sought permission from the National Council, since the Cherokee government funded and directed the newspaper, to print editorials explaining the rationale for removing and why the political climate in Washington now had turned against the Cherokees, despite the great victory in the Supreme Court, which he had himself touted to the Cherokees only a few months earlier as the resolution of their problems.

But the National Council and Principal Chief John Ross forbade Boudinot from publishing any editorials expressing pro-removal arguments. Fearing that the eloquence Boudinot had so often employed to persuade others to their cause would now be equally potent in persuading some Cherokees to desert the continuing effort, Ross and the council asserted that the Cherokee Nation could not risk the people becoming divided in their response to federal and state pressures to remove. "In prohibiting dissent, Ross expressed the traditional Cherokee approach to political disputes. Originally, the Cherokees arrived at decisions through consensus, and anyone who could not agree simply withdrew so the groups could present a united front. Since the Cherokees overwhelmingly opposed removal, Boudinot and other proremoval Cherokees should have withdrawn and maintained silence, according to traditional Cherokees ethics" (Perdue 1996, 26). In protest, Boudinot resigned the editorship. In his place, the council established Elijah Hicks, an in-law of John Ross's, as editor, but increasing pressures from Georgia soon rendered the newspaper inoperable and by 1834, without Boudinot's strong guiding hand, the *Cherokee Phoenix* ceased publishing.

With rifts now beginning to appear in the unity of the Cherokees, Georgia's actions also contributed to growing internal division. As weeks and then months passed without any federal response to the Supreme Court's decision, state officials quickly understood, as Jackson had informed them, that they had a free hand in the situation. Georgia openly defied the Supreme Court's ruling by refusing to release the imprisoned missionaries, as it had been directed by the court. As the months passed in 1832, the Reverends Samuel Worcester and Elizur Butler began to despair of being freed. Nevertheless, they held firm in their resolve not to accept pardons from the state, as the court had ruled they had done nothing improper for which to be pardoned. But as the stalemate dragged on, other national events conspired to undermine the missionaries' strong stances.

One of the Cherokees' supporters in Congress, Senator Henry Clay, had challenged Andrew Jackson in the presidential election in the fall of 1832. Although the policy of Indian removal and the Supreme Court's ruling were not among the major campaign topics or Clay's impetus for challenging Jackson, they did receive some passing remarks. Certainly, these issues were of paramount interest to the Cherokees, and the missionaries remained firm in their imprisonment, hopeful of a Clay victory. But Jackson's landslide victory over Clay dashed any prospects for a political solution. And almost immediately following the election, South Carolina took action that thrust the imprisoned missionaries into the spotlight again.

In November 1832, South Carolina passed a nullification ordinance signaling that state's resistance to federal tariff laws that many southern states felt favored northern economic interests. Thus, the states' rights debate that had also impacted the question of the removal of southern tribes continued to rear its head and threaten the unity of the American nation. At their state convention in late November, South Carolina delegates voted to nullify federal taxation within their state. Although President Jackson reacted strongly in opposition to its actions, many of the Cherokees' supporters in Congress, who saw the federalist parallels in opposing the South Carolina nullification laws and opposition to Georgia's Harassment Laws, nevertheless withdrew their promotion for the Cherokees' cause. These legislators, who had been integral to the Cherokees' strategy, "believed that if the missionaries should persevere in their suit, and the Supreme Court of the United States should attempt to enforce its decision in their favor, Georgia would join the nullifiers and that Alabama and Mississippi where unconstitutional laws had been enacted, would follow the example; then there would be four contiguous states leagued together to resist the general Government by force" (Walker 1993, 292, 293). Secession from the union had even been mentioned.

Still others took the opportunity to pressure the missionaries to "save their country." Employing overblown rhetorical arguments, opponents of the *Worcester* decision also attempted to convince the missionaries that further appeals to the court, which were planned for the early session in 1833, would only exacerbate the sentiments of an already-divided American nation and would perhaps lead to civil war. At first, the Reverends Worcester and Butler resisted the coercion, but as another month wore on and congressional support dissipated, the resolve of the missionaries began to waver. Apparently doubting that the Cherokees would gain much more by continuing with the case, the missionaries advised their attorneys to withdraw the planned appeal. Negotiating with Governor Lumpkin of Georgia to find language that would satisfy both the state's need for the missionaries to acknowledge wrongdoing and the missionaries' desires to avoid doing just that, a letter was drafted that admitted to the state's supreme jurisdiction and only "error" on the part of the missionaries. Worcester and Butler were released in January 1833, and with their freedom, the Cherokees' victorious case also ended "with the legal, but not the political, affirmation of Cherokee rights" (Norgren 2004, 126).

The missionaries, Worcester in particular, had paid a high price for their civil disobedience. During the approximately 18 months they had been imprisoned, an infant daughter, who had been born previous to his incarceration and had always been sickly, had died before her father's release. Although both missionaries composed a letter to the Cherokee Nation and its people in explanation of their capitulation, their conducts afterward were the greatest contributors to the reactions to them on the part of the Cherokee people. Worcester, who had developed a deep friendship with Elias Boudinot prior to his incarceration, maintained that friendship and, like Boudinot, began to support removal of the Cherokee people. His changed sentiments were intuited and "he who had dared so much for this people was now perceptibly less popular than before he had done anything at all. No one said anything to him directly; but his flock, silent, unreproaching, turned inscrutable eyes away from him, as from a leader whose courage had not been equal to the final test, a shepherd who had strayed from his sheep. Sometimes when he held a meeting only strangers came to hear him; people who knew him kept away" (Starkey 1946, 208, 209). But in the end, his close friendship with Boudinot may have been the true reason the Cherokees turned away from Worcester, despite his sacrifices for their cause.

Elizur Butler, in contrast, remained aligned with the Ross Party, named after the principal chief, and representing the overwhelming majority of the Cherokee people still profoundly resistant to removal from their homelands. When he "heard Worcester urge Boudinot to promote removal in 1833, was so angry at this that he reported it to others as a gross betrayal of the Cherokees" (McLoughlin 1995, 313). Becoming more consciously activistic in the years after his release, his reputation was also elevated among the Cherokees when his skills as a physician were put to their benefit during an epidemic of 1838 and along the Trail of Tears. He was one of only four missionaries who actually walked the trail with the Cherokees, sharing their suffering and enjoying their esteem ever after for his sacrifices made alongside them.

The missionaries' sacrifice of the Cherokee cause for the greater good of the American nation appeared, in hindsight, to be unnecessary. In 1833, the former presidential candidate, Senator Henry Clay, negotiated a compromise bill that appeased South Carolina and held off the states' rights conflict for the moment. But the Cherokees' interests were in greater peril than ever, despite their victories. There had been no action to enforce the court's decision in the Worcester case and the nullification crisis had cost them most of their support. After the court cases, there didn't appear to be a real strategy. Andrew Jackson had been reelected and the best the Cherokees seemed to hope for was that they could endure the harassment for another four years and outlast his administration.

With the Jackson administration now firmly entrenched for another four years, Georgia became even more bellicose. Not only did the harassment of the Cherokees continue under Georgia laws, which had been proclaimed void by the Supreme Court, the activities of the state militia, the Georgia Guard, actually increased. Lootings and burnings of Cherokee homes escalated, and by 1833, significant emigrations of Cherokees from the homelands and to the western territory, now being called the "Indian Territory," occurred as a result of state terrorism that had led to the losses of their cabins and fields.

In addition, Georgia had wrestled for several years with questions surrounding what it regarded as *its* new wealth as a result of the discovery of gold. Despite the fact that the gold existed primarily within the Cherokee Nation's boundaries, both Georgia and the United States had made competing claims to it. Within Georgia, the politics surrounding gold also contributed to the escalating attacks on Cherokee sovereignty and property. George Gilmer, the governor at the time of the discovery, favored a measured approach to the riches, including ownership of the mineral resources to the state government, which would then advance the well-being of all the state's citizens by state acquisition of wealth. But in 1831, Gilmer's opponent in his bid for reelection was Wilson Lumpkin, a man who enticed the citizens with promises of disbursements of the wealth directly to individuals, rather than expansion of state-sponsored opportunities for the citizens. "The temptation proved too great for Georgians to overcome. On Oct. 3, 1831, they sold their votes for the promise of Cherokee land and gold, and Wilson Lumpkin became the new governor" (Williams 1993, 51).

In 1832, ignoring the Cherokees' victory that had proclaimed that the lands over which Georgia had asserted its jurisdiction were, in fact, under Cherokee jurisdiction and required their permission for Georgians to enter,

Governor Lumpkin implemented a state lottery of 160-acre parcels of land lying within the Cherokee Nation. Suddenly, every inch of Cherokee territory within the boundaries of Georgia was subject to occupation by the common white men who believed they had "won" it and now owned it. As no treaty had been made by which Cherokees had agreed to relinquish their territory and remove, and as thousands of Cherokees were still occupying their cabins, working their crops, and tending their stock, the Georgia legislature passed laws requiring those lottery winners to wait until the Cherokees had vacated their properties before occupying them, and if a Cherokee vacated before a treaty was made, to pay the Cherokee for his improvements to the property—cabins, outbuildings, and wells. But "legislation protecting Cherokee property rights was worth little more than the paper it was written on. No sooner were the winners told of their good fortune than they rushed to take possession of their prizes without compensation to the previous occupants" (Williams 1993, 56). And by establishing an only woefully inadequate force to patrol the Cherokee territory and expel intruders, state officials—by their nonenforcement of their own state laws—effectively gave permission for private citizens to assert the same powers to remove Cherokees from their homes that they had granted the state militia.

As rough individual frontiersmen and their families now began to appear at Cherokee homesteads, holding a deed in hand stating that they now owned the property and its improvements, Cherokees began to be systematically dispossessed of all their belongings, including their stores of food. While some Cherokees decided to immigrate to the west and start over, many others still refused to give up the fight for the homelands and retreated to the depths of the Smoky and Blue Ridge Mountains, existing in conditions of homelessness and exposure and surviving on what could be gathered from the woods.

Some Cherokees were "allowed" by the new lottery winner to remain in their cabins—for a price. Some Cherokees were "lucky" enough to be able to pay rent on their own homes in order to not be evicted. With Cherokees now coerced into making payments to be exempted from the harassment levied by the Georgia Guard, some lottery winners had discovered that even if they didn't occupy the lands they had received, the parcel could still be a lucrative property for them. Nevertheless, by the mid-1830s, the Cherokees were overrun by lottery winners, prospectors, and speculators. Numbering only about 9,000 within their Georgia lands, the Cherokees were soon overwhelmed by the more than 50,000 Georgians, both white and black, who had poured into their territory.

Among those dispossessed of their homes during the winter of 1832–1833 was Joseph "Rich Joe" Vann, the wealthiest Cherokee of his era. Vann, a plantation owner and slaveholder like his father, resided in an opulent, three-story brick home at Spring Place, Georgia (presently Chatsworth, Georgia). Invaded by the Georgia Guard, the plantation "became a battlefield between two Georgia factions who were engaged in a gunfight over the property. As bullets whizzed back and forth, Vann, his wife, and children trembled for their safety in a room of the home. The family was eventually driven out into the winter snow and cold, fleeing to Tennessee, where they found shelter in a dirt-floored log cabin" (Hoig 1998, 149). Georgians salivated similarly over the homes of other wealthy Cherokees, as well as those of the chiefs of the National Committee and Council, who faced similar dispossessions as did the everyday Cherokee citizen.

The Vann House near Chatsworth, Georgia, was the home of Joseph "Rich Joe" Vann, who was evicted with his family in 1833 by the Georgia Guard. (Photo courtesy of the Georgia Department of Natural Resources—State Parks and Historic Sites Division)

Even the principal chief of the Cherokee Nation, John Ross, was subjected to the harassment of the Georgia Guard and the loss of home and property. In 1835, while he was on official business in Washington, Ross's home at the Head of Coosa (at the confluence of the Etowah and Oostanaula Rivers, presently Rome, Georgia) was also raided by Georgia Guardsmen. His entire family confined to one room of the sumptuous plantation dwelling, all were cast out upon Ross's return. The John Ross family withdrew to southeastern Tennessee and reoccupied an old cabin that had been built by his trader grandfather, John McDonald, and "in a rough-hewed log house of barely two rooms, the chief shared the common sufferings of his people" (Moulton 1978, 62). The Ross family remained at the cabin until their removal three years later.

Two additional wealthy Cherokees, Major Ridge and John Ridge, also resided near the Head of Coosa. As the activities of the Georgia Guard and lottery winners escalated against resistant Cherokees—both the wealthy and subsistence farmers—the homes of the Ridges were not touched. (Both homes are still standing today in Rome, Georgia.) Seen as cooperating and collaborating with the United States to effect the removal of their people, the Georgia Guard demonstrated their approval and sent a strong message to other Cherokees that cooperation would bring relief from state persecution. The exemption of the Ridges and others who were cooperating with federal and state entities promoted increased resentment of their political party and stance, and entrenched the majority of the Cherokees even further in their resistance and their growing distrust of the Ridges.

Principal Chief John Ross's greatest fear, as the persecution of Cherokees increased and the pressures from both state and federal officials mounted, was that some Cherokees, probably from the Ridge Party, would place their signatures on a removal treaty. Ross was well aware of the historic pattern of unscrupulous tribal leaders signing documents of land cession without the consent or agreement of the tribal government, and of the United States commissioners and Senate ratifying such documents. The Ridge Party—one of whose leaders, John Ridge, had devised the legal language of the 1829 Cherokee statute that prohibited cessions of Cherokee land without permission from the entire National Council, and who had written the long-standing death penalty associated with the breaking of the law into Cherokee legal codes—had been unwilling thus far to take that step. But by early 1835, with indications that U.S. commissioners were indeed willing to work with Cherokees who were willing to collaborate, Chief Ross took a delegation to Washington, D.C. While

outward appearances suggested that Ross intended to open treaty negotiations for relinquishment of the remaining Cherokee lands in the east
and removal of the Cherokee people to the Indian Territory, in reality he
was using the negotiation as a stalling tactic. "Ross and his colleagues
were driven to desperation" and "moved ahead with exaggerated propositions" (Moulton 1978, 60). Ross's primary strategy was in asking for ex-
cessive terms and monies in payment for the last 12,316 square miles of
Cherokee territory in the east. Initially asking for $20 million, five years
to prepare, compensation to the nation, and indemnification to individual Cherokees for all losses in violation of former treaties and federal
protection throughout the process, Congress offered merely a flat $5 mil-
lion total. Ross felt the amount was too little, suspecting what was later
demonstrated—that the estimated worth of the gold mines alone was
more than that (they ultimately produced about $6 million in gold). The
Senate's offer was rejected.

Although not part of the delegation, John Ridge had followed the group
to Washington, suspicious of the Ross group's intentions. When Ridge communicated to the U.S. commissioners that there were other Cherokees
in the capital who were amenable to working with them on a treaty, they
"found themselves courted and flattered in contrast with the cool reception
accorded Ross's deputation" (Wilkins 1986, 266). This, of course, had been
Ross's fear, and John Ridge certainly realized the seriousness of the action
he was taking. But although Ridge believed the Cherokees' only hope to
save their nation, culture, and society was in removing, he nevertheless felt
that any treaty made should be a very strong instrument in asserting Cherokee interests and gaining as many concessions from the United States as
possible. He believed that although they would lose their land, the avari-
cious desire of Georgia and the other states to acquire the land, and of the
United States to appease the southern states, placed the Cherokees in a
relatively strong bargaining position to receive favorable terms from the
United States.

Ridge was as concerned as Ross about the possibility that unauthorized Cherokees would enter into a treaty negotiation and would not seek
the most advantageous possible settlement from the United States. Their
fears were real, as only a year earlier they had witnessed an attempt by,
ironically, Andrew Ross, the principal chief's younger brother, to approach
federal commissioners and draft a document that even the Ridges believed
was far too accommodating of U.S. interests without adequately asserting
Cherokee concerns. Fortunately, that document had not been accepted
by the U.S. Senate, and when Ridge contacted federal commissioners

expressing a willingness to enter into a negotiation with them, he was steeled to gain as much as possible for the Cherokees and their nation, and to forestall any further rash attempts by others to offer an ineffectual surrender.

In the winter of 1835, John Ridge and others worked with U.S. commissioners—William Carroll and a Dutch Reform minister, Reverend John Schermerhorn—to fashion a treaty of Cherokee cession and removal. The document they crafted included the bases for many institutions the Cherokees relied on throughout the remainder of the century, as well as a more secure financial base. It envisioned the foundation of a Cherokee republic, a true nation of the sort in which the younger leadership had been raised to invest their emotions and intellects. The Ridge Party accepted $4.5 million in payment for the land, and to allow $150,000 for "spoliations"—claims to property lost or left behind as a result of the forced relocation. These amounts were later increased to $5 million and $300,000, respectively. The treaty also allocated $600,000 to cover the expenses of removing a nation of 18,000 people to the west, initially thought to be a generous offer, but that proved to be entirely inadequate. "In addition, a tract of 800,000 acres of land west of the Mississippi was to be added to the territory already promised them, amounting in the aggregate, including the western outlet, to about 13,800,000 acres" (Royce 2006, 156). Most of this acreage had, in fact, already been ceded to the Cherokee Nation seven years earlier by the 1828 Treaty, and the only additional lands truly received by the treaty were the 800,000 acres in present-day southeastern Kansas, known as the "Neutral Lands."[1]

The treaty also stipulated that, in accordance with the Indian Removal Act of 1830, the new lands would be granted by a fee simple patent, meaning that the Cherokee Nation's ownership of the lands would be recognized in a real-estate sense as private property owned exclusively by the Cherokee national government. This was a particularly significant provision of the treaty as it insured the Cherokees (and the others of the Five Tribes who also held similar patents) a minimum of federal intrusion into the affairs of the Cherokee Nation. Unlike other tribes, for whom "reservations"—properties held in trust by the United States on behalf of the tribe and in which the United States could therefore assert a continuing interest and interference—were being developed, the fee simple lands of the Cherokee Nation would not be in trust to the United States. The United States would have no legal basis by which it could interfere with Cherokee administration of its own land base. It would allow the Cherokees the freedom to develop their economy, society, culture, and their government in the new lands as they wished.[2]

The fifth article of the treaty assured the Cherokees that their lands would never be included within the limits or jurisdiction of a state or territory, and assured them of the greatest possible level of independence of the Cherokee government. The sixth article promised "perpetual peace and friendship" between the United States and the Cherokee Nation, and to protect the Cherokees from intruders who might trespass into their country. The United States promised to remove such intruders, but the article may also have effectively denied the Cherokees the ability to assert their own jurisdiction over citizens of the United States who were trespassing by removing them themselves.[3]

Expanding and making specific the treaty promise contained in the Hopewell document of 1785, the Ridge Party negotiators reaffirmed the Cherokees' right to seat a "deputy to Congress."[4] Updating the language of the 1700s, Article 7 of the Treaty of 1835 "stipulated that [the Cherokee Nation] shall be entitled to a delegate to the House of Representatives of the United States whenever Congress shall make provision for the same."[5] Following the advice of Justice McLean, the Cherokee negotiators were attempting to position the Cherokee Nation to use the federal legislative structure to assert their rights from within.

Endeavoring to secure the financial stability of the nation, which recently had been undermined by the United States' refusal to pay the promised annuities as a method of bankrupting the Cherokee Nation into removal, the Cherokee negotiators proposed another mechanism for funding the nation. In Article 10 of the treaty, they secured from the United States over $400,000 to be invested in three funds for general operational expenses, for orphans, and for schools. The United States would invest in public stocks and would act as the fund manager for what would be permanent investment funds of the Cherokee Nation. In the article, the Cherokee negotiators specified particular projects that would be supported from the interest earned, including orphan asylums, a system of public coeducational instruction, and two "literary institutions of a higher order" within the Cherokee Nation. The high regard for educational attainment that had been developing among the Cherokees of all strata had led to dreams of a national school system and perhaps even a Cherokee university. The negotiators hoped to bring these dreams to fruition via the monetary awards and investments provided in Article 10.[6]

The Ridge Party negotiators also sought to remedy a promise made by Andrew Jackson at Horseshoe Bend that had later been denied. In Article 14 of the treaty, they at last secured the pensions that had been promised to Cherokee veterans who had been wounded at that battle.[7]

While the treaty achieved strong support for reestablishing the Chero-kee Nation in a new land, it was, in the end, a relinquishment of the an-cient homelands and all that they meant to the Cherokees—their identities, spiritual beliefs, and ways of life. In Article 16, the treaty gave the Chero-kees two years from the date of its ratification to pack their belongings and move to the west.[8] The United States, in its justification that removal would be beneficial to the tribes, nevertheless did not wish to wrest the people immediately from their homes. They felt that two years would be adequate time for people to make the physical, psychological, and spiritual adjust-ment to leaving the area they had lived in for centuries and take up life in a strange place.

When the Ridge Party negotiators and the U.S. commissioners, William Carroll and Reverend John Schermerhorn, had completed the draft docu-ment, the question arose as to how to proceed. Knowing the National Coun-cil would not sanction such a document and knowing there was a death

Portrait of John Ridge after an 1825 painting by Charles Bird King. (Courtesy of the Research Division, Oklahoma Historical Society)

sentence awaiting any Cherokee citizen who entered into a treaty of land cession without the council's permission, the challenge to the negotiators was in finding a way to gain public support for the treaty, thus giving it legitimacy and saving their own lives. Feeling that they had been unfairly maligned and that they had never been given the opportunity to fully explain to the Cherokee people why they had shifted their position on the question of Cherokee removal, they sought a way to approach the Cherokee people directly. Elias Boudinot, in particular, whose inspiring rhetoric had been silenced when the National Council prohibited him from editorializing in the *Cherokee Phoenix*, was eager to make the case to the Cherokee people, confident in their intelligence and his own ability to present the arguments to them from the perspective of those most experienced with the political realities of Washington and the federal government. "At this point, and on the advice of Schermerhorn, [John] Ridge tried really revolutionary action. Inasmuch as there had been no election since 1828, Council was unconstitutional in any case. He would go over its head to the people and summon a council of his own" (Starkey 1946, 256).

Throughout the summer of 1835, the Ridge Party and its supporters invited Cherokee citizens to join them in deliberative meetings at John Ridge's home, Running Waters, at the Head of Coosa. Although several meetings were called, few Cherokees attended, except in July and only to vote down a proposed scheme to distribute the national annuity per capita, rather than paying it to the Cherokee government. Even this thinly veiled attempt to bribe the Cherokee people did not dissuade them from their opposition to a removal treaty.

As the year moved into the fall, U.S. commissioners became increasingly frustrated with their inability to move the treaty forward. But they saw another opportunity in the annual meeting of the National Council, which was to be held at Red Clay, Tennessee, in October of the year. Typically, thousands of Cherokees were present for the several weeks, visiting and feasting and listening to the debates and discussion carried out by the legislators, and this year's meeting was no different. At this particular council, Reverend Schermerhorn had a number of proposals to offer to the assembly. He was an unfortunate choice to do so, as by this time he had already irritated the Cherokees, including John Ridge, with his arrogance as well as his propensity to visit the grog shops and womanize. They had already developed a nickname for him: Devil's Horn.

But events did not transpire as Schermerhorn had hoped. The council refused to hear from him and he was only able to present his petitions to an ad hoc committee that had formed. When the votes on his petitions were taken, the committee resoundingly rejected them, including the proposition that they should enter into a removal treaty with the United States. Even John Ridge and Elias Boudinot voted publicly against it. It may be that their vote was "done purely for the effect it created. Both Ridge and Boudinot, aware of the penalty one must pay for participation in the cession of lands without the full consent of the Nation, feared assassination and were, therefore, not courting death while attending Council with Ross' party" (Woodward 1963, 187). Subsequent events indicated that there had been no change of heart on the part of the Ridge Party adherents.

In his most arrogant move yet, Schermerhorn advised the National Council of the Cherokee Nation that he would proceed without their permission to convene a council within their boundaries, at their capital of New Echota, Georgia, in December of that year. Although the Georgia Guard had driven the Cherokee legislature and judiciary out of the state, the commissioner knew that for the Cherokees, the location represented their aspirations for full nationhood and hoped to exploit that sentiment in enticing them to the meeting. At this meeting, the commissioner stated, the treaty would be presented to the Cherokee people for their approval. All Cherokees who were interested in learning and discussing the document should attend, they stated, "and those who did not come they should conclude gave their assent and sanction to whatever should be transacted at this council."[9] With this, Schermerhorn left little, if any room for dissent.

Again, fearing that the December 21 meeting would result in a document illegally signed by unauthorized Cherokees that could be taken to Washington and placed before the Senate for its consideration, Principal Chief Ross assembled another official governmental delegation to the capital in early December. Ross hoped to forestall any consideration of what he considered to be a fraudulent document, negotiated without approval of the National Council, and in violation of Cherokee law and the Constitution, but Schermerhorn and the Ridge's, who had experienced the Chief's delaying tactics earlier in the year, were skeptical. However, the delegation that left with Ross included men of his own political party, but it also represented a final effort to regain a semblance of Cherokee unity. Among those asked by the principal chief to attend were John Ridge and Elias Boudinot. Both had initially accepted the offer, but when Boudinot's wife fell gravely ill, requiring him to remain at home, his younger brother, Stand Watie, was substituted in his place as a delegate. Hoping that their inclusion would result in the treaty meeting at New Echota being cancelled, the group left the Cherokee Nation to travel to the American capital.

However, Schermerhorn was not to be deterred or undermined, and the meeting in New Echota carried on. Although attended by only about 300 people, almost all Ridge Party supporters who favored a removal treaty, the council began on December 21 as those present familiarized themselves with the draft document and as designated representatives made additional refinements. In only a little more than a week, the final version was ready and, on December 29, 1835, was presented to the crowd—a paltry minority within the Cherokee Nation's citizenry—for its approval. Upon its receipt, those designated as signers placed their signatures on the document. Among the 20 men who signed the infamous Treaty of New Echota were Major Ridge and Elias Boudinot. As they signed, legend has it that each stated, "I have just signed my death warrant."

Notes

1. See Primary Documents, Treaty of New Echota.
2. See Primary Documents, Treaty of New Echota.
3. Ibid.
4. See Primary Documents, Treaty of Hopewell, Article 12.
5. See Primary Documents, Treaty of New Echota.
6. Ibid.
7. Ibid.
8. Ibid.
9. See Primary Documents, Treaty of New Echota, preamble.

References

Davis, Kenneth Penn. "Chaos in the Indian Country: The Cherokee Nation 1828–1835." In *The Cherokee Indian Nation, a Troubled History*, edited by Duane King, 129–47. Knoxville: University of Tennessee Press, 1979.

Hoig, Stanley W. *The Cherokees and Their Chiefs, in the Wake of Empire*. Fayetteville: University of Arkansas Press, 1998.

Jahoda, Gloria. "White Bird's Last Stand." In *The Trail of Tears, the Story of American Indian Removals 1813–1855*, Chapter 11, 209–42. New York: Henry Holt & Co., Inc, 1995.

Kilpatrick, Jack and Anna Gritts Kilpatrick. *Friends of Thunder, Folktales of the Oklahoma Cherokees*. Norman: University of Oklahoma Press, 1995.

McLoughlin, William G. *Cherokees and Missionaries, 1789–1839*. Norman: University of Oklahoma Press, 1995.

Moulton, Gary E. *John Ross, Cherokee Chief*. Athens: University of Georgia Press, 1978.

Norgren, Jill. *The Cherokee Cases, Two Landmark Federal Decisions in the Fight for Sovereignty*. Norman: University of Oklahoma Press, 2004.

Perdue, Theda. "The Conflict Within: Cherokees and Removal." In *Cherokee Removal, Before and After*, edited by William L. Anderson, 55–74. Athens: University of Georgia Press, 1991.

Perdue, Theda. *Cherokee Editor, the Writings of Elias Boudinot*. Athens: University of Georgia Press, 1996.

Perdue, Theda and Michael D. Green. *The Cherokee Nation and the Trail of Tears*. New York: Viking Penguin, 2007.

Royce, Charles C. *The Cherokee Nation of Indians* (Fifth Annual Report of the Bureau of Ethnology, Smithsonian Institution, 1883–1884). Whitefish, MT: Kessinger Publishing, 2006 (reprinted).

Starkey, Marion. *The Cherokee Nation*. New York: Alfred A. Knopf, 1946.

Walker, Robert Sparks. *Torchlight to the Cherokees* (1931). Johnson City, TN: Overmountain Press, 1993.

Wilkins, Thurman. *Cherokee Tragedy, the Ridge Family and the Decimation of a People*. Norman: University of Oklahoma Press, 1986.

Williams, David. *The Georgia Gold Rush, Twenty-Niners, Cherokees, and Gold Fever*. Columbia: University of South Carolina Press, 1993.

Woodward, Grace Steele. *The Cherokees*. Norman: University of Oklahoma Press, 1963.

SIX

The Trail Where We Cried

IN HIS LETTER PENNED in May 1838, perhaps on the last evening he would spend in his home at Candy's Creek in Tennessee, the Reverend Steven Foreman, a Cherokee Christian minister and member of the National Council, reflected on the issue of his people's removal from their homelands:

> Indeed, ever since the 23rd of May, we have been looking almost daily for the soldiers to come, and to turn us out of our houses. They have already warned us to make preparations, and to come in to camps, before we were forced to do so. But I have already stated distinctly to some of the officers at Head Quarters, what I thought of this, so called treaty, and what course I intended to persue [*sic*] in the event no new treaty was made, and see no reasons why I should change my mind. My determination, and a determination of a large majority of the Cherokees, yet in the Nation is never to recognize this fraudulent instrument as a treaty, nor remove under it until we are forced to do so at the point of the bayonet. It may seem unwise and hazardous to the fraimers [*sic*] and friends of this instrument, that we should persue such a course, but I am fully satisfied it is the only one we can persue with clear consciences.[1]

Reverend Foreman's sentiments exemplified the Cherokee response to the events of the previous 10 years. In that time, a society that had been peaceful and prosperous, gaining in literacy and education, economic stability, and sophisticated government had experienced the withholding of federal annuities in an attempt to bankrupt the Cherokee government, the passage of state laws that allowed a state-sponsored military force to violently intimidate Cherokee citizens, the ejection of their government from its capital, the quasi-legal occupation of their lands by squatters and lottery "winners," the ignoring of an order of the highest American court, and the sanction of a treaty illegally signed. In those 10 years, there had been ample time for Cherokee citizens to reflect on the conditions of their lives and society and to make decisions about their own actions and reactions. Some had decided to emigrate from their homelands and start fresh in western areas. But many more had determined to stay, to endure the harassment directed at them, and refuse to capitulate in the face of injustice. As with Reverend Foreman, it was a decision made consciously by individual Cherokees across their nation.

"Ethnic cleansing" has been defined as "the planned deliberate removal from a specific territory, persons of a particular ethnic group, by force or intimidation, in order to render that area ethnically homogenous."[2] Another definition states more simply, "The systematic elimination of an ethnic group or groups from a region or society, as by deportation, forced emigration, or genocide."[3] Although some deny that Indian removals met the standard to be called "ethnic cleansing," the federal Indian removal policy was similar enough that it has inspired debates among contemporary scholars and the public, many of whom feel it is valid to apply the term. How do a people react to removal, possibly identified as ethnic cleansing? For those who have not actually experienced such an atrocity, imagination may lead to images of horror and terror on the part of those subjected to it. Fictional or dramatic representations of the Trail of Tears often offer traumatized, screaming victims at the hands of brutal oppressors. But the enactment of ethnic cleansing is often a relatively subdued affair, and those who are subjected to it frequently display a dignity that inspires pride in the human spirit, even as the deed also elicits shame in human actions. In theory, the Cherokees had had years to accept that they would be removed, by force if necessary, from their lands and homes. But how does one actually internalize that as a reality? Even when the moment arrives, can the mind and soul truly grasp what is happening?

The actual recorded responses of Cherokees indicate that they understood very well and were prepared to face the consequences of their resistance, as much as any people could be prepared. In May 1838, federal troops in the Cherokee Nation began to post handbills notifying residents of the various communities of the exact time frame when troops will be in that area collecting people from their homes and moving them into nearby stockades to be held for deportation to the west. Despite being notified of the time of their removal, and thus knowing they had time to flee should they wish to, most Cherokees entrenched themselves in their cabins and went about their daily lives to the extent they still could. Just as Reverend

Foreman would not, for the most part the Cherokee people also did not heed the military's urgings to bring themselves into the stockades, determined to force the military to bring them in. They would not voluntarily relinquish their homes and homeland, and they would not relinquish the higher moral ground they knew they held. Their consciences would be clear.

Rather than reacting in terror and trauma, the actuality of the military roundup of Cherokees from their homes was relatively quiet and dignified on the part of the Cherokees. "One old patriarch, when thus surprised, calmly called his children and grandchildren around him, and kneeling down, bid them pray with him in their own language, while the astonished soldiers looked on in silence. A woman, on finding the house surrounded, went to the door and called up the chickens to be fed for the last time, after which, taking her infant on her back and her two other children by the hand, she followed her husband with the soldiers" (Mooney, quoted in Moulton 1978, 96). Attempting normalcy in the last moments before the world as they had known it was shattered, the Cherokees insisted that their relationships and responsibilities to their Creator and all living things would continue to define their humanity. They would not lessen the impact of their forced removal by collaborating with it, and they hoped that by forcing the military to take them in, that the entire world would see and that future generations would remember the injustice and reflect upon it.

* * * * * * * * * * *

Principal Chief John Ross had arrived in Washington in December 1835 hoping to forestall the signing of an illegal treaty by a handful of Cherokees who were to meet with U.S. commissioners later in the month. But shortly after arriving in Washington, Ross and his delegation received word that the deed was done. Commissioner Schermerhorn and a Cherokee contingent led by Major Ridge would soon be returning to Washington from the Cherokee Nation with a treaty that they intended would be placed in front of the Senate for ratification. With the possibility of further negotiations with the United States now closed, and the stalling strategy now eliminated, the Ross delegation's efforts shifted to discrediting and preventing the passage of the fraudulent treaty.

Two members of the delegation had no desire to participate in its revised goals. John Ridge and his cousin Stand Watie had accompanied the Ross group in a final attempt to regain some degree of unity in the face of a deepening schism within Cherokee leadership. But when members of their party remaining at home followed through in signing a treaty, the younger Ridge and Watie broke with the Ross delegation and, when it arrived in Washington, affixed their signatures to it as well, for a total of 22 signers. Still seeking reconciliation, the "New Echota treaty group sought to involve Ross and his delegation with their efforts, but Ross was bitterly opposed" (Ehle 1988, 296).

Protest of the treaty began by February 1836, as the Senate considered its ratification. The Cherokees returned to their previous supporters among the federalists in Congress and the northern states. Former champions returned to the cause, as did missionary societies and reform-minded Americans. Reports and letters flooded the Congress as officials and citizens began to lobby the Senate once more, just as they had during the debate over the Indian Removal Act. Among the most impressive documents received by the Senate were two petitions signed by thousands of Cherokee citizens. The first, signed by 3,352 residents of the Aquohee and Taquohee political districts of the Cherokee Nation (districts located in Tennessee), appealed to the "august body" to refute the proposed treaty, as it had been made by "persons who are represented as acting in behalf of the Cherokees [who], in this matter, are wholly unauthorized."[4] But the more extraordinary document was a petition circulated among all the people of the Cherokee Nation, stitched together in segments as they had been collected in the various communities and districts. This document contained almost 16,000 signatures, a number greater than the living adult population of the Cherokee Nation. On close inspection, it was noted that the "signatures" of children and infants were contained on the petition, as well as "signatures" of some already deceased. As stated by Starkey, "One visualizes an artless delegate saying to a mother: 'And the baby on your back, have you signed for him? For him it is even more important than for us who have lived our lives. He, too, must sign'" (1946, 271). But although the skeptical "inference in Washington was that so many names could have been collected only by duplication and forgery" (Starkey 1946, 271), the document included as well the signatures of virtually all of the adult citizenry of the nation, excluding the 5–10 percent that comprised the Ridge's Treaty Party adherents. It was an overwhelming testimony to the sentiment of the vast majority of Cherokee citizens.

The Senate was offended that an Indian nation would deign to address it in such a fashion, and the Cherokee attempt to petition the Senate actually rebounded on them, earning a degree of enmity for their cause from some senators. But Cherokee Indians were not the only petitioners some senators chose to ignore. Confidential agents of the War Department, within which Indian Affairs was housed in the early 1800s, also reported widespread Cherokee objection to both the treaty and its signers, as did military personnel in the field.

Although the tactic of persuading (or bribing) a few Indian leaders to sign a document not sanctioned even by the majority of leaders, much less the citizenry, was a proven tactic employed for a century or more by Britain and the United States, the previous decentralized structure of Cherokee government that had lent legitimacy to the ploy was in the past. By this time, the Cherokee Nation government was well-defined by its constitution and statutes and the action of the treaty signers was in clear violation of those governing documents. It was inconceivable that the members of the U.S. Senate in 1838 were unaware of these facts. And if they had been at the outset the months of debate, they could not possibly have remained uninformed by the time of the vote for ratification six months later. The Cherokees' supporters in the Senate repeatedly pointed out the reality, as did government representatives and military officers. But the majority in the Senate chose to ignore the staggering amount of evidence of the facts.

Nevertheless, ratification of a treaty requires more than a simple majority. Two-thirds of the body was required to vote in the affirmative to insure passage, and the Cherokees felt this was a high threshold, one that could possibly be overcome. As the lobbying effort intensified, the Cherokees and their supporters counted the promised votes in opposition to the treaty, including those of two southern senators—Henry Wise of Virginia, who had long been an ally, and Hugh Lawson White of Tennessee. Many of their former supporters from northern states—Senators Clay, Everett, Frelinghuysen, Sprague, Storrs, and Webster—rejoined the cause with vigor as success seemed within reach once again. With the commitments for and against informally tallied, the Cherokees were hopeful that the ratification would fail by a vote or two, if everyone held to the pledges they had made.

But once again, events conspired to go against the Cherokees. In May 1836, the hotly contested and fiercely debated treaty came up for ratification. As Cherokee leaders awaited the vote, their nervousness was increased by the fact that one of the senators who had promised to vote against it was absent due to illness. In itself, this would not result in ratification of the treaty, but it did mean the very slight cushion they had was gone. Now every other member of the Senate who had agreed to vote against would have to keep their promises in order for the Cherokees to succeed in holding the last of their homelands. The vote, taken alphabetically, went much as expected and Cherokee hopes were rising, until one of the last few votes to be tallied, that of Senator White of Tennessee, was not what had been promised. Senator White—although an anti-Jacksonian, perhaps bowing to intense pressure from constituents in a state that had previously removed David Crockett from office for voting against the Indian Removal Act—reversed his commitment to the Cherokees and voted to ratify. In that instant, Cherokee hopes were dashed. Ratification of the Treaty of New Echota, the 1835 removal treaty of the Cherokee Nation, was achieved by a difference of only one vote. Approximately a week later, on May 23, 1836, the treaty was decreed as ratified by President Andrew Jackson.

As with the Creeks and Choctaws before them, the Cherokees, too, were undone by unauthorized individuals among them placing their signatures on a document and the Senate, despite knowing the treaties were not sanctioned by the legitimate leadership or the people, moving forward to ratification. The Cherokees certainly knew that the Creeks and Choctaws had been unable to undo the action, and that each had been removed on brutal marches to the Indian Territory in which each had lost from one quarter to one third of their populations. But the Cherokees differed from the Creeks and Choctaws in that they had employed additional strategies with some degree of success. They had used their newspaper to garner support among sympathetic Americans and they had entered the federal courts and had won. Despite the evidence from former removals of neighboring tribes that had already occurred, the Cherokees still were unwilling to relinquish the fight. Only six months after the treaty's ratification, another presidential election was to take place. By custom, Andrew Jackson would not run again and the Cherokees hoped that with a new president, the tide might turn in their favor. The treaty gave the nation two years to self-remove before they were removed by force, if required. The Cherokees viewed this as two more years in which they could press their cause to a new administration.

Members of the Treaty Party regarded the continuation of the fight as not only futile, but also foolish at that point, and as risking the well-being of the Cherokee people. Twenty-two of them were also aware that, in signing the treaty, they had committed an act that, under Cherokee law, was illegal and carried a death penalty. Having anticipated the acceptance of the treaty by the Senate, many had been preparing to remove (which some hoped would also save their lives), and by late 1836–1838, a number of pro-treaty families—including those of the party's leadership, Major Ridge, John Ridge, Elias Boudinot, and Stand Watie—as well as those who had been "virtually shanghaied or tricked into leaving their homes, . . . lured into migrating by the expense money paid them by the government" (Hoig 1998, 164) left the Cherokee Nation en route to the Cherokee lands in the

Political cartoon of Andrew Jackson, 1832. The Cherokees would have agreed with the expression that Jackson had trampled the U.S. Constitution. (Courtesy of the Library of Congress)

Indian Territory. As some of these families were among the more well-to-do business people and plantation operators among the Cherokees, they also took with them a number of the slaves that had been held by Cherokee families in the nation. In removing as the federal government had intended that all Cherokees would, they were able to take most of their personal property and were accompanied by a military escort for their protection. Traveling in groups of 300–600 each, they experienced some illness and death, but proportionately not as much as was suffered by the majority who traveled later.

As they arrived in the Indian Territory, they were met by the western Cherokees, some descended from the "Chickamaugan" warrior confederation who had moved west as early as 1794, others who had come west in 1809 as a result of the land cessions by chiefs of the Lower Towns, Old Settlers who had moved in 1817–1819 as a result of additional cessions of land, and still other Cherokees who had self-removed throughout the 1820s and particularly the 1830s after harassment had dispossessed them of their homes and property. Throughout the decades, there had been continuous communication and interaction between Cherokees in the east and the Cherokees who had moved west, and for the most part, the Treaty Party were greeted as family. The Western Cherokees had established governing structures of their own and had lived under them for two decades, first in Arkansas and then in the Indian Territory after their own removal to that area in 1828. The Treaty Party families melded easily into the society in the west and began to establish businesses and plantations once again as they rebuilt their lives and their prosperity.

But for the vast majority of the Cherokee people, the more than 16,000 who remained in the east, the ratification of the treaty resulted in an increased federal presence in their territory. Southerners in the four states where the remaining Cherokee lands were located, especially Georgians and Alabamans, now salivated at the thought of the Cherokees' imminent departure. The ratification of the treaty led to persistent rumors of an Indian uprising, although there had never been any evidence to support the gossip, and gave justification to escalating attacks on Cherokee homes. Federal troops sent to quell the alleged attacks on whites frequently discovered the case to be exactly the opposite—that it was the Indians who required their protection. "Particularly irritating to Jackson was the fact that agents and military men now sent to maintain order and prepare the Cherokees for removal showed a disposition to turn pro-Cherokee" (Starkey 1946, 269). As the military became increasingly involved in the two years from 1836 to 1838, the reports of the officers on the scene began to echo what had been reported by confidential agents in the months prior to the treaty's ratification: the Cherokee people were in genuine and widespread opposition to the terms of the treaty.

The officers of the U.S. Army who oversaw the occupation of the Cherokee Nation in these years were initially directed by General John Wool. Although Wool and those under him had federal troops at their command, the beliefs held by many of the army officers of their role, and their reflections about how to enact it with honor, were often in sharp contrast to the goals of the state militias, particularly the Georgia Guard and the Alabama Militia whose main assignments for years had been to enact terror on Cherokee families. In contrast, the officers of the army frequently felt that their assignment to occupy the region and, ultimately, to round up Cherokees from their homes and remove them was dishonorable. This sentiment was most overtly expressed by Brigadier General R. G. Dunlap, who commanded the East Tennessee volunteers, stating "I had determined that I would never dishonor the Tennessee arms in a servile service by aiding to carry into execution at the point of a bayonet a treaty made by a lean minority against the will and authority of the Cherokee people" (from the *National Intelligencer* [Philadelphia], May 22, 1838, as quoted in Royce 2006, 164).

The army found a Cherokee population that was impoverished by the events of recent years, but still defiant. They were uniformly described as holding their leadership to the fixed course of resistance, even as Principal Chief Ross was, probably unbeknownst to them, pursuing other possibilities— becoming a separate state or removing to Mexico, hoping, as previous generations as Cherokees had before him, to simply get out of the borders of the United States and its persistent demands for more land. But nothing was viable, and as tensions increased, the chief's options became progressively restrained by intractable Cherokees. As confidential agent for the War Department John Mason, Jr. stated in a report, "The officers say that, with all his power, Ross cannot, if he would, change the course he has heretofore pursued and to which he is held by the fixed determination of his people. He dislikes being seen in conversation with white men, and particularly with agents of the Government" (report dated September 25, 1837, as quoted in Royce 2006, 165).

Many Cherokees who had been systematically impoverished by state harassment had immigrated to the west. But others had attempted to remain in their homelands, retreating as refugees into the deep wooded areas of the Smoky Mountains, just as they had during the scorched earth burnings of their towns in the 1700s. Knowing there was a significant population living in conditions of hunger and exposure, the army, under General Wool's command, tried to provision the Cherokees existing in these circumstances. Universally, the reports of the officers to General Wool were that the Cherokees in the mountains were refusing the food and blankets offered them by the army. They feared that in accepting any provision from the United States, they would be accepting the terms of the treaty. After all, in the past, treaties had often been accompanied by exchanges of gifts, including food and goods. To their way of thinking, this was no different. Their response was powerful. They would rather go hungry.

In 1830, federal troops had tried to quell the chaos and hysteria that existed around the Georgia gold fields by replacing the presence of the Georgia Guard in the situation. The resulting protest had finally caused the army to withdraw, leaving the mines to the continuing disturbance of state politicians and their vigilante force. In 1836 and 1837, General John Wool attempted again to impose order in the Cherokee territory by endeavoring "to protect the Indians in their homes and to suppress the sale of whisky, and thereby incurred the hostility of state authorities" (Foreman 1932, 279). For his efforts, General Wool faced virulent protest, this time from Alabama officials who pressured the United States to bring charges against him. In the fall of 1837, the U.S. Army again relented to state pressures and brought an action of court martial against Wool. Although he was acquitted of all charges, Wool asked to be relieved of his command in protest of the orders he had been given to carry out, and disgusted with the capitulation to state demands. With Wool's resignation, General Winfield Scott became the top commander in the field.

The election in late 1836 had brought Martin Van Buren into the office of president. Inaugurated in March 1837, Van Buren actually oversaw the majority of the interim, two-year period between the ratification of the treaty and the removal deadline. The Cherokees' slim hopes for reconsideration by a new administration of the Supreme Court victory and the fraudulent treaty were disappointed. Van Buren had been Jackson's vice president. There were no changes to the policy or the federal response to events that had transpired thus far.

As 1838 opened and the deadline neared, Cherokees were uncertain as to their fate. Last minute appeals for a temporary reprieve had been heard and apparently were under consideration. By spring, the Cherokees wondered, should they put crops in this year or not? If they did not and the last-minute reprieve was granted, what would they live on in the coming year? If they did and the reprieve was not granted, then they had wasted valuable resources that would be needed during the forced march.

The insecurity of their existence weighed more heavily than ever in its immediacy.

By late April 1838, barely a month before the roundup of the Cherokees in preparation for removal was to begin, stockades were constructed throughout their nation. These four-walled holding pens, 31 in number, were tangible evidence of the intent of the federal government to move forward with the policy and the treaty, despite the recent appeals for delay. Cherokee despair rose and decisions were silently made. No crops would go in this year, or ever again in this place. Despair was also rising among the American supporters of the Cherokees. The lobbying effort and endeavors to inform the sympathetic public had not diminished. There was a growing sense of shock among many northerners in particular as they watched their government slowly moving to act in a manner they would not have believed it could. A letter received by President Van Buren demonstrated the growing concern:

> These hard times, it is true, have brought the discussion home to every farmhouse and poor man's house in this town; but it is the chirping of grasshoppers beside the immortal question whether justice shall be done by the race of civilized to the race of savage man, whether all the attributes of reason, of civility, of justice, and even of mercy, shall be put off by the American people, and so vast an outrage upon the Cherokee Nation and upon human nature shall be consummated . . . there exists in a great part of the Northern people a gloomy diffidence in the moral character of the government.[5]

Penned by Ralph Waldo Emerson, the letter was written at a time before he had become a noted American literary figure. Emerson did not write the letter of his own volition, but in respect to his recently deceased brother who had been a strong supporter of the Cherokees' cause. Emerson, by some accounts, was irritated at the request others had made of him to appeal to the president, but the rhetoric is strong nevertheless, and one suspects Emerson's intellect and compassion were genuine. His sentiments accurately mirrored those of many of his neighboring citizens, "men and women with pale and perplexed faces [who] meet one another in the streets and churches here, and ask if this be so."[6]

Two weeks before the expiration of the two-year deadline to remove, the president waffled in the face of such pressures. In early May, a reprieve was offered to the Cherokees. In an executive order, Van Buren extended the date for removal by another two years. Relief and jubilation swept through the Cherokees, marked by hasty efforts to put in crops at the late date in order that they not starve in the coming year. Their desire to remain overwhelmed any sense of cautiousness that might have been prudent at the moment. But the elation on the part of the Cherokees was matched by outrage on the part of Georgians and Alabamans, in particular, whose citizens and legislators now applied vocal and vehement pressure on the president to rescind the reprieve. Within another week, Van Buren had done so, and only a week later, notices began to appear around the Cherokee Nation informing the people of the dates when soldiers would be in their particular region to take people from their homes and herd them into the stockades. It is difficult to comprehend the emotional ride the Cherokees must have experienced in the month of May 1838.

On May 26, 1838, almost exactly two years from the date of ratification of the New Echota Treaty, the first Cherokees began to be rounded up by the U.S. Army. Over 7,000 federal and state troops had been sent into the Cherokee Nation to accomplish the task of bringing into the stockades over 16,000 Cherokees still remaining in their homes. Among the first to be taken, mostly from Georgia, were those regarded by the military as most intransigent and most prone to physical resistance. Herded to departure points along the Tennessee River, at Ross's Landing (present-day Chattanooga, Tennessee) and Gunter's Landing (near present-day Guntersville, Alabama), these perceived troublemakers were shipped out by boat within days after being rounded up. In all, as the roundup continued in other areas of the Cherokee Nation, about 2,800 individuals were sent by boat in three detachments leaving within the first weeks of June. They were guarded by military escort, but nevertheless, in one detachment, hundreds managed to escape. Traveling by riverboat and barge, the water route along the Tennessee River dropped into northern Alabama and then wound north again into Tennessee and Kentucky. The route then continued on the Ohio River at the Kentucky–Illinois border and headed west for a short time, all the while moving with difficulty in shallow water resulting from the drought. At the confluence of the Ohio and the Mississippi Rivers on the western border of Illinois, the boats now moved south on the Mississippi, flowing more easily with the river current, and finally caught the Arkansas River, heading upstream across that state, where conditions finally became so bad that some detachments abandoned the boats and walked the remainder of the way through swamp and forest. By the time the journey ended in the Indian Territory, the losses, either through death or escape, were very high.

Rather than fleeing, the majority of Cherokees stayed in their cabins and stubbornly continued to tend their fields and stock. They made little preparation to leave, other than mental notes, perhaps, about what they might hastily put together if given the opportunity by the troops. Historic accounts of the actions of federal troops are varied. Some allowed the Cherokees to feed their animals or kneel in prayer before leaving, and also allowed them to gather a few personal belongings for the long journey. But still others, often with a mob of state citizens egging them on, forced Cherokees from their homes "at bayonet point" as was frequently stated, allowing them to take little but the clothes on their backs. As the Cherokees were herded along the paths that crisscrossed their lands, they often saw Georgians, Alabamans, Tennesseans, or North Carolinians plundering their homes for the possessions they were leaving behind. Fields were set afire and stock was stolen, as squabbles and sometimes violence broke out among the rabble that now fought over occupation of deserted Cherokee cabins and lands.

There were relatively few deaths of Cherokees during the roundup, but one of the most heartbreaking stories of a killing resulting from the process was that of any man who when ordered to go left by soldiers, went right instead and was subsequently shot and killed. The man had been a deaf-mute and had not heard nor understood the orders of the soldiers. Families, whose members were going about their routines, were often separated by the roundup. Men who had been tending to their stock, women who had been gathering foods in the woods, or children who had been playing at a distance returned home to discover the remainder of the family was missing. Soldiers often scoured the area later as families reported members still absent, and usually found the others and took them into the stockades as well. But they weren't necessarily reunited with their own family members at that point, and sometimes did not reconnect with them until weeks or months later, and some did not find their missing relatives until the end of the journey had brought all of them to the Indian Territory. Occasionally, the reunification never occurred, as some who had been separated lost their lives during the removal.

In North Carolina, neighboring communities in the old Valley Towns area (which was still within the Cherokee Nation boundary) and communities higher in the mountains, in areas that had been ceded in 1819 (and thus had not been within the Cherokee Nation's borders for almost 20 years), had still engaged in a high degree of natural interaction due to their relative geographic proximity. They still shared language and cultural customs, after all, even though no longer politically connected. The Cherokees who had detribalized and taken reserves in 1819, often referred to as the Oconoluftee Cherokees, had existed nevertheless in ambiguity as to their own status. Would they be among those who would also be rounded up, even though they were no longer officially a part of the Cherokee Nation and its citizenry? And if not, what were their obligations to their neighbors slightly west and south who clearly would be among those taken?

As the roundup moved into North Carolina, some Cherokees in that area fled to their neighbors to the northeast who were technically outside the Cherokee Nation boundaries. Federal troops entered the area of the Oconoluftee communities in search of those who had escaped, leading to increased consternation among the reservees as to their own security. After all, there were those who desired to wrest all Cherokees from the southeast, even those who had, by treaty, a legal right to stay as they had been promised U.S. citizenship. Fearing that their own status would be jeopardized, the Oconoluftee Cherokees agreed that they would not conceal escaping Cherokees. They were thus placed "in the uncomfortable position of watching their brothers being tracked down while at the same time wondering whether they themselves would remain immune from the pressures of removal" (Finger 1991, 102).

One family who had fled included a man called Tsali (Charlie), his wife, two grown sons, and two younger children. On October 30, 1838, after all but one detachment of Cherokees had been removed to the west, the army apprehended a group of 12 Cherokees who had evaded the roundup, including Tsali and his family. As the group was being taken into the nearest fort, Cherokees within the group attacked the soldiers, killing two of them and wounding a third. The group fled again into the mountains, triggering a massive federal manhunt, which was joined by about 60 Oconoluftee Cherokees. Within two weeks, the force had located all but one of the fugitives, Tsali. Three of them, who had been identified as the killers of the soldiers (including Tsali's two adult sons), were executed by the Oconluftees after the military had judged them guilty. A few days later, Tsali was also apprehended and executed by Oconluftee Indians, even though there was little, if any, evidence that he had been involved in the killings. With this, the army announced that the removal was over, and any Cherokees who were still fugitive could come out of the mountains and join with the Oconoluftees, who were allowed to stay. "As runners carried the happy news throughout the mountains, little knots of Cherokees materialized like apparitions in the cold mist, taking the trails to Quallatown. There were enough of them to challenge the colonel's blithe assumption that only a few remained" (Finger 1984, 27). The North Carolina communities in the mountains thus became a permanent haven for about 400 Cherokees who escaped the roundup, who joined with the 600–800 reservees who were already there to form what would later be known as the Eastern Band of Cherokee Indians.

Throughout the late spring of 1838, in the remainder of the Cherokee Nation, communities in various regions were rounded up in consecutive days and taken to the nearest stockade. The stockades were hastily constructed structures, intended merely to be holding pens for a few days or weeks, as it was thought that those imprisoned would be shortly underway on the journey west. But as the spring shifted to summer, the heat intensified and the normal rainfall, which had been delayed, failed to come at all. Very quickly, reports began to come back to the military officers in the stockades of the wretched traveling conditions of the first detachments that had left by water. The water levels on the rivers had lowered and they had struggled to advance. There had been difficulty in finding potable water along the way and the supplemental foods for which they had foraged along the riverbanks had begun to wither. In the blazing heat of summer, the people traveling on the rivers had died in great numbers from the blistering conditions and related diseases.

By mid-June 1838, the removal was halted as drought had been officially declared and the impossibility of carrying it out under these conditions was acknowledged. "For the land at large the drought was unfortunate; for the Cherokees it was a calamity" (Wilkins 1986, 322). With no contingency plan in place and the Cherokees' homes already reoccupied by whites, there was nowhere to contain the more than 13,000 people who still remained in the stockades. The rudimentary structures were not designed for a longer period of inhabitation, and significant problems of sanitation were developing. As deaths from diseases related to contaminated conditions began to occur, the Cherokees were moved out of the stockades and transferred to internment camps. Encampments were established close to the departure points at Ft. Payne and Ross's Landing, but the largest was around Charleston, Tennessee, an area south of Ft. Cass on the Hiwassee River in the southeastern part of the state. This area was actually dotted with at least seven encampments scattered over an area that was 4 miles wide and 12 miles long. Almost 5,000 Cherokees were held in this area, with another 2,000 nearby around Calhoun, Tennessee.[7] While the transfer to encampments offered more space, it did little to alleviate exposed and contaminated conditions. Soon, disease—fevers and whooping cough, in addition to cholera and dysentery—afflicted all of the encampments, and Cherokee deaths began to occur, even before they had begun their arduous journey.

Under these conditions, Principal Chief John Ross, by a resolution of the National Council, approached the commanders of the military with a request that the Cherokees be allowed to manage their own removal. Promising no further resistance, but simply asking that they be allowed to logistically plan the operation themselves, the request was transmitted to Congress, and was approved by the body. Although the military would remain on scene at the encampments, they would not accompany the Cherokees on their march to the west. Ross also lobbied for additional monies to be allocated for the removal. With the unexpected expense of holding the Cherokees in the encampments throughout the summer, the $600,000 that had been awarded by the New Echota Treaty was being rapidly consumed. Surely, Ross argued, it was not Congress's intent that the Cherokee should remove without adequate financial provision? To do so would undoubtedly result in tremendous hardship and high death rates. Congress reluctantly allowed an additional $1 million, but strongly cautioned Ross that any expenses above that amount would be deducted from the $5 million that was to be paid to the Cherokee Nation for the last piece of land they were relinquishing in the east. With additional funds now available, the Cherokees began to address the logistics of the endeavor. Cherokee "captains" were designated who would lead multiple detachments across the route, with a land route now seen as most feasible. These men were leaders in the National Council or aides to the principal chief. "The migration thus became a national movement on the part of the Indians, and for the first time occurred 'a unanimity of feeling and concurrence of the whole tribe'" (Wilkins 1986, 323). The responsibility for contracting supplies along the route was given to Lewis Ross, the principal chief's brother. Lewis Ross was an astute businessman of the Cherokee Nation and one of the wealthiest of its citizens. He had the necessary experience required for making such contracts, but the huge task was surely daunting, even to him.

As the summer dragged on without any relief from the drought, Chief John Ross and his advisors from the National Council realized that even to start the journey so late in the year ran the risk of Cherokees being on the trail during the depths of winter. By late summer, they were anticipating and requesting that they be allowed to remain in the east until the following spring when a journey of this magnitude could be undertaken without such a heightened risk of hardship and death. But as the expenses of holding the people in the camps escalated, Congress became increasingly concerned about what was becoming a financial debacle. By August 1838, the Cherokees were ordered to get underway. Although there had been some rains, it was not enough to declare an end to the drought, and the broiling heat had not abated. The late date also meant that the detachments would almost certainly encounter winter weather along the route. Nevertheless, the Cherokees began to be transferred to the departure point, which was—for the thousands encamped in the southeastern area of that state—Charleston, Tennessee. Still others would join them on this route by traveling north from Ross's Landing. Those in Alabama would leave from Ft. Payne and travel a different northwestern route, although one roughly parallel to that taken by most detachments.

In addition, a small group of Treaty Party families who had not yet been removed to the west would gather in their own detachment led by John Bell, one of the treaty signers. Fearing for their safety if consolidated with the Ross Party Cherokee majority, these families, who were seen as having cooperated with the federal government, would go under military escort/ protection. Also leaving out of the Ross's Landing area, they would take a direct westward route across Tennessee and Arkansas, transferring to the Arkansas River at Little Rock to complete their journey by water. Regarded as having cooperated with the United States, they were allowed to take much of their personal property and their slaves, since many were plantation owners and business people, even as most Cherokees were losing everything they had.

Although the majority of the Ross Party Cherokees who traveled the Trail of Tears were everyday Cherokee subsistence farmers, there were wealthy families, plantation operators, and businesspeople, among the Ross Party as well. Those families who had been able to retain much of their financial, although not material, wealth were able to make the journey to the west using private funds and taking their slaves with them. Many of them went by water, which was easier and more comfortable for small parties of people than it had proven to be for the first detachments of thousands that had left in early June. But the men from some of these families were among those leading detachments, and in their roles, they shared the hardships experienced by the majority of the Cherokees.

It wasn't only the wealthier Cherokees who owned slaves. The 1835 Cherokee census indicated many small households who held one or two slaves, clearly not used as field laborers, but probably regarded much as other Indians who had been held as captives in previous centuries—as household help, perhaps even seen as actual members of the household.[8] These slaves were also on the long march, and of the approximately 1,600 slaves that were held by Cherokee families and among the over 13,000 Cherokees in total that traversed the Trail of Tears were about 400 African slaves.

Missionaries were also among those who walked the Trail of Tears with the Cherokees. Although most had already gone west before the actual removal, four missionaries—Daniel Butrick and Elizur Butler (Congregati onalists/Presbyterians), Evan Jones (northern Baptist), and David Cumming (Methodist)—also shared the people's hardships, and Reverend Butrick kept an extensive diary along the journey, which is one of the best first-hand accounts existing about the Trail of Tears. Likewise, "Evan Jones never had any doubt that he would march along the Trail of Tears with the Cherokees" and many records of the event produced by Reverend Jones also exist (McLoughlin 1990, 181). These missionaries were not obligated to travel on the march nor experience the suffering, but they felt it was part of their calling to stay with the people through good times and bad. In making the great sacrifice of their time and comfort when they need not have done so, they remained the most esteemed among the Cherokees during their remaining years in the Indian Territory.

As Cherokees and those who would travel with them gathered at the departure points, Lewis Ross was finalizing preparations. It took almost a month before everyone was gathered and the first detachments did not leave until late September, with others following throughout the month of October. Clearly, this was extremely late in the year to be undertaking an almost 900-mile journey. As the detachments started out, they took a northwestern route that led them to the outskirts of Nashville, a road that has since been incorporated into the city's limits. At Nashville, despite the first groups not yet needing them, "the parties were met by Lewis Ross who issued rations and supplies which—as the winter was quickly setting in—included cloaks, bearskins, blankets, overcoats, thick boots, and heavy socks" (Moulton 1978, 100). By the end of the journey, the boots had often worn through and the blankets had been rubbed threadbare, but initially all were well-supplied.

Thirteen detachments, ranging in size from approximately 200 to approximately 1,800, were organized. Most traveled what came to be known as the "northern route," and each was led by Cherokee captains, including Hair Conrad (a member of the National Council) and Daniel Colston with 729 in their group, Elijah Hicks (former editor of the *Cherokee Phoenix* and an in-law of John Ross's) with 858 in his, Reverend Jesse Bushyhead with 950, Situwakee with 1,250, Old Field with 983, Moses Daniel with 1,035, Choowalooka and Thomas N. Clark with 1,150, James Brown with 850, George Hicks with 1,118, Richard Taylor (whose group originated at Ross's Landing, rather than Charleston) with 1,029, and Peter Hilderbrand with 1766. Another detachment, that of John Benge with 1,200, left from Fort Payne and traversed a route parallel, but south of the route taken by 11 groups.

A final detachment comprised of 231 people and led by John Drew, a nephew-in-law of Chief John Ross, left in December and traveled by water

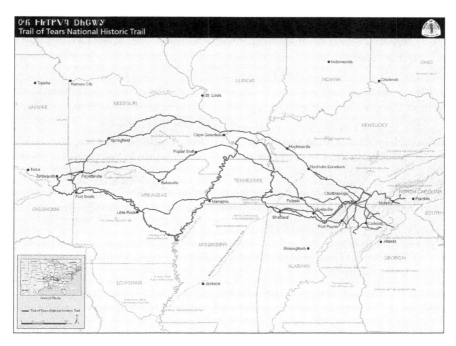

Map of the various routes of the Trail of Tears. (Courtesy of the National Park Service, National Trails Association)

as the earliest groups had. This detachment was comprised of Principal Chief John Ross and his extended family, as well as persons who had been too ill to travel earlier. Ross had overseen the departure of all the people before he and his family finally left. He had been indefatigable during the exodus, offering encouragement and uplift to those about to embark, and managing a tremendous logistical challenge. In these months, the heart and strength of their principal chief became more evident to the Cherokee people than it had ever been and Ross earned a deep and uncompromising loyalty from the overwhelming number of Cherokee people as his leadership was tested and found true.

The detachments were spaced a few days apart as they traveled, and as they headed northwest from Nashville, traveling a mere 8 or 10 miles a day, they strove to reach Hopkinsville, Kentucky, which had been designated as a site where they would take a more prolonged rest. As the first group arrived, they set up camp to stay for a few days to a week. A few days later, another group arrived, and still another a few days after that. It was a good opportunity for the people in the detachments to share their experiences thus far, to search for missing family members among the other detachments, and to regain a sense of cultural normalcy as they visited with each other and provided mutual emotional support. But the impacts were already being felt, even a few weeks into the journey. Two members of the National Council, Fly (or Flea) Smith and the venerated elder, White Path, both died as a result of the physical rigors of the journey and were buried at Hopkinsville.

From Hopkinsville, the detachments traveled northwest across Kentucky and ferried across the Ohio River into southern Illinois. The cold of late fall was setting in and the rains were beginning. The journey west across southern Illinois finally led the detachments to the banks of the Mississippi River. As the first detachments arrived, they were able to cross the river without incident, but as later detachments traversed the state and approached the crossing, snowstorms began to strike the region. By early December, ice floes in the Mississippi River prevented further crossings. Riders were dispatched back along the line of detachments stretched across southern Illinois to instruct them to halt and hold their positions until the weather improved. Unfortunately, the Ohio Valley winter was as harsh as the southeastern summer had been and the blizzards continued unabated for almost three weeks. The conditions became desperate as people agonized from exposure and contracted pneumonia. Those who had suffered from tuberculosis even before leaving found their illness greatly exacerbated, and at the least, no one was able to get their clothing dry or to be warm throughout the brutal weeks of delay.

The weeks in southern Illinois throughout December 1838 were unquestionably the most miserable portion of an inevitably miserable march, and many of the deaths that occurred on the Trail of Tears happened in this time and region. As Christmas approached and Congress was anticipating its recess in celebration of the holiday, it asked for a report from President Van Buren as to the progress of the Cherokees toward their new lands. As Cherokees were stranded in Illinois and dying of exposure and illness, the president stated happily to the Congress that

> It affords me sincere pleasure to apprise the Congress of the entire removal of the Cherokee Nation of Indians to their new homes west of the Mississippi. The measures authorized by Congress at its last session have had the happiest effects. By an agreement concluded with them by the commanding general in that country, their removal has been principally under the conduct of their own chiefs, and they have emigrated without any apparent reluctance. (quoted in Brown 1938, 515)

At about the same time, the weather was beginning to improve and the ice in the Mississippi River at last began to recede. The detachments began to move again and within a couple of weeks, all were able to make the river crossing, landing at a point slightly north of present-day Cape Girardeau, Missouri. But the road ahead was not any easier. Now, in the last few weeks of the march, they would face some of the most rugged terrain thus far as they inched through the Ozark Mountains of southern Missouri.

They Cherokees often traveled on roads that were already developed, at river crossings that were already established, and through or near towns that already existed. But as the autumn rains fell and the roads became more rutted, the journey became a quagmire. Lewis Ross had arranged for supplies to be available along the way, but provisions ran short and had to be supplemented. "To alleviate their distress, Lewis Ross . . . hurried to St. Louis to purchase [additional supplies]. The money for these supplies was borrowed by Lewis Ross in St. Louis by pledging his own securities" (Woodward 1963, 216). Local merchants often compounded the Cherokees' financial strains, engaging in price gouging as the Cherokees attempted to procure food and other necessities of the march, including caskets.

The reception of the Cherokees by Americans in the towns along the way was varied. Some accounts describe sympathetic people, surprised at what they described as the "civilized" character of the Cherokees in their dress and demeanor, particularly the women, and of the appearance of some they would have presumed to be white people had they met them on the street. Nevertheless, they were all citizens of a nation and a culture that had been ousted from their homelands and, no matter what their appearance, were also suffering the arduous trek. Some Americans invited Cherokees into their homes and provided supper, sometimes inviting the captains to sleep in a warm bed for the night as their guest. Other towns asked the detachments to detour around the outskirts so that the delicate sensibilities of their citizens were not exposed to the harshness of the event.

As they inched across southern Missouri, the detachments finally turned into the extreme northwestern corner of Arkansas, coming through an area that later was the Pea Ridge Battlefield, and west to enter the Indian Territory. The march was over, and for those who had survived it, the sense of gratitude was surely dulled by the realization that they had left thousands behind, buried in the encampments or along the trail. Those who had perished had primarily been their elders and their youngest children. Although they did not name it at the time, those who had experienced the removal knew the description was accurate when Cherokee people later spoke of it as "The Trail Where We Cried." American history knows it as "The Trail of Tears."

Notes

Political cartoon of Andrew Jackson, 1832. The Cherokees would have agreed with the expression that Jackson had trampled the U.S. Constitution. (Courtesy of the Library of Congress)1. From papers of the American Board of Commissioners for Foreign Missions, Houghton Library, Harvard University, ABC: 18.3.1, V. 10, Item 205. Provided to the author by Cherokee Nation Tribal Councilor Jack Baker.

2. U.N. Security Council Resolution 819 (1993).

3. *The American Heritage® Dictionary of the English Language*, 4th ed. (Boston: Houghton Mifflin Company, 2000, updated in 2009).

4. H. R. No. 286, 24th Congress, 1st Session, 107–108 (No. 74, Cherokee petition to the Senate). Provided to the author by Cherokee Nation Principal Chief Chad Smith as part of the supplemental text used in the Cherokee Nation History Course.

5. Excerpted from a letter from Ralph Waldo Emerson to President Martin Van Buren, 1838.

6. Ibid.

7. "History and Significance of the Trail of Tears," in *Comprehensive Management and Use Plan, Trail of Tears National Historic Trail* (U.S. Department of the Interior, National Park Service, Denver Service Center, September 1992), 7.

8. *The 1835 Cherokee Census* (Park Hill, OK: Trail of Tears Association, Oklahoma Chapter, 2002).

References

Brown, John P. *Old Frontiers, the Story of the Cherokee Indians from Earliest Times to the Date of Their Removal to the West, 1838*. Kingsport, TN: Southern Publishers, Inc., 1938.

Carter, Samuel III. *Cherokee Sunset, a Nation Betrayed, a Narrative of Travail and Triumph, Persecution and Exile*. New York: Doubleday, 1976.

Corn, James F. "Conscience or Duty: General John E. Wool's Dilemma with Cherokee Removal." *Journal of Cherokee Studies* 3, no. 1 (Winter 1978): 35–39.

Ehle, John. *The Trail of Tears, the Rise and Fall of the Cherokee Nation*. New York: Anchor Books, 1988.

Finger, John R. *The Eastern Band of Cherokees, 1819–1900*. Knoxville: University of Tennessee Press, 1984.

Finger, John R. "The Impact of removal on the North Carolina Cherokees." In *Cherokee Removal, Before and After*, edited by William L. Anderson. Athens: University of Georgia Press, 1991.

Fitzgerald, David G. and Duane King, with a foreword by Principal Chief Chad Smith. *The Cherokee Trail of Tears*. Portland, OR: Graphic Arts Center Publishing Co., 2007.

Foreman, Grant. *Indian Removal, the Emigration of the Five Civilized Tribes of Indians*. Norman: University of Oklahoma Press, 1932.

Gilbert, Joan. *The Trail of Tears across Missouri*. Columbia: University of Missouri Press, 1996.

Hicks, Brian. *Toward the Setting Sun, John Ross, the Cherokees, and the Trail of Tears*. New York: Atlantic Monthly Press, 2011.

Hoig, Stanley W. *The Cherokees and Their Chiefs, in the Wake of Empire*. Fayetteville: University of Arkansas Press, 1998.

Jahoda, Gloria. *The Trail of Tears, the Story of the American Indian removals 1813–1855*. New York: Wings Books, 1975.

King, Duane. "The Origin of the Eastern Cherokees as a Social and Political Entity." In *The Cherokee Indian Nation, a Troubled History*, edited by Duane King. Knoxville: University of Tennessee Press, 1979.

King, Duane and E. Raymond Evans. "Tsali: The Man Behind the Legend." *Journal of Cherokee Studies* 4, no. 4 (Fall 1979): 194–201.

McLoughlin, William G. *Champions of the Cherokees, Evan and John B. Jones*. Princeton, NJ: Princeton University Press, 1990.

Moulton, Gary. *John Ross, Cherokee Chief*. Athens: University of Georgia Press, 1978.

Perdue, Theda and Michael D. Green. *Cherokee Removal, a Brief History with Documents*. Boston: Bedford/St. Martin's, 2005.

Perdue, Theda and Michael D. Green. *The Cherokee Nation and the Trail of Tears*. New York: Viking Penguin, 2007.

Royce, Charles C. *The Cherokee Nation of Indians* (Fifth Annual Report of the Bureau of Ethnology, Smithsonian Institution, 1883–1884). Whitefish, MT: Kessinger Publishing, 2006 (reprinted).

Rozema, Vicki. *Voices from the Trail of Tears*. Winston-Salem, NC: John F. Blair, 2003.

Smith, Daniel Blake. *An American Betrayal, Cherokee Patriots and the Trail of Tears*. New York: Henry Holt and Company, LLC, 2011.

Starkey, Marion. *The Cherokee Nation*. New York: Alfred A. Knopf, 1946.

Walker, Robert Sparks. *Torchlights to the Cherokees*. Johnson City, TN: Overmountain Press, 1993.

Wilkins, Thurman. *Cherokee Tragedy, the Ridge Family and the Decimation of a People*. Norman: University of Oklahoma Press 1986.

Woodward, Grace Steele. *The Cherokees*. Norman: University of Oklahoma Press, 1963.

SEVEN

Resurrections of a Nation

LATE IN THE EVENING OF JUNE 21, 1839, a group of conspirators secretly met to plan their next moves. In a meeting that Cherokee oral history says was fueled by alcohol, the plotters devised and assigned action to the group of more than 100 men who had gathered. These men were accustomed to logistical planning. Many of them were members of the Cherokee National Council and leaders of both prominent and grassroots Ross Party families. Some had been among the captains that had recently led the Cherokee people from the southeastern homelands to the Indian Territory.

In the hours before daybreak the next morning, June 22, 1839, they began to unfurl their plan. Striking first at Honey Springs, the home of John Ridge, having ridden through the night to reach its location (near present-day Grove, Oklahoma), more than 20 assailants rousted Ridge from his bed, dragged him into the front yard of the home, and repeatedly stabbed him until he was dead.

A few hours later, in far western Arkansas, just a mile from the border of the Indian Territory, another group of men accosted John's father, Major Ridge. Ridge had been in Van Buren, Arkansas, where a sick slave was being tended to, and, accompanied by a servant boy, was returning to his home, located in the same area as John's, when he was ambushed and was shot to death by men firing from bluffs above the road. The killers dispersed, leaving Ridge's body in the road. The boy was left unharmed.

At approximately the same time, at Park Hill, 40 miles south of the Delaware District, where the Reverend Samuel Worcester had located his mission in the Indian Territory, Elias Boudinot was staying at the home of his good friend Worcester while his own home was being constructed nearby. As Boudinot arrived to visit the construction site that morning, he was approached by several men who claimed they had relatives who were ill and in need of Boudinot's assistance, since he was in charge of the public medicines. Thus drawn away by the ruse, Boudinot was subsequently attacked, knifed, and killed by blows from a hatchet to the back of his head.

But the third attack was heard by the workmen on his house. Hastening back to Worcester's home, they alerted Boudinot's family as to the killing. The family, realizing immediately that Boudinot's statement at the moment he signed the 1835 Treaty, "I've just signed my death warrant," was being enacted, dispatched a rider to alert Stand Watie, Boudinot's brother, that as a signer himself, he too might be targeted. Watie received the warning in time and was able to escape and draw a bodyguard of men around him before any attack upon him could be made. His survival insured a trajectory of events that plagued the Cherokee Nation for decades to come.

The split that had occurred between Ross Party and Ridge Treaty Party supporters within the Cherokees had driven deep wedges among the people. The situation between the adherents of each party had been tense even before the removal, but after the thousands of deaths that had occurred, both in the camps and along the trail, many Cherokees, in their rage and grief, sought to place blame for the event. At that moment of high emotion, most Cherokees could not intellectually reflect upon the colonizing tactics that had been employed against them—the divisions that had resulted only from President Jackson's lack of enforcement of a Supreme Court decision in the Cherokees' favor, and a removal treaty that had been achieved only after the Senate chose to accept a document that was considered by the Cherokee government and people to be fraudulent and illegally signed. These kinds of actions are familiar strategies that imperializing nations have repeatedly employed to render subordinate the peoples they are attempting to colonize. And they were certainly known to the southeastern Indian nations, all of whom had had such tactics employed against them, first by Great Britain and later by the United States.

But in 1839, barely 3 months after the last detachments had arrived in the Indian Territory after the brutal 900-mile trek, the Cherokees were in emotional turmoil. Seeking to take control of their lives again, the first instinct of many was, understandably, to strike at those who had done this to them. They were powerless to strike at the ones who had truly done it, two American presidents and Congress, and so they turned on themselves. They felt they knew who was to blame—the Treaty Party, those who had negotiated and signed a document that 90–95 percent of the Cherokee people had not agreed with. For the most part, Treaty Party families had not borne the losses of personal property that the thousands who had marched the trail had experienced. They had not endured the exposed conditions in the broiling summer and the brutal winter. They had not seen their elders and children suffer to their deaths and had not laid their bodies into the ground in a strange place where those who loved them would never be able to attend to them again. The members of the Treaty Party, the signers in particular, were easy and obvious targets, and in their grief, the Cherokees took aim.

But the men who were killed on June 22, 1839, and many others who were killed in the years following had been among the most respected and ardent proponents of a rising Cherokee Nation in the southeast. They had built their lives and careers in service to its social and political sovereignty. In these goals, they had been united for many years with those from the Ross Party. In the end, all wanted the same—a strong and vibrant Cherokee Nation, society, and culture. They simply had different ideas about where that could best be achieved. In the end, those involved in this critical time, both in Ross and Treaty parties, gave their all for the continuance and well-being of the Cherokee Nation. In the words of a character from a script by Cherokee screenwriter Shane Smith, "John Ross knew the hearts of the people; but John Ridge saw the future of the Nation."[1] In hindsight, many Cherokees today agree that there was no villain among the Cherokees. The villainy lay elsewhere.

* * * * * * * * * * *

The last detachments arrived in the Indian Territory in late March 1839 after a journey of four to six months and several months spent in stockades and internment camps previous to that. For many, it had been almost 10 months since they had been rounded up from their homes. Cherokee captains had done their best to keep records of the numbers of deaths that had occurred in their detachments, but also recognized that the numbers did not square. Since there had not been any military personnel guarding the marchers, people had been quite free to move between detachments. Some had remained in Arkansas after meeting up with relatives who were already there from earlier dispersions and who had not moved west to the Indian Territory. Others had dropped off and returned to the east, often to join with the Oconoluftee Cherokees in North Carolina, later to be known as the Eastern Band of Cherokee Indians. It was difficult to know what had happened to those who had not arrived. Those who had died were known, but almost as many more were simply missing.

Popular belief and many historic texts have placed the number of Cherokee deaths on the Trail of Tears at 4,000. But as contemporary scholars and researchers have delved more deeply into the subject, the number "seems highly speculative. It appears to be only a suggested estimate, one without hard factual basis, but one that subsequent scholars have cited and recited" (Thornton 1991, 85). The work of the National Trails Association, a branch of the National Park Service, in mapping the trail used by the Cherokees, has also called into question the number of 4,000 deaths. The available evidence does not indicate the number of deaths as being that high. Today, the best estimates are that somewhere between 2,000 and 2,500 Cherokees died, either in the camps, on the march itself, or after arriving in the Indian Territory, but as a result of the conditions of the march. However, researchers also acknowledge that there are probably 1,000–1,500 people who simply could not be accounted for. They left the southeast with a detachment, but did not arrive in the Indian Territory. Although it is likely that most of these people did not die, but simply dropped off the trail to stay with relatives or return to the eastern Cherokees, by the action of choosing not to complete the journey, they had effectively relinquished their citizenship in the tribal government. The loss of citizenry to the Cherokee Nation was indeed somewhere between 3,000 and 4,000 people, about 2,000 and 2,500 of which resulted from deaths.

The Cherokees had been rounded up in the southeast as communities, and they had been held as communities in regional stockades. The detachments were usually comprised of people from neighboring communities, and when they were dispersed to locations within the Indian Territory to reestablish, they did so as communities. Thus, the Cherokee communities of the southeast were transported somewhat intact as associations of families that had lived near each other for decades, sometimes centuries, and who often would continue to do so.

The detachments reached their destination from January through March 1839. Conditions were still very difficult, however, for those who had just arrived. They had no homes, no stores of food, and very little of personal possessions. All the tools and implements that would allow them to restart their lives had been left behind. Cherokee oral history says some people again lived in caves as they were trying to rebuild. The Congress had promised the Cherokees that they would be provisioned with food during the first year after their arrival, and the army was tasked with making those supplies available. Lewis Ross had contracted for supplies along the way, and most indications are that the food they had was adequate and of decent quality, even though they were often charged exorbitantly high prices for it. But as the army began to provision them out of Fort Gibson, there was widespread complaint that the "provisions were unfit for human consumption—the flour and meal being infested with weevils and the meat, according to Chief Ross, 'poor and unhealthy'" (Woodward 1963, 219). There was little relief until the following year when Cherokees were at last able to plant crops from seed supplied by the army, and began to develop self-sufficiency once again.

"In many ways the immediate postremoval era proved more disruptive than the tormented years preceding the forced migration. In the old Cherokee Nation, tribal divisions had centered largely on ideological differences, while the new factionalism grew out of struggles for power, both political and economic" (Moulton 1978, 125). A competitive situation was inevitable, since western Cherokees had already inhabited the region—for 10 years in the Indian Territory and as much as 20 years more in Arkansas previous to that—and had already established governing structures. But the recent "emigrants numbered more than twice as many as the remainder of the tribe, and they had a code of laws for their government. . . . Each faction was accustomed to looking to their respective chiefs and officers for advice and guidance in their tribal affairs; neither could have been expected to abandon their laws and chiefs for those of the other" (Foreman 1934, 291). The government of Principal Chief John Ross, supported by those just arrived after the Trail of Tears, moved swiftly to consolidate its authority in the situation, bolstered as it was by what was suddenly the great majority of the Cherokees in the Indian Territory.

In the summer of 1839, a meeting was held at an encampment on the Illinois River, which ran through the Cherokee Nation, at which the eastern (meaning those who had just arrived from the Trail of Tears) and western (meaning those Cherokees, predominantly Old Settlers, who had already been in the Indian Territory) Cherokee governments were unified into one. That government was legally established and named "The Cherokee Nation" in a very poetic document entitled the "Act of Union," regarded today as the organic document of the contemporary Cherokee Nation. Although the "acting" principal chief of the western Cherokees, John Looney, was present and ultimately agreed to the unification, many members of the western council objected and boycotted the meeting. It would be several more years before a true unification was achieved.

Just as hastily, elections followed at which John Ross was reelected to the chieftaincy by his constituency, before any concerted opposition from either western Cherokees or the Treaty Party could be organized. By September 1839, a superseding constitution of the Cherokee Nation had been adopted and the Ross government continued to consolidate its authority in the situation supported by the majority of the Cherokees. Most Cherokees had more pressing concerns at those moments—building new cabins, procuring the tools and other goods they needed to start a new life, and simply being able to feed themselves. Family members were still ill and dying from the rigors of the march and people needed help. The quick reestablishment of a strong government such as they had known in the east and the minimizing of internal political competition and turmoil served the most immediate needs of the people, but it would be several years before this too was accomplished. In no small part, the delay occurred as a result of the War Department, within which Indian Affairs was housed, refusing to acknowledge the Ross government supported by the majority, thus pursuing "a vicious and dangerous course in the Cherokee country, keeping alive the rancor and unrest in that nation instead of allaying it" (Foreman 1934, 311).

In hindsight, the psychological and spiritual effects of the journey on Cherokees were evident. Many seemed to be almost in an emotional stupor upon arrival. As children and elders had died in disproportionate numbers along the way, the hopes and beliefs that sustain any people had eroded. Some Cherokees today state that "we lost our past and we lost our future" as a result of the Trail of Tears, and at the time, it must certainly have seemed so for many people. While some went about the business of building homes and putting in crops, there were reports of many others who chose instead to self-medicate. Rates of alcohol abuse escalated dramatically for a time, and tempers flared as Cherokees attempted to escape the trauma that was still fresh in their hearts and minds.

On June 22, 1839, grief and anger overcame the Cherokees. According to Cherokee oral tradition, the strikes against the Treaty Party leadership were carried out in haste, and in great secrecy. For historians, the questions linger: Were the killings ordered by anyone in authority? Did Principal Chief John Ross know about them? Some accounts indicate that although many men who were close to Chief Ross were involved, Ross himself was deliberately not informed. Ross's son Allan was involved and later stated that his assignment on this day was to distract his father's attention so that he would not hear of the events until after the deeds were done, suggesting that the chief did not know and that the conspirators may have intuited that, had he known, he would not have approved. Or perhaps, his allies were simply giving him deniability and thus political protection, realizing that their plans would have dramatic impacts. It is likely the degree of the chief's knowledge and involvement, or not, will never be known.

Some feel it was irrelevant whether the chief knew or not as the killers were simply carrying out Cherokee law. Because blood law has been mischaracterized by many historians as based in revenge, the attacks on the

Treaty Party leadership have often been misidentified as occurring under blood law, even though they clearly did not follow the rules of clans or philosophies of balance as proscribed by blood law. But blood law had been abolished in the Cherokee Nation for about 30 years by that time and was no longer much in evidence. The killings, in fact, were almost certainly in response to a written statute of the Cherokee Nation, passed in 1829 and authored, ironically, by John Ridge, which contained a death penalty for anyone ceding Cherokee land without permission from the National Council. However, the killings clearly were not carried out in legal fashion by Cherokee law enforcement and courts as "no public trial preceded the execution of Boudinot and the Ridges; the all-important question of their guilt was left open for endless generations to wrangle over" (Starkey 1946, 313), and so disagreement continues among contemporary Cherokees as to whether these were "executions" or "assassinations."

Ross's actions afterward imply that he did not know in advance of the plot. Within a few weeks of the killings, Ross pardoned those involved in the killings, and offered to also pardon any treaty signer who would recant their action, as eight signers ultimately did. But some regarded his conciliatory efforts as uneven. Treaty Party signers were required to offer concessions; the killers were not. "Perhaps he later regretted these harsh terms as they had much to do with the civil strife that haunted the Cherokee Nation for the next half-dozen years" (Moulton 1978, 116). The tensions escalated and violence between Treaty Party and Ross Party supporters erupted. Additional treaty signers were also killed in the months and years afterward, and Treaty Party adherents responded with killings of Ross Party proponents.

The dispute, which has been called the "Cherokee Civil War," carried on for seven years between 1839 and 1846, intensifying in particular when the Ross government conducted its regular election in 1843, and again in late 1845 when the "Cherokee Nation reeled as it was buffeted by internal turbulence. Murders were common, armed bands roamed the countryside, and hundreds of Cherokees (especially Treaty Party people) left the Nation seeking refuge in Arkansas" (Reed 1979, 157). Although never of the scale that most people would truly describe as a "war," the violence nevertheless was critical, particularly for families who were actively engaged in Cherokee politics. But it was also used as a pretext for the United States to declare martial law in the Cherokee Nation and position troops at Ft. Smith, Arkansas, just over the border with the Indian Territory, who were ready to occupy the Cherokee Nation should matters become uncontrollable by the Cherokees themselves.

Although the issue never became uncontainable by Cherokee authorities, it was also not resolved. After seven years of such infighting, during which as many as 500 people were killed, the United States was becoming exasperated. It was receiving constant appeals from Treaty Party families who felt that, having cooperated with the United States and having received its protection during the removal, they should also be federally protected under present conditions. By 1846, President James Polk was threatening to permanently divide the Cherokee Nation, giving a portion of the territory to the western Cherokees–Treaty Party faction and the remainder to the Ross government and its supporters, the majority of the Cherokee people. "This ultimatum was a blow to Chief Ross, who set to work to avert such a catastrophe. Heretofore he had not recognized the validity of the Treaty of 1835 and the opposition to his administration had been unable to make inroads upon his influence, but now he was faced with disruption of his plans unless he made concessions" (Wardell 1977, 69). Under this very serious threat of division, something Ross had striven for years to prevent on the question of removal, the principal chief entered into negotiations with representatives of the Treaty Party and the western Cherokees to resolve all outstanding disputes and close the internal discord.

In the Treaty of August 6, 1846, the Ross government of the Cherokee Nation made concessions to both groups in order to keep the nation intact. The United States also imposed terms to resolve the dispute. They insisted that the land had been given to the Cherokee Nation (not just the western Cherokees) and that the $5 million, minus overages of removal costs, was to be paid per capita to all Cherokee citizens (not just the eastern emigrants). The Treaty Party was also indemnified for their cooperation in the matter of removal, which they believed had cost them the lives of significant leaders. The families of the Ridges and Boudinot were paid $5,000 each and a remaining $100,000 was allocated to be divided among Treaty Party families who had lost family members during the Cherokee Civil War that had broken out after the removal. Ross Party families, who had also lost family members, neither asked for nor received compensation from the United States.

In many respects, the 1846 Treaty signals the end of the Cherokee removal era. A famous handshake occurred between Principal Chief John Ross and Stand Watie, the treaty signer who had been targeted but had evaded the attempt on his life, even as his brother, uncle, and cousin had been killed. "John Ross had kept the Cherokee Nation together once again. Now, seven years after removal, the Cherokee people looked forward to a quiet future with the funds and stability for revitalization" (McLoughlin

1993, 58). Although many issues related to the removal still plagued the Cherokee Nation, including the settlement of claims for lost property and the amount of removal costs to be deducted from the $5 million the Cherokee Nation was to be paid for the last piece of land in the southeast (claims that were not resolved until the early 1850s), a great era of rebuilding opened, which is known as the Cherokee Golden Age. Between 1846 and 1861, the Cherokee Nation established most of the institutions for which it would be known afterward—the Cherokee National Male and Female Seminaries (college preparatory schools operated by the Cherokee Nation itself), the first system of public coeducation known to the world, the first newspaper in the Indian Territory, numerous public buildings and roads, as well as private homes and enterprises such as businesses and plantations, and most especially, thousands of small family farms. The Golden Age resulted in widespread self-sufficiency and prosperity for the Cherokee people as a more peaceful existence than they had known for decades emerged. Literacy and education were prioritized and flourished through the generation.

But the Treaty of 1846 and the closing of the Cherokee removal was an imposed solution by the United States, and, not having been initiated by the Cherokees themselves, it thus did not represent a true resolution of their internal differences. As the 1850s inched toward internal conflict in the United States that ultimately resulted in the American Civil War, opposition leaders in the Cherokee Nation—led by Stand Watie, Chief Ross's old nemesis—saw an opportunity to wrest power from the chief and his supporters. Ross had continued to be reelected throughout the 1840s and 1850s and was clearly loved and respected by the majority of the Cherokee people. But many of the old Treaty Party families had continued to seethe under his leadership, particularly those of the Waties, Bells, and Adairs who were either signers or descendants of signers of the removal treaty and who had never recanted. As the Civil War broke out, Watie raised a regiment of Cherokees who aligned themselves with the Confederacy, protecting business interests as well, and who threatened the government of John Ross. Placed in an untenable situation, Ross was forced to bring the Cherokee Nation into an alliance with the Confederacy to prevent what he suspected would be an attempted military toppling of his government by Watie's forces. Most Cherokees did not agree with the southern alliance, since these were exactly the states that had persecuted the Cherokees and other tribes and driven them from their homelands, but understood the strategy behind it. But as circumstances of the war changed and Union troops strengthened their presence in the region, the Cherokee Nation was able to repudiate the alliance by early 1863 and the majority of its fighting men ultimately joined Union forces. The alliances, however, were very indicative of the internal fissure among the Cherokees. Instead of being driven by overriding concerns about slavery or states' rights as was the case for the United States and the Confederacy, the Cherokee alignments in the American Civil War largely evidenced the old Treaty Party–Ross Party divisions. And the ferocity of the fighting that ensued in the Cherokee Nation indicated that this was the true source of the conflict for the Cherokees.

By the end of the war, the Cherokees had once again lost about a third of their population, not only soldiers and civilians who were killed in battle, but even more who had perished in refugee camps once again as disease and conditions of exposure, hunger, and contamination had taken them. The nation was then comprised of staggering numbers of widows and orphans, and its infrastructure was wrecked. Its homes, woods, and fields had been burned in scorched earth campaigns that had been carried out not by foreign forces, but by their own Cherokee warriors battling against each other. The nation was devastated, and without exception, historians of the Cherokees regard the devastation of the American Civil War on the Cherokee Nation as largely the result of unresolved internal divisions among the Cherokees resulting from the removal.

The Cherokee Nation was forced by treaty at the conclusion of the Civil War to accept significant losses of land and sovereignty. The short era of relatively minimal interference in Cherokee affairs by the United States ended. In the decades afterward, the Cherokee Nation was overrun once again by outsiders and intruders who squatted on its land and began to make demands on the United States to take land from the Cherokee Nation and open it to white homesteading. It was also increasingly subjected to federal oversight, despite the fact that it owned its land as private property, rather than as a reservation, and had successfully defended its right in court to administer its territory as it chose. In 1893, even though the Cherokees owned their property outright, the United States asserted an interest it did not legally have and extorted another piece of land from the Cherokee Nation, the Cherokee Outlet. On September 16 of that year, it opened it to homesteading in the greatest land run in Oklahoma history— an action that recalled, in the minds of many Cherokees, the Georgia lottery and the gold rush. Throughout the last decades of the 1800s, the parallels to the actions of Georgia and events leading to the Cherokee removal 60 years earlier were too obvious for Cherokees to overlook. Many feared they knew what the result would be yet again.

And just as had happened before, Cherokee Nation land was taken again from 1893 through 1906 by extremely questionable quasi-legal actions on the part of the U.S. Congress. Land that had been held "in common" by the Cherokee government for all Cherokees to use was forcibly divided up and deeded to individual Cherokees in a process known as "allotment." Although most Cherokees objected to the process, and the United States had no right to dictate to a private property owner such as the Cherokee Nation that it had to divide and divest itself of its land, the policy was forced by political and judicial mechanisms. In 1890, "Oklahoma Territory" had been legally created out of the western part of the Indian Territory, and by 1907, the eastern part of the territory—the lands of the Five Tribes including the Cherokee Nation—had also been subsumed into the new state of Oklahoma. This violated all the treaties these tribes had with the United States in that they had been promised they would never become part of a state.

Although the Cherokee people were not physically forced from their land at that time, swindles and economic pressures resulted, by the 1920s, in a loss of 90 percent of the land that had been allotted to individual Cherokees. Cherokees began to fall into dire poverty as the region was economically dominated by white Americans, and by the 1930s, mass emigrations of Cherokees resulted from the area of northeastern Oklahoma that was the Cherokee Nation. As many as 50 percent of the Cherokees left, many relocating to California in particular in an economic event that is known to the Cherokees as the "Second Trail of Tears."

The 20th century was a desperate time for the Cherokee Nation. For more than 60 years beginning with Oklahoma statehood in 1907, it endured oppressive oversight of its nominal government by the Bureau of Indian Affairs (BIA). Chiefs were appointed by the president of the United States, and in an era between 1917 and 1936, were appointed only occasionally to serve a term of office lasting a mere 24 hours each as they did the bidding of the BIA—signing documents that had accumulated that required the legal signature of a Cherokee chief. The remaining deeply cultural Cherokee communities faced racial discrimination and economic and political marginalization. Cherokees, who had been among the most literate and highly educated populations in the country, if not the world, in the 1800s began to be socially excluded from state public educational systems, and in the 1900s were often sent instead to federal boarding schools where their language was prohibited and the instruction demeaned their culture, history, and identity. Cherokee educational attainment dropped precipitously in the 20th century and in certain areas of northeastern Oklahoma, remains among the lowest in the state—a state that itself ranks among the bottom five in the country in educational achievement.

By the 1960s, civil rights movements began to sweep across the United States, and Indian people participated, including Cherokees. But for Native Americans, who had strong remembrances of themselves as governments with historic treaty relationships with the United States, the desire was not for integration, as for many other minority groups, but for increased political and cultural sovereignty. Toward those ends, the last decades of the 20th century have been marked in the Cherokee Nation by increased assertions of governmental authority. Several pieces of federal legislation and important court cases have opened the way for the Five Tribes to re-establish elections and tribal councils in the 1970s, tribal judicial systems in the 1980s, and regulatory authority for purposes of law enforcement and taxation in the 1990s. A Cherokee constitution was developed in 1975 to update and supersede the 1839 document, which had become archaic, and a superseding constitution to the 1975 document was adopted in 2003.

In 1985, Wilma Mankiller became the first woman to be principal chief of the Cherokees, and in the years afterward became one of the most famous Indian chiefs of any tribe in any era. Chief Mankiller was especially noted for an administration that aggressively pursued available federal funding and tribal self-governance contracts, and the Cherokee Nation made enormous strides under her leadership. Tribal law enforcement was established, tax codes to regulate smoke shops and motor fuels sales were developed, and prosperity began to increase once again.

But internal tensions continue to exist among the Cherokees. The Mankiller administration was followed by that of Chief Joe Byrd, who was defaulted into office when his opponent in the 1995 election was ruled ineligible by the Cherokee Supreme Court to run in the runoff election, and after the court also disallowed the third-place candidate from stepping into the runoff instead. The Byrd administration was marked by financial chaos and political turmoil, including the firing of over 200 employees of the Cherokee Nation, the boycotting of council meetings by an oppositional block on the council, the retroceding of tribal law enforcement back to the BIA, and protests in the streets by Cherokee Nation citizens. There was no resolution of the governmental disarray until the election of 1999 in which Chad Smith defeated Joe Byrd.

The administration of Chief Smith from 1999 to 2011 was characterized by a perspective that emphasized the governmental nature of the Cherokee Nation beyond its social services functions, a more corporate approach to economic development, and aggressive revitalization efforts of Cherokee language, culture, history, and community. Initial audits attempting to assess the financial disorder of the previous years revealed about $6 million that could not be accounted for from the Byrd administration, but in the ensuing 12 years, Smith and the enhanced business board brought the Cherokee Nation and its business entities from a $100 million a year operation to a $1.2 billion a year operation, including an almost 300 percent increase in jobs. Cherokee prosperity achieved its highest level since Oklahoma statehood.

Although not related to the divisions that emerged during the removal era, strong disagreements exist about the nature of the Cherokee Nation in contemporary times. Chief Smith's conservative approach to the Cherokee Nation's social services as existing for those who needed them rather than as entitlement programs for all provoked a backlash from some quarters. In the 2011 election for chief, opposition candidate Bill John Baker epitomized the perspective that emphasizes the Cherokee Nation's social service functions and that year was elected on a campaign slogan that "It's Time to Serve the People" and promises of per capita payments to elders and free homes. The atmosphere of the extremely contentious and controversial campaign has carried into the Baker administration as the contest over the direction of the Cherokee Nation continues. Although many rue the nastiness of the debate, in the end, the debate itself is evidence that a vital and engaged Cherokee citizenry still remains.

The descendants of the people who walked the Trail of Tears are alive and kicking in northeastern Oklahoma and all around the United States. In 2013, the Cherokee Nation counted over 320,000 citizens who reside in every state of the country, although the greatest concentration still remains in Oklahoma. The nation is the largest employer in northeastern Oklahoma and provides over 9,000 jobs. Through its gaming, hospitality, recreation, technology, manufacturing, environmental solutions, and other businesses, it is an economic and political force in the state and exercises a strong ability to defend its citizens and their sovereign rights. Although the region in which it is located still has high rates of poverty and unemployment (among its residents overall, not just the Cherokees), the situation for many, if not most, Cherokee Nation citizens is greatly improved from what it was even 20 years ago. If their history teaches anything to the present citizens of the Cherokee Nation, it is that reenvisioning themselves has often been a contested process, and it sometimes has taken decades to arrive at and perfect their new vision. But time and again, the Cherokees have emerged to demonstrate a state of excellence, despite the almost total devastation that has sometimes preceded it.

And if the story of the Trail of Tears teaches anything to not only the Cherokees, but also to all peoples, it is that the grandeur of the human spirit is recognizable to all of us. Like others who have experienced injustices, the Cherokees demonstrated endurance and the refusal to submit. They engaged in smart and strategic maneuvers and carried themselves with dignity, even in the face of great indignities. They aligned themselves with other Americans of good character who were willing to stand up beside them. Although they appeared at the time to have lost their cause, it is important to remember that the Cherokee people, who have existed on this continent for thousands of years, have a long view of themselves. From the Cherokee perspective, this story is not over. As former Principal Chief Chad Smith has often stated, the Cherokee legacy is to face adversity, survive, adapt, prosper, and excel. For the Cherokees, the triumph is in the long run, and prosperity and excellence are still within reach.

Note

1. Shane Smith, "The Trail of Tears" (2006, original script, unpublished). Used with permission from the author.

References

Carter, Samuel III. *Cherokee Sunset: A Nation Betrayed, a Narrative of Travail and Triumph, Persecution and Exile.* New York: Doubleday, 1976.

Foreman, Grant. *The Five Civilized Tribes.* Norman: University of Oklahoma Press, 1934.

Gilbert, Joan. *The Trail of Tears across Missouri.* Columbia: University of Missouri Press, 1996.

Hicks, Brian. *Toward the Setting Sun, John Ross, the Cherokees, and the Trail of Tears.* New York: Atlantic Monthly Press, 2011.

Hoig, Stanley W. *The Cherokees and Their Chiefs, in the Wake of Empire.* Fayetteville: University of Arkansas Press, 1998.

King, Duane, ed. "The Murder of John Ridge" from the *Daily Albany Argus. Journal of Cherokee Studies* 4, no. 2 (Spring 1979a): 109–10.

King, Duane, ed. "A Tribute to John Ridge" from the *Daily Albany Argus. Journal of Cherokee Studies* 4, no. 2 (Spring 1979b): 111–17.

McLoughlin, William G. *Champions of the Cherokees, Evan and John B. Jones.* Princeton, NJ: Princeton University Press, 1990.

McLoughlin, William G. *After the Trail of Tears, the Cherokees' Struggle for Sovereignty 1839–1880.* Chapel Hill: University of North Carolina Press, 1993.

Moulton, Gary E. *John Ross, Cherokee Chief.* Athens: University of Georgia Press, 1978.

Perdue, Theda and Michael D. Green. *The Cherokee Nation and the Trail of Tears.* New York: Viking Penguin, 2007.

Reed, Gerald. "Postremoval Factionalism in the Cherokee Nation." In *The Cherokee Indian Nation: A Troubled History,* edited by Duane King. Knoxville: University of Tennessee Press, 1979.

Royce, Charles C. *The Cherokee Nation of Indians* (Fifth Annual Report of the Bureau of Ethnology, Smithsonian Institution, 1883–1884). Whitefish, MT: Kessinger Publishing, 2006 (reprinted).

Rozema, Vicki. *Voices from the Trail of Tears.* Winston-Salem, NC: John F. Blair, 2003.

Smith, Daniel Blake. *An American Betrayal, Cherokee Patriots and the Trail of Tears.* New York: Henry Holt and Company, LLC, 2011.

Starkey, Marion L. *The Cherokee Nation.* New York: Alfred A. Knopf, 1946.

Thornton, Russell. *The Cherokees: A Population History.* Lincoln: University of Nebraska Press, 1990.

Thornton, Russell. "The Demography of the Trail of Tears Period: A New Estimate of Cherokee Population Losses." In *Cherokee Removal, Before and After,* edited by William L. Anderson. Athens: University of Georgia Press, 1991.

Wardell, Morris L. *A Political History of the Cherokee Nation, 1838–1907.* Norman: University of Oklahoma Press, (1938) 1977.

Wilkins, Thurman. *Cherokee Tragedy, the Ridge Family and the Decimation of a People.* Norman: University of Oklahoma Press, 1986.

Woodward, Grace Steele. *The Cherokees.* Norman: University of Oklahoma Press, 1963.

Biographical Profiles of Key Figures

Elias Boudinot
(1804?–1839)

Boudinot was editor of the *Cherokee Phoenix*, the first newspaper ever printed by an Indian tribe, and the author of numerous antiremoval and social tracts. Born in Oothcaloga (near present-day Calhoun), Georgia, Boudinot was the eldest of nine children of a Cherokee man named Oo-watie and his wife, Susanna Reese, also a Cherokee. Named Gallegina (Buck) at birth, he grew up in a newer Cherokee community established by many of its inhabitants as a project in "civilization." As devotees to the policy, as well as the educational attainment of Cherokees, his parents sent him at the age of six to the Moravian mission at Spring Place (near present-day Chatsworth), Georgia, where he remained in school until 1817. Gaining in acculturation, English language usage, and general education, Buck Oo-watie (having taken his father's name as a surname) was noticed by a visiting missionary, Elias Cornelius, from the American Board of Commissioners for Foreign Mission (ABCFM). Cornelius invited Buck to attend a college-preparatory school that the board had established in Cornwall, Connecticut. While there, Buck encountered an elderly benefactor, Elias Boudinot, and to honor him took his name, by which he was known ever after. Boudinot also met and married one of the townswomen, Harriet Gold, causing violent dissension in the town over the interracial relationship. His piety and idealism thus tempered, Boudinot became a strong advocate for a Cherokee Nation, still on the path to "civilization" and refining its nationality, but doing so independent of the United States. As one of the more articulate and acculturated young men of the nation, Boudinot was used strategically by the Cherokees on speaking tours to raise funds for their antiremoval efforts, and ultimately, as editor of their newspaper, which provided him with a broader audience through exchanges with metropolitan dailies in the United States. As pressures for Cherokee removal intensified throughout the late 1820s and early 1830s, Boudinot became the literary voice of

Cherokee resistance through his many nationalist political tracts, which impressed American audiences with not only their critical arguments, but also their rhetorical eloquence. But the appearance of victory in the Supreme Court in 1832 brought only further disillusionment with the American system for Boudinot. When it became evident that the president would not enforce the court decision, Boudinot thereafter believed the continuance of the Cherokee Nation was possible only in the west, out of the reach of encroaching American settlers. His reversal of position to one advocating removal was denounced by the Cherokee citizens, however, and Boudinot was prevented by the National Council from printing his arguments in the *Phoenix*. He resigned in protest, and the tenor of his writings afterward became increasingly embittered and defensive. Ultimately, he was one of the 22 signers of the Treaty of New Echota, which ceded the remaining Cherokee lands without the permission of the national government. Soon after, his wife died, leaving him with six children. Ever faithful and connected to the ABCFM, he was remarried within a year to one of their missionaries, Delight Sargent. In 1836, Boudinot self-removed to the Indian Territory in advance of the majority of the Cherokee Nation. But his second marriage and life in the west were short-lived. On June 22, 1839, he was killed by a mob of Cherokees who regarded his action in signing the treaty as traitorous as defined by Cherokee statute.

Elizur Butler
(1794–1857)

Butler was a missionary among the Cherokees who was arrested by Georgia for violating its "harassment laws" and who subsequently became a codefendant in the Supreme Court case, *Worcester v. Georgia*, which upheld Cherokee sovereignty and territorial jurisdiction. Born in Connecticut, Butler became a missionary with the interdenominational American Board of Commissioners for Foreign Missions (ABCFM). In 1820, he was assigned to the Brainerd Mission to the Cherokees in present-day Chattanooga, Tennessee. He later served at Creek Path Mission in present-day Guntersville, Alabama, as well as the Haweis Mission near present-day Rome, Georgia, where he settled in 1826. But in 1831, he was arrested, along with 10 other missionaries of the ABCFM, for failing to be licensed by the state of Georgia to work in the Cherokee Nation. Although most of the missionaries capitulated to state pressures, Butler and a colleague, Samuel Worcester, believing the state laws infringed on Cherokee sovereignty, refused to acquiesce to state jurisdiction and forced a trial. They were found guilty and sentenced to imprisonment at the Georgia State Penitentiary at Milledgeville. They subsequently became the plaintiffs in a federal case against Georgia that was heard by the Supreme Court, which ruled in their favor, and thus the Cherokee Nation's, in early 1832. However, President Andrew Jackson and the state of Georgia refused to obey the court's ruling and the missionaries languished in prison until 1833. Finally released after accepting a pardon from the state, Butler continued to support Cherokee resistance. His position was shared by another colleague, Daniel Butrick, but caused schisms among the ABCFM missionaries who worked among the Cherokees. However, because Butler, who was also a physician, was one of the only four missionaries who traveled the Trail of Tears with the Cherokees, he enjoyed their esteem for years after in the Indian Territory. There he was assigned the Fairfield Mission and later became the superintendent of the Cherokee National Female Seminary. He died in 1857 in Arkansas.

Jeremiah Evarts (1781–1831)

Evarts served as a director of the American Board of Commissioners for Foreign Missions (ABCFM) and wrote a series of anti-Jacksonian essays in support of the Cherokees' cause. Born in Vermont, he attended Yale University and initially practiced law, but was also drawn to religious affairs and the connections between religion and politics in American life. In 1810, Evarts accepted the editorship of the *Panoplist*, a journal of social reform, and became devoted to moral reform and missionary work. In 1811, he was elected treasurer of the burgeoning ABCFM, and within a year had been elected to its board of directors. By 1817, ABCFM efforts had extended to the southern Indian tribes, and Evarts immersed himself in the conflicts around federal Indian policy. In the 1820s, Evarts was drawn into the politics of Indian removal, which culminated in his authorship of the *William Penn* essays, a series of anti-Jacksonian tracts that challenged the morality of federal removal policy. Widely circulated and reprinted, the essays were influential in solidifying support throughout New England for the Cherokee cause. Unfortunately, Evarts, who had suffered with bouts of ill health throughout his life, did not witness the victory, or the ultimate betrayal, of the Cherokees. He died in 1831, the year in which two of his missionaries were imprisoned and the beginning of the seminal *Worcester v. Georgia* case that defined Cherokee rights.

Andrew Jackson (1767–1845)

Jackson, president of the United States from 1829 to 1837, aggressively promoted the policy of Indian removal and refused to obey a Supreme Court ruling protecting the rights and territory of the Cherokees. Born in the Waxhaws area, a region straddling North and South Carolina, Jackson's father had died a few weeks before his birth, and his two brothers died during the Revolutionary War. His mother passed away when Jackson was 14, leaving Jackson without any immediate family. Jackson studied law and was admitted to the bar in North Carolina in 1787. He became a planter, slave owner, and merchant, and a major land speculator in western Tennessee involving lands he had been instrumental in taking from the Chickasaw Nation. He was appointed commander of the Tennessee militia in 1801 and is best known for his service in the War of 1812, including a campaign against dissident Creeks known as "Redsticks." Although most Creeks did not oppose the United States and Cherokees actually fought alongside Jackson at the Battle of Horseshoe Bend, Jackson forced land cessions from both tribes within the next two years. Regarded as a betrayal of their friendship, Cherokee opinion against Jackson solidified throughout the 1820s, particularly as Jackson was elected to the Senate again and then brought the policy of Indian removal to the forefront of his campaign, and after his election in 1828 to the presidency. In 1830, his supporters in Congress shepherded the Indian Removal Act through Congress, which required Jackson to make deals with several legislators to change their votes to effect its passage. As president, Jackson also ignored an 1832 Supreme Court decision in the Cherokees' favor, giving support to the unlawful and violent activities of state vigilante groups in Georgia. Ultimately, the illegal Treaty of New Echota was ratified under Jackson's administration, but he left office over a year before the terms of the treaty went into effect, leaving it to his successor Martin Van Buren, who had been Jackson's vice president, to actually enact the removal of the Cherokees. Jackson retired in 1837 to The Hermitage, his home near Nashville, and remained there until his death from tuberculosis and heart failure in 1845.

John Marshall (1755–1835)

Marshall, chief justice of the Supreme Court, wrote the opinions in *Cherokee Nation v. Georgia* (1831) and *Worcester v. Georgia* (1832) that reaffirmed Cherokee sovereignty and established the foundation for federal Indian law. Born on the Virginia frontier where no schools existed, he was home schooled through most of his youth, including the study of law. During the Revolutionary War, he served in the Continental Army, and afterward held several state political positions in Virginia. As a delegate of the U.S. Constitutional Convention, he led the fight for ratification and advocated in particular for Article III, which established a federal judicial branch. Marshall had a successful law practice and was elected to the House of Representatives in 1799, but was selected later that year by President Adams to be secretary of state. He finally accepted a Supreme Court appointment in 1801 by the outgoing president and a lame duck session as a political maneuver to establish a strong federalist on the bench. Under his tenure, the weak court was greatly enhanced as the final arbiter of constitutional matters. His opposition to the harassment laws passed by Georgia may have come primarily from his federalist sensibilities, but his decisions in the two Cherokee cases resulted in both restraints to and enhancements of Indian sovereignty. They have been mulled by both courts and law students for almost 200 years as the parameters of Indian rights continue to be refined. Marshall's health declined between 1831 and 1835, and he died in 1835 in Philadelphia, Pennsylvania, where he had gone to seek medical treatment.

John Ridge
(1803–1839)

Ridge, member of the Cherokee National Council, was instrumental in defending the Cherokee position in Washington, but was later ejected from the council for shifting his position to support removal. Born in Oothcaloga (near present-day Calhoun), Georgia, to Kah-nung-da-tla-geh (later to be known as The Ridge and still later as Major Ridge) and his wife, Sehoya (known in English as Susannah Wickett), John Ridge, like his cousin Elias Boudinot (Buck Oo-watie, see above, whose father was Major Ridge's brother), grew up in a community and family dedicated to American ideals of "civilization." The oldest son, the family raised John as a Cherokee nationalist, preparing him to one day become the principal chief. He spoke only Cherokee and lived a typical Cherokee childhood until the age of seven when his parents sent him to the Moravian mission school at Spring Place, Georgia, where he learned English and excelled as a student, although never as pious as his cousin Boudinot. Troubled periodically by ill health resulting from a hip condition, John was frequently frail, and at his mother's insistence, John was removed after a few years and schooled at home until he reached the age of 14. He then transferred to Brainerd Mission at present-day Chattanooga, Tennessee, operated by the American Board of Commissioners for Foreign Missions (ABCFM) and was subsequently selected to attend their academy in Cornwall, Connecticut. By 1818, John had joined his cousin at the ABCFM's academy, where he soon became their best student, and like Boudinot, John also met and ultimately married one of the townswomen, Sarah Northrup. The couple was condemned and vilified by the townspeople for their marriage, and they settled in the Cherokee Nation, where John became an attorney and a member of the National Council, as was selected to be the National Clerk. Regarded by many as a rising star among the Cherokees, his deep devotion to Indian sovereignty as well as his brilliance led to his work in the mid-1820s as a lobbyist for the Creek Confederacy, on whose behalf he proved to be a wily and tough advisor and negotiator. He was used strategically by the Cherokees as an orator and negotiator in Washington, cultivating public sentiment in opposition to Indian removal. But like Boudinot, he was disillusioned by the refusal of President Jackson to enforce the ruling of the Supreme Court in the 1832 *Worcester v. Georgia* case, and changed his position on the issue, believing that the only hope of continuance of an independent, sovereign Cherokee Nation rested in removal to the west. Having convinced his father of the same, the two were expelled from the National Council and went on to become the leaders of a small political party of the Cherokee people favoring removal, known as the Ridge Party, and later as the Treaty Party; after John, his father and cousins signed the infamous Treaty of New Echota in 1835. John and his family moved to the Indian Territory prior to the Trail of Tears, but on June 22, 1839, shortly after the arrival of the majority of the Cherokee Nation from the Trail of Tears, John was ambushed in his home and killed by a mob who regarded him as a traitor and as having broken Cherokee law that placed a death penalty on anyone who ceded Cherokee land without permission of the National Council—a law that, ironically, John had authored.

Major Ridge
(1771?–1839)

Ridge was a venerated senior member of the National Council and mentor of John Ross who later broke with the Ross government to support his son, John's, position in support of removal. Born at Hiwassee in present-day

Polk County, Tennessee, the individual later known as Major Ridge had several names throughout his lifetime. His mother was the daughter of intermarried Cherokee and Scots parents, and his father's identity cannot be definitively proven, although certainly a renowned Cherokee hunter. Raised in an era of perpetual conflict between Cherokees and Tennessee frontiersmen, Ridge's family moved several times attempting to evade the harassment. Having learned the traditional skills of hunters and warriors of his people, Ridge joined the Chickamaugan warrior confederation after his village was attacked in 1788. Ridge continued to engage in warfare into the early 1790s, until he was at last disgusted when a colleague, Double-head, murdered a white family, including several children, without provocation. Leaving the warrior life, Ridge was chosen by his community to represent it at council, where he became recognized as a skilled orator. He was also one of the first adherents among the Cherokees to the tenets of "civilization" as it was being introduced to the Cherokees by federal Indian agents. He married and moved with his wife, Sehoya (Susannah Wickett), to the Oothcaloga Valley in Georgia, where he began to build his wealth, acquiring horses, livestock, and slaves; developing orchards and fields; and growing food as well as cotton for export. He and Susannah had four children who lived—including John, who they hoped would become the principal chief someday. Ridge stood strongly against cessions of land, and in 1807 was one of the assigned killers of Doublehead who had ceded Cherokee land in violation of Cherokee law. He was also a strong advocate of abolishing the ancient blood law among the Cherokees, and was successful in helping pass a statute to that end in 1810. Ridge joined American forces under Andrew Jackson's command in 1814 at the Battle of Horseshoe Bend, where he earned the rank of major, which he took as his first name. Ridge never learned to speak or write English, but his influence on the National Council only rose throughout his lifetime. When Principal Chiefs Pathkiller and Charles Hicks died in 1827, Ridge should have been next in line to become principal chief, but feeling the Cherokee Nation needed a more acculturated leader at that time, he threw his support to his protégé, John Ross, who was elected chief in 1828 under the terms of the new Cherokee Constitution. Ross and Ridge worked in concert to resist removal until 1832 when President Jackson refused to uphold the Cherokees' Supreme Court victory. When it appeared to Major Ridge's son John that all hope was lost, he was also convinced and together they and other family members broke with the Ross Party and began to advocate removal. Ejected from the National Council for their views, Ridge was particularly vilified after signing the 1835 Treaty of New Echota, which sanctioned Cherokee removal. Major Ridge removed to the Indian Territory in 1837, but when the majority of the nation arrived a year later after the Trail of Tears, he was targeted for assassination and was killed in an ambush on June 22, 1839.

John Ross
(1790–1866)

Ross was principal chief of the Cherokee Nation, 1828–1866, who represented the resistance of the majority of the Cherokee people to removal. Born in Turkey Town on the Coosa River (present-day Center), Alabama, he was the third of nine children born to Daniel and Mollie Ross, a Scotsman and his Cherokee/Scots wife. The Shoreys and McDonalds from whom Mollie was descended had remained with the Cherokees over the generations, and by the time John was born, were well integrated as traders. As a maternal clan flowed within the family from generation to generation, the Cherokees of the time likely regarded John and his siblings as full Cherokees, and from an early age, John displayed a deep love for the land, traditions, and people of the Cherokees. The family moved several times during Ross's youth, finally settling at the northern end of Lookout Mountain (near present-day Chattanooga), Tennessee. Ross gained his education at home with tutors hired by his father, and also attended Reverend Gideon Blackburn's mission school at Chickmauga as well as an academy at present-day Kingston, Tennessee. Ross entered into trade also and worked for several traders in his early adulthood. But he seemed to prefer more adventurous endeavors through government contracts that allowed him to travel and interact with the Creeks to the south and western Cherokees in Arkansas, among others. In partnership with his brother Lewis, and even with his brother Andrew for a short time, Ross became increasingly involved in politics in the 1820s and moved to the Head of Coosa (present-day Rome), Georgia, to be nearer the Cherokee political center at Ustenali, by then called New Echota (near present-day Calhoun), Georgia. Still, his early career in business helped him to hone many skills that would be invaluable to him as he moved through his remarkable political career. Under the mentorship of Major Ridge, Ross was a rising star among the Cherokees and was selected by the National Council to be the principal chief of the Cherokee Nation in 1828, a remarkable accomplishment for a relatively young man and particularly one who spoke only passable Cherokee. But his devotion to the people was unwavering and trusted and Cherokee faith in him deepened as the nation moved into the era of the removal crisis. For 38 years, Ross was a strong hand at the helm of the Cherokee Nation, guiding it through the many pressures in the years before removal, the Trail of Tears, the internal conflicts in the Indian Territory after the removal, the Golden Age, and the devastations of the Civil War. When Ross passed away in 1866, he ached at the sight of a Cherokee Nation that had been shattered once again by the Civil War, but was pleased that in the Reconstruction Treaty of 1866, the Cherokees had once again been able to stave off permanent division of the nation, which had threatened it so many times during his career, but which he had always been able to thwart. In his sickbed during the negotiations of the treaty, he held on long enough to see the relationship with the United States restored and the Cherokee Nation government kept intact, but a week after its ratification, Ross passed away in Washington, D.C. As a result of the war, he died impoverished, having outlived two wives and several children, having seen his home burned and his plantation ruined. But his grateful nation was poised to rebuild once again, and Cherokees today regard John Ross as the greatest chief they have ever had.

General Winfield Scott
(1786–1866)

Scott commanded 7,000 troops and carried out the order to round up the Cherokees from their homes. Born in Dinwiddie County, Virginia, he attended William and Mary College, studied law, and served with the Virginia militia. He was commissioned in 1808 as a captain with the U.S. Army, but was court-martialed two years later for insubordination. His commission suspended for a year, Scott returned and a year later was promoted to lieutenant, fighting in the war of 1812. Captured by the British, he was released in a prisoner exchange, even as other Americans imprisoned with him were executed. In 1813, he was promoted to colonel, and in 1814, to brigadier general, making him, at age 27, one of the youngest generals in American history. In 1838, Winfield Scott was given command of the army that was to round up the Cherokees for removal after General John Wool resigned. The roundup under Scott began on May 26, 1838, in Georgia, where Scott used 4,000 state troops—the very people who had been harassing the Cherokees—because federal troops had not yet arrived. Although he ordered that the Cherokees be treated humanely and not be fired upon unless offering resistance by force, his orders were ignored by many of the state troops under his command. Scott, like Wool before him, found the orders to roundup and remove the Cherokees distasteful, but carried out his duty. When Cherokees negotiated to manage their own removal, Scott supported their effort, and when the march got underway, he traveled as far as Nashville with one of the early detachments. From there, he was ordered back to Washington and reassigned. Scott continued to have a prominent career, promoted to major general a few years later and distinguishing himself in the Mexican–American War. Too aged and ill to be a field commander in the Civil War, he was an early strategist but resigned in November 1861. Scott was buried at West Point after his death.

Sequoyah
(1776?–1840)

Sequoyah invented the written Cherokee language, called a syllabary, from the spoken language. He is the only person ever known who could neither read nor write to have invented a written language. Sequoyah's origins are shrouded, but he grew up in the Cherokee village of Tuskegee of a mother who was related by clan to the Chickmaugan Chiefs Doublehead and Old Tassel, who were brothers. Sequoyah's father is not definitively known, but may have been either a German trader or an English officer named Gist, sometimes spelled Guess. Sequoyah's English name was George (Jaji, in Cherokee), and so he is also known as George Gist or George Guess. Sequoyah never attended school, but spent his youth tending stock and working in the family's gardens. He became lame early in life, but it is unknown whether it resulted from illness or an injury. As an adult, he learned smithing and became a silversmith, and later a blacksmith. After moving to Alabama, he fought alongside other Cherokees and under the command of Andrew Jackson in the campaigns of 1813 and 1814 against the Red Stick Creeks. But within a few years, he had turned to other interests, including the puzzle of developing a writing system for the Cherokee language. Beginning in 1809, Sequoyah spent the next 12 years experimenting and perfecting a system based not on words or isolated sounds, but on combinations of sounds, syllables. Over the years, he identified and assigned symbols to 86 characters that encompassed all of the sounds of the Cherokee language. Later reduced to 85 characters (1 being found redundant), the syllabary was introduced first to Cherokees who had immigrated to Arkansas, but also spread quickly among the majority who still remained in their eastern lands. It took the average Cherokee about two weeks to learn the characters at which time they became instantly literate in their own language. The development opened innumerable possibilities for the Cherokees, including the development of a newspaper, the printing of their own laws, and the translation of the Bible into a Cherokee texts, all of which the Cherokees and missionaries undertook. The syllabary thus became an important tool that facilitated Cherokee popular resistance and nationalism. Sequoyah immigrated to Arkansas in 1825, and moved with the western Cherokees to the Indian Territory in 1828, establishing a cabin in what is today the county in Oklahoma named after him, Sequoyah County. He died somewhere near the present-day Texas–Mexico border, searching for Cherokees who had fled to Mexico after having been routed from their east Texas communities in 1839, still trying to unify his people.

William Wirt
(1772–1834)

Wirt, former U.S. attorney general, argued the Cherokee cases in the Supreme Court and was successful in defending Cherokee territory and sovereignty in the 1832 *Worcester v. Georgia* case. Born in Bladensburg, Maryland, Wirt was orphaned by the time he was eight years old and was raised by an uncle. He received a classical education and became a tutor and a lawyer. In 1792, he was admitted to the bar in the state of Virginia. He became acquainted with Thomas Jefferson and James Monroe, and became clerk of the Virginia House of Delegates. In 1807, he was asked to be the prosecutor in the trial of Aaron Burr on the charge of treason, and made a name for himself. He was elected the following year to the Virginia legislature, where he served for eight years. In 1817, he was named attorney general by President James Monroe, and was continued in that office under President John Quincy Adams, leaving the position in 1829 after the election of Andrew Jackson. During his tenure, Wirt strengthened the office of attorney general into one of great influence. In 1830–1831 and again in 1832, Wirt took two cases to the Supreme Court, *Cherokee Nation v. Georgia* and *Worcester v. Georgia*, on behalf of the Cherokee Nation and its supporters. The cases established several of the foundational cornerstones of federal Indian law and Wirt's victory on behalf of the missionaries, but by extension, the Cherokee Nation made him a hero to the Cherokees, who named their children after him for generations to come. He made an unsuccessful bid for president in 1832 against Andrew Jackson, and afterward retired to private practice until his death two years later.

General John E. Wool
(1784–1869)

Wool commanded the troops that occupied the Cherokee Nation after the ratification of the Treaty of New Echota in 1836. Wool was born in New-burgh, New York, and orphaned at an early age. He attended public school, however, and was later hired by a law firm where he read and studied their cases, and thus learned the law and was admitted to the bar. He fought in the War of 1812 and was wounded, which led to his promotion to major in 1814 and then to colonel at the end of the war. He was sent to Europe as an observer and on his return was made inspector general of the U.S. Army. In 1836, he was sent to command the troops, many of them state militiamen, who were sent to keep the peace between the Cherokees and the southerners who encroached on their territory in anticipation of their removal. Wool had great sympathy for the Cherokee cause and tried to restrain many of the abuses of state citizens and militias that were perpe-trated on the Cherokees. He was accused of interference in the enforcement of state laws and state military activities, and after strenuous complaint from Alabama, the army court-martialed Wool in 1837. Exonerated of all charges, Wool was nevertheless disgusted with the orders he had been given and the abuses of the states. In July 1837, he resigned rather than continue with his role in the removal of the Cherokee Nation. Nevertheless, Wool was promoted to brigadier general in 1841, and fought in the Mexican–American War and in the American Civil War. In 1863, he retired, the oldest general having an active command in the war. He returned to New York, where he lived until his death a few years later.

Samuel Worcester
(1798–1859)

Worcester was arrested by Georgia in 1832 and became the plaintiff in the *Worcester v. Georgia* case that successfully defined Cherokee rights and sovereignty in their own territory. Born in Peacham, Vermont, Worcester came from a family of preachers. As his father was also a printer, Worcester learned to set type, which served him well as he later worked with his good friend, Elias Boudinot, in printing the *Cherokee Phoenix*, the Cherokee Bible, and other texts. He attended school at the Peacham Academy under the tutelage of Jeremiah Evarts, and afterward attended the University of Vermont. He graduated from Andover Theological Seminary in 1823 and went to work for the American Board of Commissioners for Foreign

Missions (ABCFM). As a new missionary, he was assigned to the Cherokee Nation and arrived at Brainerd Mission in present-day Chattanooga, Tennessee, in late 1825. Worcester's first intensive efforts were in learning the Cherokee language and syllabary. Working closely with Boudinot, Worcester's efforts were directed toward teaching and translating Christian values and texts into the Cherokee language. He was recruited to oversee the operation of the new Cherokee press at New Echota, Georgia, the Cherokee capital where the printing office was to be located. But as the pressures on the Cherokees to remove mounted and the Cherokees expressed their resistance through the new instrument, the *Cherokee Phoenix*, Worcester came under fire from Georgians for "allowing" the Cherokees to freely express their objections in their own newspaper. As the state passed its harassment laws in 1829–1830, Worcester and other missionaries became the targets of certain sections of the law, which sought to bring them under Georgia's control. In the summer of 1831, Worcester and a number of other ABCFM missionaries were arrested by the state. Worcester and his colleague, Dr. Elizur Butler, forced the state to put them on trial, seeking to help the Cherokee Nation define and defend its sovereignty within the limits of Georgia. In 1832, Worcester and Butler's case was heard by the Supreme Court and determined in their favor. But the missionaries remained imprisoned until early 1833, when they became convinced that the Nullification Crisis required their acknowledgment of wrongdoing in order to save the country, a highly overblown charge. As part of the agreement he had made for his release, Worcester thereafter advocated for Cherokee removal. As a result, the man who had been so highly regarded by the Cherokees was now vilified for his changed position. Worcester's sermons were shunned by the Cherokees, and he removed to the Indian Territory in 1835, convinced that Cherokee removal was inevitable, and preparing to reestablish their press in the new lands. He was at the Presbyterian Dwight Mission, moved to the Union Mission on Grand River, and finally to Park Hill in present-day Oklahoma. Boudinot joined him there in 1837 and prepared to build a house nearby. But it was not to be. Boudinot was killed in an ambush not far from Worcester's home in 1839. Worcester remained among the Cherokees, but his influence among them was severely reduced, primarily, perhaps, because of his continuing friendship with Boudinot, who had come to be viewed as a traitor. Worcester died at Park Hill and is buried there.

Primary Documents

EXCERPTS FROM THE TREATY OF HOPEWELL, NOVEMBER 28, 1785

The Treaty of Hopewell was the first treaty made between the Cherokees and the new United States of America. These excerpts indicate the many issues that needed to be resolved between the Cherokees and the United States at the conclusion of the American Revolution. Prisoners were exchanged, jurisdictions were defined, a deputy to Congress was established, and peace was declared between the two former enemies. The most important articles of the treaty in subsequent years relating to the removal are numbers 3 and 9, in which the Cherokees placed themselves as a protectorate of the United States, and the United States asserted exclusive regulatory authority over the relationships with the tribes. This article was reiterated a few years later in the Commerce Clause of the United States Constitution, and effectively prevents the states from asserting regulatory authority over tribes within their borders.

The Commissioners Plenipotentiary of the United States in Congress assembled, give peace to all the Cherokees, and receive them into the favor and protection of the United States of America, on the following conditions.

Art. 1. The Head-Men and Warriors of all the Cherokees, shall restore all the prisoners, citizens of the United States, or subjects of their allies, to their intire (*sic*) liberty: They shall also restore all the negroes, and all other property taken during the late war from the citizens, to such person, and at such time and place, as the commissioners shall appoint.

Art. 2. The commissioners of the United States in congress assembled, shall restore all the prisoners taken from the Indians, during the late war, to the Head-Men and Warriors of the Cherokees, as early as is practicable.

Art. 3. The said Indians for themselves, and their respective tribes and towns, do acknowledge all the Cherokees to be under the protection of the United States of America, and of no other sovereign whosoever.

Art. 5. If any citizen of the United States, or other person not being an Indian, shall attempt to settle on any of the lands westward or southward of the said boundary which are hereby allotted to the Indians for their hunting grounds, or having already settled and will not remove from the same with six months after the ratification of this treaty, such person shall forfeit the protection of the United States, and the Indians may punish him or not as they please.

Art. 8. It is understood that the punishment of the innocent under the idea of retaliation, is unjust, and shall not be practiced on either side, except where there is a manifest violation of this treaty; and then it shall be preceded, first by a demand of justice, and if refused, then by a declaration of hostilities.

Art. 9. For the benefit and comfort of the Indians, and for the prevention of injuries or oppressions on the part of the citizens or Indians; the United States in Congress assembled shall have the sole and exclusive right of regulating the trade with the Indians, and managing all their affairs in such manners as they think proper.

Art. 12. That the Indians may have full confidence in the justice of the United States respecting their interests, they shall have the right to send a deputy of their choice, whenever they think fit, to Congress.

Art. 13. The hatchet shall be forever buried, and the peace given by the United States, and friendship re-established between the said states on the one part, and all the Cherokees on the other, shall be universal; and the contracting parties shall use their utmost endeavours to maintain the peace given as aforesaid, and friendship re-established.

Source: Treaty with the Cherokee, 1785. November 28, 1785, 7 Stat., 18. *Indian Affairs: Laws and Treaties. Vol. II, Treaties.* Compiled and edited by Charles J. Kappler. Washington, DC: Government Printing Office, 1904, 8–11.

EXCERPTS FROM THE TREATY OF HOLSTON, JULY 2, 1791

The Treaty of Holston was the second treaty made between the United States and the Cherokee Nation. Negotiated at the conclusion of several years of continuing frontier warfare between the Tennesseans, led by John Sevier, and the Chickamaugan Cherokee warrior confederation, the treaty again calls for a prisoner exchange, acknowledges Congress's exclusive regulatory rights toward the tribes, reiterates the protectorate status of the Cherokee Nation under the United States, guarantees the Cherokees all lands not previously ceded, and addresses jurisdictions, hunting rights, and blood law. One of the most interesting articles of the treaty is number 14, which establishes the infrastructure for a "civilization" program among the Cherokees. Indian agents were appointed and small parcels of land were loaned to them to educate the Cherokees in the arts of farming—a practice in which they had already engaged for centuries. But the most notable aspect of this treaty is subtle: the use of the word "nation" for the first time in regard to the Cherokees. Thereafter, "the Cherokee Nation" was the official usage of the tribe. The Treaty of Holston thus marks the era of rising nationalist sentiment among the Cherokees.

A Treaty of Peace and; Friendship made and concluded between the President of the United States of America, on the Part and Behalf of the said States, and the undersigned Chiefs and Warriors, of the Cherokee Nation of Indians, on the part aide Behalf of the said Nation.

The parties being desirous of establishing permanent peace and friendship between the United States and the said Cherokee Nation, and the citizens and members thereof, and to remove the causes of war, by ascertaining their limits and making other necessary just and friendly arrangements: The President of the United States, by William Blount, Governor of the territory of the United States of America, south of the river Ohio, and Superintendent of Indian affairs for the southern district, who is vested with full powers for these purposes, by and with-the advice and consent of the Senate of the United States. And the Cherokee Nation, by the undersigned Chiefs and Warriors representing the said nation, have agreed to the following articles, namely:

Art. 1. There shall be perpetual peace and friendship between all the citizens of the United States of America, and all the individuals composing the whole Cherokee nation of Indians.

Art. 2. The undersigned Chiefs and Warriors, for themselves and all parts of the Cherokee nation do acknowledge themselves and the said Cherokee nation, to be under the protection of the said United States of America, and of no other sovereign whosoever; and they also stipulate that the said Cherokee nation will not hold any treaty with any foreign power, individual state, or with individuals of any state.

Art. 3. The Cherokee nation shall deliver to the Governor of the territory of the United States of America, south of the river Ohio, on or before the first day of April next, at this place, all persons who are now prisoners, captured by them from any part of the United States: And the United States shall on or before the same day, and at the same place, restore to the Cherokees, all the prisoners now in captivity, which the citizens of the United States have captured from them.

Art. 6. It is agreed on the part of the Cherokees, that the United States shall have the sole and exclusive right of regulating their trade.

Art. 7. The United States solemnly guarantee to the Cherokee nation, all their lands not hereby ceded.

Art. 8. If any citizen of the United States, or other person not being an Indian, shall settle on any of the Cherokees' lands, such person shall forfeit the protection of the United States, and the Cherokees may punish him or not, as they please.

Art. 9. No citizen or inhabitant of the United States, shall attempt to hunt or destroy the game on the lands of the Cherokees: nor shall any citizen or inhabitant go into the Cherokee country without a passport first obtained from the Governor of some one of the United States, or territorial districts, or such other person as the President of the United States may from time to time authorize to grant the same.

Art. 12. In case of violence on the persons or property of the individuals of either party, neither retaliation or (*sic*) reprisal shall be committed by the other, until satisfaction shall have been demanded of the party of which the aggressor is and shall have been refused.

Art. 14. That the Cherokee nation may be led to a greater degree of civilization, and to become herdsmen and cultivators, instead of remaining in a state of hunters, the United States will from time to time furnish gratuitously the said nation with useful implements of husbandry and further to assist the said nation in so desirable a pursuit, and at the same time to establish a certain mode of communication, the United States will send such, and so many persons to reside in said nation as they may judge proper, not exceeding four in number, who shall qualify themselves to act as interpreters. These persons shall have lands assigned by the Cherokees for cultivation for themselves and their successors in office; but they shall be precluded exercising any kind of traffic.

Source: Treaty with the Cherokee, 1791. July 2, 1791, 7 Stat., 39; Proclamation, February 7, 1792. *Indian Affairs: Laws and Treaties. Vol. II, Treaties.* Compiled and edited by Charles J. Kappler. Washington, DC: Government Printing Office, 1904, 29–33.

EXCERPTS FROM THE TRADE
AND INTERCOURSE ACT, 1802

The U.S. Congress passed a series of Trade and Intercourse Acts regulating trade with the tribes beginning in 1790 and continuing through 1834. The following sections are from the 1802 statute, the first in the series that did not have an expiration date attached. The acts established that in addition to its exclusive constitutional authority to regulate trade with the Indians, Congress also had the exclusive right to accept Indian land in a transfer from the tribe. Sec. 12 forbids a state, a consortium, or an individual from purchasing or leasing Indian land. Even today, this restriction exists, and tribes must get approval from the Bureau of Indian Affairs before they can lease portions of their reservations. Sec. 5 was included in anticipation that tribes would be transferring their lands to the United States, and tried to insure that when that happened, few or no trespassers or squatters were on the lands claimed by the United States. It had previously been the United States' intention to pay Revolutionary War veterans with parcels of land, rather than money, since the country did not have much of that. The provision was continued in later years in anticipation of settlement by a growing American population. The acts came into play when Georgia made an agreement in 1802 to have the United States extinguish all Indian land titles within state boundaries, as Georgia could not do it by itself.

Sec. 5. *And be it further enacted,* That if any such citizen, or other person, shall make a settlement on any lands belonging, or secured, or granted by treaty with the United States, to any Indian tribe, or shall survey or attempts to survey, such lands, or designate any of the boundaries, by marking trees, or otherwise, such offender shall forfeit a sum not exceeding one thousand dollars, and suffer imprisonment, not exceeding twelve months. And it shall, moreover, be lawful for the President of the United States to take such measures, and to employ such military force, as he may judge necessary, to remove from lands, belonging or secured by treaty, as aforesaid, to any Indian tribe, any such citizen, or other person, who has made, or shall hereafter make, or attempt to make a settlement thereon.

Sec. 12. *And be it further enacted,* That no purchase, grant, lease, or other conveyance of lands, or of any title or claim thereto, from any Indian, or nation, or tribe of Indians, within the bounds of the United States, shall be of any validity, in law or equity, unless the same be made by treaty or convention, entered into pursuant to the constitution: and it shall be a misdemeanor in any person, not employed under the authority of the United States, to negotiate such treaty or convention, directly or indirectly, to treat with any such Indian nation, or tribe of Indians, for the title or purchase of any lands by them held or claimed, punishable by fine not exceeding one thousand dollars, and imprisonment not exceeding twelve months: *Provided nevertheless*, that it shall be lawful for the agent or agents of any state, who may be present at any treaty held with Indians under the authority of the United States, in the presence, and with the approbation of the commissioner or commissioners of the United States, appointed to hold the same, to propose to, and adjust with the Indians, the compensation to be made, for their claims to lands within such state, which shall be extinguished by the treaty.

Source: Library of Congress, Seventh Congress, Sess. I, Ch. 13, 1802. *An Act to Regulate Trade and Intercourse with the Indian Tribes, and to Preserve the Peace on the Frontiers.* Found online at http://memory.loc.gov/cgi-bin/ampage?collId=llsl&fileName=002/llsl002.db& recNum=176.

———

EXCERPTS FROM THE ARTICLES OF AGREEMENT AND CESSION BETWEEN THE UNITED STATES AND THE STATE OF GEORGIA, 1802 (THE GEORGIA COMPACT)

Georgia owned lands to the west of Georgia proper, the current states of Alabama and Mississippi, which had been given to the state in a charter in 1730. The United States wanted to incorporate those lands into its territory, but before they could purchase them from Georgia, a land speculation company entered into an agreement with the state to purchase the lands. Georgia held the land for ransom, forcing the United States to compensate the land speculation company and to promise Georgia that it would extinguish Indian titles within the state limits and, by implication, remove the tribes within its borders. Georgia needed the United States to do this as, under the Trade and Intercourse Acts, Georgia had no right to accept Indian land in a transfer. In the Georgia Compact, the United States is agreeing to act as a middleman on behalf of the state, who then was granted a preemption right (right of first ownership) after the United States had taken Cherokee and Creek lands.

Art. 1. The state of Georgia cedes to the United States all the right, title, and claim, which the said state has to the jurisdiction and soil of the lands situated within the boundaries of the United States south of the state of Tennessee, and west of a line beginning on the western bank of the Chatahouchee river, where the same crosses the boundary line between the United States and Spain; running thence, up the said river Chatahouchee, and along the western bank thereof, to the great bend thereof, next above the place where a certain creek or river, called "Uchee" (being the first considerable stream on the western side, above the Cussetas and Coweta towns), empties into the said Chatahouchee River; thence, in a direct line, to Nickajack, on the Tennessee river; thence, crossing the said last mentioned river, and thence, running up the said Tennessee river, and along the western bank thereof, to the southern boundary line of the state of Tennessee; upon the following express conditions, and subject thereto, that is to say:

First. That out of the nett (*sic*) proceeds of the sales of the lands thus ceded, which nett proceeds shall be estimated by deducting, from the gross amount of sales, the expenses incurred in surveying, and incident to the sale, the United States shall pay, at their Treasury, one million two hundred and fifty thousand dollars to the state of Georgia, as a consideration for the expenses incurred by the said state, in relation to the said territory; and that, for the better securing as prompt a payment of the said sum as is practicable, a land office for the disposition of the vacant lands thus ceded, to which the Indian title has been, or may hereafter be, extinguished, shall be opened within a twelvemonth after the assent of the state of Georgia to this agreement, as hereafter stated, shall have been declared.

Fourthly. That the United States shall, at their own expense, extinguish, for the use of Georgia, as early as the same can be peaceably obtained, on reasonable terms, the Indian title to the county of Talassee, to the lands left out by the line drawn with the Creeks, in the year one thousand seven hundred and ninety-eight, which had been previously granted by the state of Georgia; both which tracts had formerly been yielded by the Indians; and to the lands within the forks of Oconee and Oakmulgee rivers; for which several objects, the President of the United States has directed that a treaty should be immediately held with the Creeks; and that the United States shall, in the same manner, also extinguish the Indian title to all other lands within the state of Georgia.

Art. 2. The United States accept the cession above mentioned, and on the conditions therein expressed; and they cede to the state of Georgia whatever claim, right, or title, they may have to the jurisdiction or soil of any lands, lying within the United States, and out of the proper boundaries of any other state, and situated south of the southern boundaries of the states of Tennessee, North Carolina, and South Carolina, and east of the boundary line hereinabove described, as the eastern boundary of the territory ceded by Georgia to the United States.

Source: "The Articles of Agreement and Cession," 24 April, 1802, in *American State Papers, Public Lands* (Washington, DC: Duff Green, 1834), vol. 1, 114.

EXCERPTS FROM THE CONSTITUTION
OF THE CHEROKEE NATION, 1827

The height of Cherokee nationalist endeavors is represented by the 1827 Constitution. By this time, the Cherokees had been moving toward centralized government for almost 40 years. Taking their inspiration from the U.S. Constitution, the Cherokees nevertheless ratified a document that addressed their particular cultural values and pragmatic needs in that moment and for the future. In Article I, Sec. 2, the system of collective tribal landholding is described and set, as is a residency requirement, that a Cherokee must reside within the boundaries of the nation to be regarded as one of its citizens. Article III establishes the legislative branch, sets up a system of elections, and acknowledges treaties and the exclusive negotiating power of the council. It also establishes standards and procedures for impeachment of any elected or appointed official, processes that were presumably employed against Major Ridge and John Ridge a few years later. Article IV establishes the executive branch, and Article V the judicial. In Article VI, the Cherokees also established a rudimentary Bill of Rights. The ratification of this document provoked a fierce response from the state of Georgia, who felt it was "superb effrontery" for an Indian nation to declare its own nationality within its borders, a situation that the Cherokees had dealt with for a century or more, from Georgia and six other states, whom they paradoxically regarded as the foreigners within Cherokee territory.

Formed by a Convention of Delegates from the several Districts, at New Echota, July 1827.

WE THE REPRESENTATIVES of the people of the CHEROKEE NATION in Convention assembled, in order to establish justice, ensure tranquility, promote our common welfare, and secure to ourselves and our posterity the blessings of liberty, acknowledging with humility and gratitude the goodness of the sovereign Ruler of the Universe, in offering as an opportunity so favorable to the design, and imploring his aid and direction in its accomplishment, do ordain and establish this Constitution for the Government of the Cherokee Nation.

Article I

Sec. 2. The Sovereignty and Jurisdiction of this Government shall extend over the country within the boundaries above described, and the lands therein are, and shall remain the common property of the Nation; but the improvements made thereon, and in the possession of the citizens of the Nation, are the exclusive and indefeasible property of the citizens respectively who made, or may rightfully be in possession of them; Provided, That the citizens of the Nation, possessing exclusive and indefeasible right to their respective improvements, as expressed in this article, shall possess no right nor power to dispose of their improvements in any manner whatever to the United States, individual states, nor to individual citizens hereof; and that, whenever any such citizen or citizens shall remove with their effects out of the limits of this Nation, and become citizens of any other government, all their rights and privileges as citizens of this nation shall cease; Provided nevertheless, That the Legislature shall have power to re-admit by law to all the rights of citizenship any such person or persons, who may at any time desire to return to the Nation on their memorializing the General Council for such readmission. Moreover, the Legislature shall have power to adopt such laws and regulations, as its wisdom may deem expedient and proper, to prevent the citizens from monopolizing improvements with the view of speculation.

Article II

Sec. 1. The Power of this Government, shall be divided into three distinct departments; the Legislative, the Executive, and the Judicial.

Article III

Sec. 1. THE LEGISLATIVE POWER shall be vested in two distinct branches; a Committee, and a Council; each to have a negative on the other, and both to be styled, the General Council of the Cherokee Nation.

Sec. 3. The Committee shall consist of two members from each district, and the Council shall consist of three members from each District, to be chosen by the qualified electors of their respective Districts for two years; and the elections to be held in every District on the first Monday in August for the year 1828, and every succeeding two years thereafter; and the General Council shall be held once a year, to be convened on the second Monday of October in each year, at New Echota.

Sec. 6. In all elections by the people, the electors shall vote viva voce.

Sec. 13. Each member of the General Council, before he takes his seat, shall take the following oath of affirmation, to wit: "I A, B, do solemnly swear (or affirm as the case may be) that I have not obtained my election by Bribery, Treats, or any undue and unlawful means used by himself, or others by my desire or approbation, for that purpose; that I consider myself Constitutionally qualified as a member of _____; and that, on all questions and measures which may come before me, I will so give my vote, and so conduct myself, as may, in my judgment, appear most conducive to the interest and prosperity of this Nation; and that I will bear true faith and allegiance to the same, and to the utmost of my ability and power observe conform to, support, and defend the Constitution thereof."

Sec. 22. All acknowledged Treaties shall be the Supreme Law of the land.

Sec. 23. The General Council shall have the sole power of deciding on the construction of all Treaty stipulations.

Sec. 24. The Council shall have the sole power of impeaching.

Sec. 25. All impeachments shall be tried by the Committee; when sitting for that purpose, the members shall be upon oath or affirmation; and no person shall be convicted without the concurrence of two thirds of the members present.

Sec. 26. The Principal Chief, assistant principal Chief, and all civil officers, under this nation shall be liable to impeachment for any misdemeanor in office, but Judgment in such cases shall not extend further that removal from office, and disqualification to hold office of honor, trust or profit, under this Nation. The party, whether convicted or acquitted shall, nevertheless, be liable to indictment, trial, judgment and punishment according to law.

Article IV

Sec. 1. The Supreme Executive Power of this Nation shall be vested in a Principal Chief, who shall be chosen by the General Council, and shall hold his office for four years.

Sec. 2. No person, except a natural born citizen shall be eligible to the office of Principal Chief; neither shall any person be eligible to that office, who shall not have attained to the age of thirty-five years.

Sec. 7. Before the Principal Chief enters on the execution of his office, he shall take the following oath or affirmation; "I do solemnly swear (or affirm) that I will faithfully execute the office of Principal Chief of the Cherokee nation, and will, to the best of my ability, preserve, protect and defend, the Constitution of the Cherokee Nation."

Article V

Sec. 1. The Judicial Powers shall be vested in a Supreme Court and such Circuit and Inferior Courts, as the general Council may, from time to time ordain and establish.

Sec. 2. The Supreme Court shall consist of three Judges, any two of whom shall be a quorum.

Sec. 3. The Judges of each shall hold their Commissions four years, but any of them may be removed from office on the address of two thirds of each house of the general Council to the Principal Chief, for that purpose.

Sec. 5. No person shall be appointed a Judge of any of the Courts before he shall have attained to the age of thirty years, nor shall any person continue to execute the duties of any of the said officers after he shall have attained to the age of seventy years.

Article VI

Sec. 1. Whereas the ministers of the Gospel are, by their profession, dedicated to the service of God and the care of souls, and ought not to be directed from the great duty of their function, therefore, no minister of the gospel, or public preacher of any religious persuasion, whilst he continues in the exercise of his pastoral functions, shall be eligible to the office of Principal Chief, or a seat in either house of the general Council.

Sec. 2. No person who denies the being of a God, or a future state of rewards and punishment, shall hold any office in the civil department of this Nation.

Sec. 3. The free exercise of religious worship, and serving God without distinction shall forever be allowed within this Nation.

Sec. 9. The right of a trial by jury shall be inviolate.

Sec. 10. Religion, morality, and knowledge being necessary to good government, the preservation of liberty, and the happiness of mankind, schools and the means of education shall forever be encouraged in this Nation.

Source: Laws of the Cherokee Nation: Adopted by the Council at Various Periods. Tahlequah, Cherokee Nation: Cherokee Advocate Printing Office, 1852.

EXCERPTS FROM THE GEORGIA
STATUTE, DECEMBER 19, 1829
(FIRST GEORGIA HARASSMENT LAW)

The passage of the Cherokee Constitution in 1827 had spurred Georgia to take a more hardline position against the tribes within its borders, and compounded in 1828 and 1829 by the election of Andrew Jackson and the discovery of gold, Georgia became frenzied in its attempts to grasp control of the situation. The passage of two laws in 1829 and 1830, to-gether known as the Georgia Harassment Laws, represents the moment when the state loses all restraint and enacts controlling legislation, even in violation of federal law and the Constitution, as well as the treaties that even Georgia had previously acknowledged as supreme. The first law asserts the nullification of Cherokee boundaries and extends Georgia's jurisdiction over the Cherokee Nation by nullifying Cherokee laws and outlawing the Cherokee national government. It encourages Cherokee emigration from Georgia and declares Cherokees "incompetent to tes-tify against whites in the state courts," effectively allowing depredations against Cherokees to go unpunished.

An act to add the territory lying within the chartered limits of Georgia, and now in the occupancy of the Cherokee Indians, to the counties of Carroll, De Kalb, Gwinnett, Hall, and Habersham, and to extend the laws of this state over the same, and to annul all laws and ordinances made by the Cherokee nation of Indians, and to provide for the compensation of officers serving legal process in said territory, and to regulate the testimony of Indians, and to repeal the ninth section of the act of 1828 upon this subject.

Sec. 6. And be it further enacted, that all the laws, both civil and criminal, of this state, be, and the same are hereby extended over said portions of territory, respectively; and all persons whatever residing within the same, shall, after the 1st day of June next, be subject and liable to the operation of said laws, in the same manner as other citizens of this state, or the citizens of said counties, respectively; and all writs and processes whatever, issued by the courts or officers of said courts, shall extend over, and operate on, the portions of territory hereby added to the same, respectively.

Sec. 7. And be it further enacted, that after the 1st day of June next, all laws, ordinances, orders and regulations, of any kind whatever, made, passed or enacted, by the Cherokee Indians, either in general council or in any other way whatever, or by any authority whatever of said tribe, be, and the same are hereby declared to be, null and void, and of no effect as if the same had never existed; and in all cases of indictment or civil suits, it shall not be lawful for the defendant to justify under any of said laws, ordinances, orders or regulations; nor shall the courts of this state permit the same to be given in evidence on the trial of any suit whatever.

Sec. 8. And be it further enacted, that it shall not be lawful for any person or body of persons, by arbitrary Power or by virtue of any pretended rule, ordinance, law or custom of said Cherokee nation, to prevent by threats, menaces on other means, or endeavour to prevent, any Indian of said nation residing within the chartered limits of this state, from enrolling as an emigrant, or actually emigrating or removing from said nation; nor shall it be lawful for any person or body of persons, by arbitrary power or by virtue of any pretended rule, ordinance, law or custom of said nation, to punish in any manner, or to molest either the person or property, or to abridge the rights or privileges of any Indian, for enrolling his or her name as an emigrant, or for emigrating or intending to emigrate, from said nation.

Sec. 10. And be it further enacted, that it shall not be lawful for any Person or body of persons, by arbitrary Power, or under colour of any pretended rule, ordinance, law or custom of said nation, to prevent or offer to prevent, or deter any Indian headman, chief or warrior of said nation, residing within the chartered limits of this state, from selling or ceding to the United States, for the use of Georgia, the whole or any part of said territory, or to prevent or offer to prevent, any Indian, headman, chief or warrior of said nation, residing as aforesaid, from meeting in council or treaty any commissioner or commissioners on the part of the United States, for any purpose whatever.

Sec. 12. And be it further enacted, that it shall not be lawful for any person or body of persons, by arbitrary force or under colour of any pretended rules, ordinances, law or custom of said nation, to take the life of any Indian residing as aforesaid, for enlisting as an emigrant; attempting to ernigrate; ceding, or attempting to cede, as aforesaid, the whole or any part of the said territory; or meeting or attempting to meet, in treaty or in council, as aforesaid, any commissioner or commissioners aforesaid; and any Person or body of persons offending against the provisions of this section, shall be guilty of murder, subject to indictment, and, on conviction, shall suffer death by hanging.

Sec. 13. And be it further enacted, that, should any of the foregoing offences be committed under colour of any pretended rules, ordinances, custom or law of said nation, all persons acting therein, either as individuals or as pretended executive, ministerial or judicial officers, shall be deemed and considered as principals, and subject to the pains and penalties hereinbefore described.

Sec. 15. And be it further enacted, that no Indian or descendant of any Indian, residing within the Creek or Cherokee nations of Indians, shall be deemed a competent witness in any court of this state to which a white person may be a party, except such white person resides within the said nation.

Source: *American Annual Register for the Year 1829–30*, 2nd edition. Boston: Gray and Bowen, 1832, pp. 577, 578.

EXCERPTS FROM THE GEORGIA STATUTE, DECEMBER 22, 1830 (SECOND GEORGIA HARASSMENT LAW)

The second of the Harassment Laws was passed in 1830. It is more specific about the outlawing of Cherokee government than the previous law, particularly in regard to Cherokee courts and their orders. It specifies the penalty for violation of any section of the laws—four years at hard labor. Most importantly for the Cherokees, it attempted to regulate labor within the Cherokee Nation, particularly the activities of the missionaries, which became critically important to the Cherokees and gave them the necessary basis to enter federal courts. But the law also established the Georgia Guard, a vigilante militia that became the scourge of the Cherokees. The message of the two laws together was unmistakable: if the Cherokees did not remove from Georgia, Georgia would make their lives miserable until they did.

An act to prevent the exercise of assumed and arbitrary power; by all persons under pretext of authority from the Cherokee Indians and their laws, and to prevent white persons from residing within that part of the chartered limits of Georgia occupied by the Cherokee Indians, and to provide a Guard for the protection of the gold mines, and to enforce the laws of the state within the aforesaid territory.

Be it enacted by the senate and house of representatives of the state of Georgic in general assembly met, and it is hereby enacted by the authority of the same, that, after the 1st day of February 1831, it shall not be lawful for any person or Persons, under colour or pretence of authority from said Cherokee tribe, or as headmen, chiefs or warriors of said tribe, to cause or procure by any means the assembling of any council or other pretended legislative body of the said Indians or others living among them, for the Purpose of legislating (or for any other purpose whatever). And persons offending against the provisions of this section shall be guilty of a high misdemeanour, and subject to indictment therefor, and, on conviction, shall be punished by confinement at hard labour in the penitentiary for the space of four years.

Sec. 2. And be it further enacted by the authority aforesaid, that, after the time aforesaid, it shall not be lawful for any person or Persons, under pretext of authority from the Cherokee tribe, or as representatives, chiefs, headmen or warriors of said tribe, to meet or assemble as a council, assembly, convention, or in any other capacity, for the Purpose of making laws, orders or regulations for said tribe. And all Persons offending against the provisions of this section, shall be guilty of a high misdemeanour, and subject to an indictment, and, on conviction thereof, shall undergo an imprisonment in the penitentiary at hard labour for the space of four years.

Sec. 3. And be it further enacted by the authority aforesaid, that, after the time aforesaid, it shall not be lawful for any person or persons, under colour or by authority of the Cherokee tribe, or any of its laws or regulations, to hold any court or tribunal whatever, for the purpose of hearing and determining causes, either civil or criminal; or to give any judgment in such causes, or to issue, or cause to issue, any Process against the person or property of any of said tribe. And all persons offending against the provisions of this section shall be guilty of a high misdemeanour, and subject to indictment, and, on conviction thereof, shall be imprisoned in the penitentiary at hard labour for the space of four years.

Sec. 4. And be it further enacted by the authority aforesaid, that, after the time aforesaid, it shall not be lawful for any person or persons, as a ministerial officer, or in any other capacity, to execute any Precept, command or process issued by any court or tribunal in the Cherokee tribe, on the Persons or property of any of said tribe. And all Persons offending against the provisions of this section shall be guilty of a trespass, and subject to indictment, and, on conviction thereof, shall be punished by fine and imprisonment in the jail or in the penitentiary, not longer than four years, at the discretion of the court.

Sec. 7. And be it further enacted by the authority aforesaid, that all white persons residing within the limits of the Cherokee nation, on the 1st day of March next, or at any time thereafter, without a license or permit from his excellency the governor, or from such agent as his excellency the governor shall authorise to grant such permit or license, and who shall not have taken the oath hereinafter required, shall be guilty of a high misdemeanour, and, upon conviction thereof shall be punished by confinement to the penitentiary at hard labour for a term not less than four years: provided, that the provisions of this section shall not be so construed as to extend to any authorised agent or agents of the government of the United States or of this state, or to any person or persons who may rent any of those improvements which have been abandoned by Indians who have emigrated west of the Mississippi: provided, nothing contained in this section shall be so construed as to extend to white females, and all male children under twenty-one years of age.

Sec. 8. And be it further enacted by the authority aforesaid, that all white persons, citizens of the state of Georgia, who have procured a license in writing from his excellency the governor, or from such agent as his excellency the governor shall authorise to grant such permit or license, to reside within the limits of the Cherokee nation, and who have taken the following oath, viz. "I, A.B., do solemnly swear (or affirm, as the case may be) that I will support and defend the constitution and laws of the state of Georgia, and uprightly demean myself as a citizen thereof, so help me God" shall be, and the same are hereby declared, exempt and free from the operation of the seventh section of this act.

Sec. 9. And be it further enacted, that his excellency the governor be, and he is hereby, authorized to grant licenses to reside within the limits of the Cherokee nation, according to the provisions of the eighth section of this act.

Sec. 11. And be it further enacted by the authority aforesaid that his excellency the governor be, and he is hereby, empowered, should he deem it necessary, either for the protection of the mines, or for the enforcement of the laws of force within the Cherokee nation, to raise and organize a guard, to be employed on foot, or mounted, as occasion may require, which shall not consist of more than sixty persons which guard shall be under the command of the commissioner or agent appointed by the governor, to protect the mines, with power to dismiss from the service any member of said guard, on paying the wages due for services rendered, for disorderly conduct, and make appointments to fill the vacancies occasioned by such dismissal.

Sec. 13. And be it further enacted by the authority aforesaid, that the said guard, or any member of them, shall bet and they are hereby, authorised and empowered to arrest any person legally charged with, or detected in, a violation of the laws of this state, and to convey as soon as practicable, the person so arrested before a justice of the peace, judge of the superior or justice of inferior court of this state, to be dealt with according to law; and the pay and support of said guard be provided out of the fund already appropriated for the protection of the gold mines.

Source: *Acts of the General Assembly of the State of Georgia, Passed in Milledgeville at an Annual Session in October, November, and December 1830.* Milledgeville, GA: Camak & Ragland, 1834, pp. 114–17.

INDIAN REMOVAL ACT OF 1830

The Indian Removal Act brought to the forefront a policy that had been discussed for decades. Although many smaller tribes from the Great Lakes and Ohio Valley regions had already been removed, the powerful southeastern tribes were the targets of this legislation. The "Five Civilized Tribes" as they had become known—Cherokees, Creeks, Choctaws, Chickasaws, and Seminoles—were proving strategic and intransigent. The legislation thus has aspects that are intended to be attractive to the tribes, particularly the offer in Section 3 of a fee simple grant or patent to any tribe that removes under the terms of this act. Although it was not enough to coerce any of them, when the tribes were forcibly removed, they negotiated for the land patents as part of their removal treaties. As a result, the ownership of their new lands in the Indian Territory was legally stronger than it had been in the southeast, and it was wrested from them a second time only by outright legal force and extortion in the 1890s and first decade of the 1900s. The Indian Removal Act was one of the most controversial pieces of legislation in the early 1800s, not because people cared much about Indians, but because Georgia had passed laws apparently in violation of federal law and the Constitution. The Indian Removal Act thus became a referendum on whether one advocated for states'

rights and thus approved Georgia's action, or whether one took a strongly
federalist position and disavowed Georgia's laws. Passing a federal law
that mirrored Georgia's intent was the way out of the conundrum for
some legislators.

An Act to provide for an exchange of lands with the Indians residing in any of the states or territories, and for their removal west of the
Mississippi.

Be it enacted by the Senate and House of Representatives of the United
States of America, in Congress assembled, That it shall and may be lawful for the President of the United States to cause so much of any territory
belonging to the United States, west of the river Mississippi, not included
in any state or organized territory, and to which the Indian title has been
extinguished, as he may judge necessary, to be divided into a suitable number of districts, for the reception of such tribes or nations of Indians as
may choose to exchange the lands where they now reside, and remove
there; and to cause each of said districts to be so described by natural or
artificial marks, as to be easily distinguished from every other.

Sec. 2. *And be it further enacted,* That it shall and may be lawful for the
President to exchange any or all of such districts, so to be laid off and described, with any tribe or nation of Indians now residing within any of the
limits of the states or territories, and with which the United States have existing treaties, for the whole or any part or portion of the territory claimed
and occupied by such tribe or nation, within the bounds of any one or more
of the states and territories, where the land claimed and occupied by the
Indians, is owned by the United States, or the United States are bound to
the state within which it lies to extinguish the Indian claim thereto.

Sec.3. *And be it further enacted,* That in the making of any such exchange or exchanges, it shall and may be lawful for the President solemnly
to assure the tribe or nation with which the exchange is made, that the
United States will forever secure and guaranty to them, and their heirs or
successors, the country so exchanged with them; and if they prefer it, that
the United States will cause a patent or grant to be made and executed to
them for the same: *Provided always,* That such lands shall revert to the
United States, if the Indians become extinct or abandon the same.

Sec.4. *And be it further enacted,* That if, upon any of the lands now
occupied by the Indians, and to be exchanged for, there should be such
improvements as add value to the land claimed by any individual or individuals of such tribes or nations, it shall and may be lawful for the President to cause such value to be ascertained by appraisement or otherwise,

and to cause such ascertained value to be paid to the person or persons rightfully claiming such improvements. And upon the -payment of such valuation, the improvements so valued and paid for, shall pass to the United States, and possession shall not afterwards be permitted to any of the same tribe.

Sec. 5. *And be it further enacted,* That upon the making of any such exchange as is contemplated by this act, it shall and may be lawful for the President to cause such aid and assistance to be furnished to the emigrants as may be necessary and proper to enable them to remove to, and settle in, the country for which they may have exchanged; and also, to give them such aid and assistance as may be necessary for their support and subsistence for the first year after their removal.

Sec. 6. *And be it further enacted,* That it shall and may be lawful for the President to Cause such tribe or nation to be protected, at their new residence, against all interruption or disturbance from any other tribe or nation of Indians, or from any other person or persons whatever.

Sec. 7. *And be it further enacted,* That it shall and may be lawful for the President to have the same superintendence and care over any tribe or nation in the country to which they may remove as contemplated by this act, that he is now authorized to have over them at their present places of residence: *Provided,* That nothing in this act contained shall be construed as authorizing or directing the violation of any existing treaty between the United States and any of the Indian tribes.

Sec. 8. *And be it further enacted,* That for the purpose of giving effect to the provisions of this act, the sum of five hundred thousand dollars is hereby appropriated, to be paid out of any money in the treasury, not otherwise appropriated.

Source: Indian Removal Act. *U.S. Statutes at Large,* 4 (1830): 411.

FROM THE WRITINGS OF ELIAS BOUDINOT, EDITOR OF THE *CHEROKEE PHOENIX,* 1830 (REFLECTIONS ON THE RECENT PASSAGE OF THE INDIAN REMOVAL ACT)

As the editor of the Cherokee Phoenix, Boudinot took the responsibility to inform the Cherokee public very seriously. Even more serious was the need to inform the American public, and the many essays written by Boudinot in the hopes that they would be reprinted in a major northern

newspaper have resulted in a literary legacy of unparalleled grandeur in
an Indian nation. Many were reprinted and the Cherokee cause gained
traction, but the apathy and lack of understanding, or even to try to un-
derstand Indian sovereignty on the part of the American public that so
frustrated Boudinot is still very prevalent in the "Christian and Philan-
thropic" nation to which he and others ever since have given their faith
and trust. Boudinot's arguments attempted to call the United States back
to its ideals—of respecting legal documents that hold the highest position
in international law and of justice even for the poorest among us—and
represent arguments that are still made today, as Indians continue to
struggle to be seen and heard by the American public and government.

June 19, 1830

In our last was given the proceedings of the House of Representatives on the Indian bill, to the time when it was ordered to a third reading. In this day's paper will be found the final proceedings and the adoption of the amendment by the Senate. We stated last week that if the amendment was adopted, or the bill failed, but the refusal of the Senate to adopt it, our fears would not be realized in their full extent. But since, on mature reflection, and after reading the doings of the Senate which the reader can see for himself, we are constrained to say, the formal acknowledgment of the validity of treaties is but a mock show of justice. This is evident from the fact that the very men who have all along contended for the unconstitutionality of treaties with the Indians, were the first to agree to the amendment of the House, & (*sic*) to reject the amendments offered by Messers. Frelinghuysen, Sprague and Clayton. The bearing of the bill then on the interests of the Indians will be the same as if it had passed in its original shape.

We confess our ignorance, our utter ignorance, of the views of the majority of the members of Congress, so far as they have been developed, on the rights of the Indians, and the relation in which they stand to the United States, on the score of treaties; nor can we discern the consistency of contending for the unconstitutionality of these treaties, and yet at the same time, declaring that *they shall not be violated*, which a man of common sense would take to be the meaning of the amendment. If a treaty is unconstitutional, it is of course null and void, and cannot be violated. If a treaty may *not be violated*, it is taken for granted that it is binding; and if it is binding, the parties to it have a right to demand its enforcement. How are we then to understand the decision of the Senate on this important subject? What do they mean by adopting the proviso, and at the same breath deliberately refusing to enforce the provisions of the existing treaties? We can find no suitable answer but this, *palpable injustice is mediated against the poor Indians!*

It is somewhat surprising that many well meaning persons, who would never in other circumstances, lend their aid and influence to do injustice to the Indians should be perfectly blinded by this bill. They believe, as its advocates represent to them, that it is harmless, and that its operation cannot be otherwise than highly beneficial. But they are greatly deceived—the bill is not harmless, nor was it ever intended to be harmless. For the truth of this assertion, look at the decision of the Senate, rejecting the several amendments for the protection of the Indians? This 500,000 dollars is intended to co-operate with any other expedient, which will play at our backs like a flaming sword, while this sum will address itself to our fears & (*sic*) avarice. Compulsion behind, while the means of escape are placed before. Go or perish. And this is said when treaties are declared to be binding, and in them ample provisions are made for the protection of the Indians. Who would trust his life and fortune to such a faithless nation? No Cherokee *voluntarily* would.

At this time of much distress and darkness, the Cherokees can have some consoling thoughts—they have been ably and most manfully defended to the last, and although self-interest and party and sectional feelings have triumphed over justice, yet it has only been by a pitiful majority, and against the known will and feelings of the good people of these United States. Those worthy advocates of Indian rights in the Senate and House of Representatives will be remembered while there is a living Cherokee—and notwithstanding oppression and power may crush us and utterly destroy us, yet their laudable efforts to save us, will be estimated in their proper light, and held in pleasing recollection by the Christian and Philanthropist of future ages, and of all countries.

Source: Elias Boudinot, *Cherokee Phoenix*, June 17, 1829.

EXCERPTS FROM THE MAJORITY OPINION, *CHEROKEE NATION V. GEORGIA*, 1830–1831 (AUTHORED BY CHIEF JUSTICE JOHN MARSHALL)

The Cherokee Nation v. Georgia was among the first attempts by an Indian nation to define its rights in front of the Supreme Court. Argued by former U.S. Attorney General William Wirt, the case established important tenets of federal Indian law, such as the "domestic dependent nation" status of the tribes and the "trust responsibility" of the federal government to the tribes. In his majority opinion, Chief Justice Marshall examined the premise that the Cherokee Nation was a foreign government, the argument made by Wirt to establish that the court held original jurisdiction. But even though not contained in this work, the concurrent and dissenting opinions in the case are also as enlightening in their perspectives held across the spectrum in the United States regarding race and sovereignty, as well as the social science of the day, and students are urged to research the three additional opinions that exist. Many of those perspectives are still very present in American society, and one wonders what social science the American nation and its courts are investing in today that will also be discredited in the future. Marshall was perhaps wise in confining himself to the immediate legal question, but he also created confusion even as he attempted clarity in defining the tribal governments not as foreign but as domestic dependent nations. The parameters of that category continue to be tested.

This bill is brought by the Cherokee nation, praying an injunction to restrain the state of Georgia from the execution of certain laws of that state, which, as is alleged, go directly to annihilate the Cherokees as a political society, and to seize, for the use of Georgia, the lands of the nation which have been assured to them by the United States in solemn treaties repeatedly made and still in force.

If courts were permitted to indulge their sympathies, a case better calculated to excite them can scarcely be imagined. A people once numerous, powerful, and truly independent, found by our ancestors in the quiet and uncontrolled possession of an ample domain, gradually sinking beneath our superior policy; our arts and our arms, have yielded their lands by successive treaties, each of which contains a solemn guarantee of the residue, until they retain no more of their formerly extensive territory then is deemed necessary to their comfortable subsistence. To preserve this remnant, the present application is made.

Before we can look into the merits of the case, a preliminary inquiry presents itself. Has this court jurisdiction of the cause?

The third article of the constitution describes the extent of the judicial power. The second section closes an enumeration of the cases to which it is extended, with "controversies . . . between a state or the citizens thereof and foreign states, citizens, or subjects." A subsequent clause of the same section gives the supreme court original jurisdiction in all cases in which a state shall be a party. The party defendant may then unquestionably be sued in this court. May the plaintiff sue in it? Is the Cherokee nation a foreign state in the sense in which that term is used in the constitution?

The counsel have shown conclusively that they are not a state of the union, and have insisted that individually they are aliens, not owing allegiance to the United States. An aggregate of aliens composing a state must, they say, be a foreign state. Each individual being foreign, the whole must be foreign.

This argument is imposing but we must examine it more closely before we yield to it. The condition of the Indians in relation to the United States is perhaps unlike that of any other two people in existence. In the general, nations not owing a common allegiance are foreign to each other. The term foreign nation is, with strict propriety, applicable by either to the other. But he relation of the Indians to the United States is marked by peculiar and cardinal distinctions which exist no where else.

The Indian territory is admitted to compose a part of the United States. On all our maps, geographical treatises, histories, and laws, it is so considered. In all our intercourse with foreign nations, in our commercial regulations, in any attempt at intercourse between Indians and foreign nations, they are considered as within the jurisdictional limits of the United States, subject to any of those restraints which are imposed upon our own citizens. They acknowledge themselves in their treaties to be under the protection of the United States; they admit that the United States shall have the sole and exclusive right of regulating the trade with them, and managing all their affairs as they think proper; and the Cherokees in particular were allowed by the treaty of Hopewell, which preceded the constitution, "to send a deputy of their choice, whenever they think fit, to congress." Treaties were made with some tribes by the state of New York, under a then unsettled construction of the confederation, by which they ceded all their lands to that state, taking back a limited grant to themselves, in which they admit their dependence.

Though the Indians are acknowledged to have an unquestionable, and, heretofore, unquestioned right to the lands they occupy, until that right shall be extinguished by a voluntary cession to our government; yet it may well be doubted whether those tribes which reside within the acknowledged boundaries of the United States can, with strict accuracy, be denominated foreign nations. They may more correctly perhaps, be denominated domestic dependent nations. They occupy a territory to which we assert a title independent of their will, which must take effect in point of possession when their right of possession ceases. Meanwhile they are in a state of pupilage. Their relation to the United States resembles that of a ward to his guardian.

They look to our government for protection; rely upon its kindness and its power; appeal to it for relief to their wants; and address the president as their great father. They and their country are considered by foreign nations, as well as by ourselves, as being so completely under the sovereignty and dominion of the United States, that any attempt to acquire their land, or to form a political connexion (*sic*) with them, would be considered by all as an invasion of our territory, and an act of hostility.

These considerations go far to support the opinion, that the framers of our constitution had not the Indian tribes in view, when they opened the courts of the union to controversies between a state or the citizens thereof, and foreign states.

The Court has bestowed its best attention on this question, and, after mature deliberation, the majority is of opinion that an Indian tribe or nation within the United States is not a foreign state in the sense of the constitution and cannot maintain an action in the courts of the United States.

A serious additional objection exists to the jurisdiction of the court. Is the matter of the bill the Proper subject for judicial inquiry and decision? It seeks to restrain a state from the forcible exercise of legislative power over a neighbouring people, asserting their independence; their right to which the state denies. On several of the matters alleged in the bill, for example on the laws making it criminal to exercise the usual powers of self government in their own country by the Cherokee nation, this court cannot interpose; at least in the form in which those matters are presented.

Source: Cherokee Nation v. Georgia, 30 U.S. (5 Peters) 1 (1831).

EXCERPTS FROM THE MAJORITY OPINION, *WORCESTER V. GEORGIA,* 1832 (AUTHORED BY CHIEF JUSTICE JOHN MARSHALL)

Worcester v. Georgia represented the pinnacle of Cherokee efforts over the previous 40 years. Their attempts to learn as much as they could about the Americans' system of law and to structure a similar system had not been out of admiration for that system so much as a need to defend themselves in terms the United States could understand and respect. That moment had arrived in 1832, and the Cherokees celebrated. Boudinot stated that the case should settle the Indian question for all time, and he was right. Marshall's argument is based deeply in treaty rights and obligations and on European models of protectorates that still retain sovereignty to the protected. The argument is strong, unequivocal, and clear: within their own well-defined territories, tribes are the governing body. The decision placed the tribes on the same jurisdictional level as the United States, at least within their own lands. But almost immediately, that began to be chipped away. In 1846, in another case involving a Cherokee citizen, United States v. Rogers, Congress asserted its authority even within Indian nations, if it chose to. And the 1886 case United States v. Kagama resulted in a drastic reinterpretation of the framers' original intent in establishing Congress to regulate trade with the Indians and manage all

their affairs as they think proper. But in 1832, the Cherokees were jubi-
lant at a victory at last. It was a short-lived celebration.

The plaintiff in error was indicted to the Supreme Court for the County of Gwinnett in the state of Georgia "for residing on the 15th July 1831 in that part of the Cherokee nation attached by the laws of the state of Georgia to that county, without a license or permit from the governor of the state or from any one authorised to grant it, and without having taken the oath to support and defend the constitution and laws of the state of Georgia and uprightly to demean himself as a citizen thereof, contrary to the laws of the said state." To this indictment he pleaded that he was, on the 15th July, 1831, in the Cherokee Nation, out of the jurisdiction of the court of Gwinnett county, that he was a citizen of Vermont, and entered the Cherokee nation as a missionary under the authority of the President of the United States, and has not been required by him to leave it, and that with the permission and approval of the Cherokee nation he was engaged in preaching the gospel, that the state of Georgia ought not to maintain the prosecution, as several treaties had been entered into by the United States with the Cherokee Nation by which that nation was acknowledged to be a sovereign nation, and which the territory occupied by them was guarantied to them by the United States; and that the laws of Georgia under which the plaintiff in error was indicated are repugnant to the treaties, and unconstitutional and void, and also that they are repugnant to the act of congress of March 1802, entitled "an act to regulate trade and intercourse with the Indian tribes." The superior court of Gwinnett overruled the plea, and the plaintiff in error was tried and convicted, and sentenced "to hard labour in the penitentiary for four years." Held, that this was a case in which the supreme court of the United States had jurisdiction by writ of error, under the twenty-fifth section of the "act to establish the judicial courts of the United States" passed in 1789.

The indictment and plea in this case draw into question the validity of the treaties made by the United States with the Cherokee Indians: if not so, their construction is certainly drawn into question; and the decision has been, if not against their validity, "against the right, privilege, or exemption specially set up and claimed under them." They also draw into question the validity of a statute of the state of Georgia "on the ground of its being repugnant to the constitution, treaties and laws of the United States and the decision is in favour of its validity."

It is too clear for controversy, that the act of congress, by which this court is constituted, has given it the power, and of course imposed upon it the duty of exercising jurisdiction in this case. The record, according to the judiciary act and the rule and practice of the court, is regularly before the court.

The act of the legislature of Georgia, passed 22nd December 1830, entitled "an act to prevent the exercise of assured and arbitrary power by all persons under pretext of authority from the Cherokee Indians" etc. . . . [denies that t]he territorial power over every legislature [is] limited in its action to its own citizens or subjects, the very passage of this act is an assertion of jurisdiction over the Cherokee nation, and of the rights and powers consequent thereto.

Certain it is, that our history furnished no example, from the first settlement of our country, of any attempt, on the part of the crown, to interfere with the internal affairs of the Indians, farther than to keep agents of foreign powers, who, as traders or otherwise, might seduce them into foreign alliances. The king purchased their lands, when they were willing to sell, at a price they were willing to take; but never coerced a surrender of them. He also purchased their alliance and dependence by subsidies; but never intruded into the interior of their affairs, or interfered with their self government, so far as respected themselves only.

The third article of the treaty of Hopewell acknowledges the Cherokees to be under the protection of the United States and of no other power.

It merely bound the nation to the British crown, as a dependent ally, claiming the protection of a powerful friend and neighbor and receiving the advantages of that protection, without involving a surrender of the national character.

This is the true meaning of the stipulation, and is undoubtedly the sense in which it was made. Neither the British government, nor the Cherokees, ever understood it otherwise.

The same stipulation entered into with the United States, is undoubtedly to be construed in the same manner. They receive the Cherokee nation into their favour and protection. The Cherokees acknowledge themselves to be under the protection of the United States, and of no other power. Protection does not imply the destruction of the protected. The manner in which this stipulation was understood by the American government is explained by the language and acts of our first president.

The sixth and seventh articles stipulate for the punishment of the citizens of either country, who may commit offences on or against the citizens of the other. The only inference to be drawn from this is, that the United States considered the Cherokees a nation.

The ninth articles is in these words: "for the benefit and comfort of the Indians, and for the prevention of injuries or oppressions on the part of the citizens or Indians, the United States, in congress assembled shall have the sole and exclusive right of regulating the trade with the Indians, and *managing all their affairs*, as they think proper." To construe the expression "managing all their affairs," into a surrender of self government would be a perversion of their necessary meaning, and a departure from the construction which has been uniformly put on them. The great subject of the article is the Indian trade. The influence it gave made it desirable that congress should possess it. The commissioners brought forward the claim, with the profession that their motive was "the benefit and comfort of the Indians and the prevention of injuries or oppressions." This may be true, as respect the regulation of their trade, and as respects the management of all their affairs. The most important of these, is the cession of their lands, and security against intruders on them. Is it credible, that they could have considered themselves as surrendering to the United States, the right to dictate their future cessions, and the terms on which they should be made; or to compel their submission to the violence of disorderly and licentious intruders? It is equally inconceivable that they could have supposed themselves, by a phrase thus slipped into an article, on another and more interesting subject, to have divested themselves of the right of self government on subjects not connected with trade. Such a measure could not be "for their benefit and comfort," or for "the prevention of injuries and oppression." Such a construction would be inconsistent with the spirit of this and of all subsequent treaties; especially of those articles which recognise the right of the Cherokees to dictate hostilities, and to make war. It would convert a treaty of peace covertly into an annihilating the political existence of one of the parties. Had such a result been intended, it would have been openly avowed.

The treaty of Holston, negotiated with the Cherokees in July 1791; explicitly recognising the national character of the Cherokees, and their right of self government; thus guarantying their lands; assuming the protection, and of course pledging the faith of the United States for that protection; has been frequently renewed and is now in full force.

The treaties and laws of the United States contemplate the Indian territory as completely separated from that of the states; and provide that all intercourse with them shall be carried out exclusively by the government of the union.

The Indian nations had always been considered as distinct, independent political communities, retaining their original natural rights as the undisputed possessors of the soil, from time immemorial; with the single exception of that imposed by irresistible power which excluded them from intercourse with any other European potentate than the first discoverer of the coast of the particular region claimed: and this was a restriction which those European potentates imposed on themselves, as well as the Indians. The very term "nation," so generally applied to them, means "a people distinct from others." The constitution, by declaring treaties already made, as well as those to be made, to be the supreme law of the land, has adopted and sanctioned the previous treaties with the Indian nations, and, consequently, admits their rank among those powers who are capable of making treaties. The words "treaty" and "nation" are words of our own language selected in our diplomatic and legislative proceedings, by ourselves, having each a definite and well-understood meaning. We have applied them to Indians, as we have applied them to other nations of the earth. They are applied to all in the same sense.

In opposition to the original right, possessed by the undisputed occupants of every country, to this recognition of that right, which is evidenced by our history in every change through which we have passed, are placed the charters granted by the monarch of a distant and distinct region, parcelling out a territory in possession of others, whom he could not remove, and did not attempt to remove, and the cession made of his claims, by the treaty of peace. The actual state of things at the time, and all history since, explain these charters, and the king of Great Britain, at the treaty of peace, could cede only what belonged to his crown. These newly asserted titles can derive no aid from the articles so often repeated in Indian treaties, extending them, first, the protection of Great Britain, and afterwards of the United States. These articles are associated with others, recognising their title to self-government. The very fact of repeated treaties with them recognizes it; and the settled doctrine of the law of nation is, that a weaker power does not surrender its independence—its right to self-government, by associating with a stronger, and taking its protection. A weak state, in order to provide for its safety, may place itself under the protection of one more powerful, without stripping itself of the right of government, and ceasing to be a state. Examples of this kind are not wanting in Europe.

The Cherokee nation, then, is a distinct community, occupying its own territory, with boundaries accurately described, in which the laws of Georgia can have no force, and which the citizens of Georgia have no right to enter, but with the assent of the Cherokees themselves, or in conformity with treaties, and with the acts of congress. The whole intercourse between the United States and this nation is, by our constitution and laws, vested in the government of the United States.

The act of the state of Georgia, under which the plaintiff in error was prosecuted, is consequently void, and the judgment a nullity.

The acts of the legislature of Georgia interfere forcibly with the relations established between the United States and the Cherokee nation, the regulation of which, according to the settled principles of our constitution, is committed exclusively to the government of the union.

They are in direct hostility with treaties, repeated in a succession of years, which mark out the boundary that separates the Cherokee country from Georgia; guaranty to them all the land within their boundary; solemnly pledge the faith of the United States to restrain their citizens from trespassing on it; and recognize the pre-existing power of the nation to govern itself.

They are in equal hostility with the acts of congress for regulating this intercourse and giving effect to the treaties.

Source: *Worcester v. Georgia*, 31 U.S. (6 Pet.) 515 (1832).

EXCERPTS FROM THE TREATY OF NEW ECHOTA, DECEMBER 29, 1835

The Cherokees considered the Treaty of New Echota to be an illegal treaty, and for years afterward refused to settle claims because to do so would signal its acceptance. However, as a negotiated settlement, its terms are probably as strong as they could have been. From this treaty were derived many of the foundations of a new Cherokee Nation in the Indian Territory, and the Indian republic that was developed throughout the remainder of the 19th century. The treaty awarded the fee simple patent they had been promised in the Indian Removal Act; it arranged for investments that would drive the governmental, educational, and social welfare programs that were developed; and it established pensions for wounded veterans and reaffirmed the right to seat a delegate to Congress. But in the end, it ceded all their land in the southeast. While Cherokees blamed the signers, the real culprit was the U.S. Senate, who ratified the treaty by a single vote, even though it was abundantly evident to them that 95 percent of the Cherokee people were opposed to it, and that it had never been sanctioned by their elected officials.

Concluded at New Echota in the State of Georgia on the 29th day of Decr. (*sic*) 1835 by General William Carroll and John F. Schermerhorn commissioners on the part of the United States and the Chiefs Head Men and People of the Cherokee tribe of Indians.

WHEREAS, the Cherokees are anxious to make some arrangements with the Government of the United States whereby the difficulties they have experienced by a residence within the settled parts of the United States under the jurisdiction and laws of the State Governments may be terminated and adjusted; and with a view to reuniting their people in one body and securing a permanent home for themselves and their posterity in the country selected by their forefathers without the territorial limits of the State sovereignties, and where they can establish and enjoy a government of their choice and perpetuate such a state of society as may be most consonant with their views, habits and condition; and as may tend to their individual comfort and their advancement in civilization.

And whereas a delegation of the Cherokee nation composed of Messrs. John Ross Richard Taylor Danl. McCoy Samuel Gunter and William Rogers with full power and. authority to conclude a treaty with the United States did on the 28th day of February 1835 stipulate and agree with the Government of the United States to submit to the Senate to fix the amount which should be allowed the Cherokees for their claims and for a cession of their lands east of the Mississippi river, and did agree to abide by the award of the Senate of the United States themselves and to recommend the same to their people for their final determination.

And whereas on such submission the Senate advised "that a sum not exceeding five millions of dollars be paid to the Cherokee Indians for all their lands and possessions east of the Mississippi river."

And whereas this delegation after said award of the Senate had been made, were called upon to submit propositions as to its disposition to be arranged in a treaty which they refused to do, but insisted that the same "should be referred to their nation and there in general council to deliberate and determine on the subject in order to insure harmony and good feeling among themselves."

And whereas a certain other delegation composed of John Ridge Elias Boudinot Archilla Smith S. W. Bell John West Wm. A. Davis and Ezekiel West, who represented that portion of the nation in favor of emigration to the Cherokee country west of the Mississippi entered into propositions for a treaty with John F. Schermerhorn commissioner on the part of the United States which were to be submitted to their nation for their final action and determination:

And whereas the Cherokee people, at their last October council at Red Clay, fully authorized and empowered a delegation or committee of twelve persons of their nation to enter into and conclude a treaty with the United States commissioner then present, *at that place or elsewhere* and as the people had good reason to believe that a treaty would then and there be made or at a subsequent council at New Echota which the commissioners it was well known and understood, were authorized and instructed to convene for said purpose; and since the said delegation have gone on to Washington city, with a view to close negotiations there, as stated by them notwithstanding they were officially informed by the United States commissioner that they would not be received by the President of the United States; and that the Government would transact no business of this nature with them, and that if a treaty was made it must be done here in the nation, where the delegation at Washington last winter *urged that it should be done for the purpose of promoting peace and harmony among the people*; and since these facts have also been corroborated to us by a communication recently received by the commissioner from the Government of the United States and read and explained to the people in open council and therefore believing said delegation can effect nothing and since our difficulties are daily increasing and our situation is rendered more and more precarious uncertain and insecure in consequence of the legislation of the States; and seeing no effectual way of relief, but in accepting the liberal overtures of the United States.

And whereas Genl William Carroll and John F. Schermerhorn were appointed commissioners on the part of the United States, with full power and authority to conclude a treaty with the Cherokees east and were directed by the President to convene the people of the nation in general council at New Echota and to submit said propositions to them with power and authority to vary the same so as to meet the views of the Cherokees in reference to its details.

And whereas the said commissioners did appoint and notify a general council of the nation to convene at New Echota on the 21st day of December 1835; and informed them that the commissioners would be prepared to make a treaty with the Cherokee people who should assemble there and those who did not come they should conclude gave their assent and sanction to whatever should be transacted at this council and the people having met in council according to said notice.

Therefore the following articles of a treaty are agreed upon and concluded between William Carroll and John F. Schermerhorn commissioners on the part of the United States and the chiefs and head men and people of the Cherokee nation in general council assembled this 29th day of Decr (*sic*) 1835.

Art. 1. The Cherokee nation hereby cede relinquish and convey to the United States all the lands owned claimed or possessed by them east of the Mississippi river, and hereby release all their claims upon the United States for spoliations of every kind for and in consideration of the sum of five millions of dollars to be expended paid and invested in the manner stipulated and agreed upon in the following articles.

Art. 2. In addition to the seven millions of acres of land thus provided for and bounded, the United States further guaranty to the Cherokee nation a perpetual outlet west, and a free and unmolested use of all the country west of the western boundary of said seven millions of acres, as far west as the sovereignty of the United States and their right of soil extend:

Art. 3. The United States also agree that the lands above ceded by the treaty of February 14, 1833, including the outlet, and those by this treaty shall all be included in one patent executed to the Cherokee nation of Indians by the President of the United States according to the provisions of the act of May 28, 1830. It is, however, agreed that the military reservation at Ft. Gibson shall be held by the United States. But should the United States abandon said post and have no further use for the same it shall revert to the Cherokee nation.

Art. 5. The United States hereby covenant and agree that the lands ceded to the Cherokee nation in the foregoing article shall, in no future time without their consent, be included within the territorial limits or jurisdiction of any State or Territory. But they shall secure to the Cherokee nation the right by their national councils to make and carry into effect all such laws as they may deem necessary for the government and protection of the persons and property within their own country belonging to their people or such persons as have connected themselves with them.

Art. 6. Perpetual peace and friendship shall exist between the citizens of the United States and the Cherokee Indians. The United States agree to protect the Cherokee nation from domestic strife and foreign enemies and against intestine wars between the several tribes. The Cherokees shall endeavor to preserve and maintain the peace of the country and not make war upon their neighbors they shall also be protected against interruption and intrusion from citizens of the United States, who may attempt to settle in the country without their consent; and all such persons shall be removed from the same by order of the President of the United States. But this is not intended to prevent the residence among them of useful farmers mechanics and teachers for the instruction of Indians according to treaty stipulations.

Art. 7. The Cherokee nation having already made great progress in civilization and deeming it important that every proper and laudable inducement should be offered to their people to improve their condition as well as to guard and secure in the most effectual manner the rights guarantied to them in this treaty, and with a view to illustrate the liberal and enlarged policy of the Government of the United States towards the Indians in their removal beyond the territorial limits of the States, it is stipulated that they shall be entitled to a delegate in the House of Representatives of the United States whenever Congress shall make provision for the same.

Art. 8. The United States also agree and stipulate to remove the Cherokees to their new homes and to subsist them one year after their arrival there and that a sufficient number of steamboats and baggage wagons shall be furnished to remove them comfortably, and so as not to endanger their health, and that a physician well supplied with medicines shall accompany each detachment of emigrants removed by the Government. Such persons and families as in the opinion of the emigrating agent are capable of subsisting and removing themselves shall be permitted to do-so.

Art. 10. The President of the United States shall invest in some safe and most productive public stocks of the country for the benefit of the whole Cherokee nation who have removed or shall remove to the lands assigned by this treaty to the Cherokee nation west of the Mississippi the following sums as a permanent fund for the purposes hereinafter specified . . . the sum of two hundred thousand dollars in addition to the present annuities of the nation to constitute a general fund the interest of which shall be applied annually by the council of the nation to such purposes as they may deem best for the general interest of their people. The sum of fifty thousand dollars to constitute an orphans' fund the annual income of which shall be expended towards the support and education of such orphan children as are destitute of the means of subsistence. The sum of one hundred and fifty thousand dollars in addition to the present school fund of the nation shall constitute a permanent school fund, the interest of which shall be applied annually by the council of the nation for the support of common schools and such a literary institution of a higher order is may be established in the Indian country.

Art. 14. It is also agreed on the part of the United States that such warriors of the Cherokee nation as were engaged on the side of the United States in the late war with Great Britain and the southern tribes of Indians, and who were wounded in such service shall be entitled to such pensions as shall be allowed them by the Congress of the United States to commence from the period of their disability.

Art. 16. It is hereby stipulated and agreed by the Cherokees that they shall remove to their new homes within two years from the ratification of this treaty and that during such time the United States shall protect and defend them in their possessions and property and free use and occupation of the same and such persons as have been dispossessed of their improvements and houses.

Art. 17. All stipulations in former treaties which have not been superseded or annulled by this shall continue in full force and virtue.

Art. 18. Whereas in consequence of the unsettled affairs of the Cherokee people and the early frosts, their crops are insufficient to support their families and great distress is likely to ensue and whereas the nation will not, until alter their removal be able advantageously to expend the income of the permanent funds of the nation it is therefore agreed that the annuities of the nation which may accrue under this treaty for two years, the time fixed for their removal shall be expended in provision and clothing for the benefit of the poorer class of the nation; and the United States hereby agree to advance the same for that purpose as soon after the ratification of this treaty as an appropriation for the same shall be made.

Source: Treaty with the Cherokee, 1835. Dec. 29, 1835, 7 Stat., 478; Proclamation May 23, 1836. *Indian Affairs: Laws and Treaties. Vol. II, Treaties.* Compiled and edited by Charles J. Kappler. Washington, DC: Government Printing Office, 1904, 439–449.

CHEROKEE PETITION TO CONGRESS, 1836

The Cherokees collected signatures on several petitions throughout the winter and spring of 1836. Presented to the Senate, they made clear to that body that the Treaty of New Echota was fraudulent and had not been approved by the Cherokee government. It was impossible for any Senator to have missed the message. This particular petition was signed by over 3,300 people. Another, which is preserved at the National Museum of the American Indian in Washington D.C., has over 15,000 signatures! Stitched together in segments with each segment comprised of several columns of signatures, the Cherokees signed as they knew how, and the document evidences the diversity that was already present within Cherokee society. Some signed with X marks, others in syllabary, and still others in flowing cursive signatures, complete with flourishes. The strategy backfired. Although the Cherokees engaged in extravagant flattery toward the Senate, the Senate was affronted at the audacity of an Indian nation to petition it in such a fashion. More likely, the Senate was angered that now they would not be able to claim ignorance of the Cherokees' sentiments on the matter of the treaty.

WHEREAS, we, the citizens of the districts of Aquohee and Taquohee, in the Cherokee nation, are informed that, on the 21st of December, 1835, certain individual Cherokees assembled at New Echota, and without any authority from the council or people of the nation, entered into an agreement with the Rev. Mr. Schermerhorn, under the name of a treaty, by the provisions of which, all the lands of the Cherokees are ceded, their government and laws abolished, their private improvements, the property of individuals alienated from their rightful owners, without their consent, and all their rights, as freemen, wrested from them, and left to the discretionary disposal of strangers.

And WHEREAS, we are further informed, that this compact is to be presented to the Senate of the United States for ratification, as a treaty, we, the undersigned, do, with the deepest anxiety and the most respectful earnestness, appeal to the Senate of the United States against the ratification of the same; and in entering our protest before the honorable and august body, we again humbly solicit their attention to the following points, on account of which we so urgently deprecate the ratification of said instrument. viz. the persons who are represented as acting in behalf of the Cherokees, in this matter, are wholly unauthorized, and the circumstance of a few individuals making a treaty vitally affecting their liberties, the property, and the personal rights of a whole people, appears to us so utterly repugnant to reason and justice, and every dictate of humanity, that we come to the Senate of the United States with full confidence that, under such circumstances, the voice of weakness itself will be heard in its cry for justice. To the basis of said instrument, and most of its details, we entertain insuperable objections; but being fully persuaded that an instrument so unwarranted will not be sanctioned by the Senate, we deem it unnecessary to recite the particular provisions which it contains, as we feel all assurance of the justice and magnanimity of the august body before whom we humbly presume to present our grievances.

Source: Protest of the New Echota Treaty by the Cherokee People of the Aquohee and Taquohee Districts, 1836. President's messages relating to treaties with the Cherokees (SEN 24B-C4), 24th Congress, Record Group 46, Records of the U.S. Senate. National Archives.

RALPH WALDO EMERSON'S LETTER
TO PRESIDENT MARTIN VAN BUREN, 1838

Although Emerson was not yet famous when this letter was penned, the genius is evident nevertheless. Emerson did not have deep sympathy for the Cherokees; it was his brother who had taken up their cause. His brother's death spurred other supporters to approach Emerson and appeal the removal, in tribute to his brother's memory. No matter that Emerson held not the sentiments himself. As he wrote, they seem to have entered him anyway. The letter is a challenge to every citizens, but particularly to the agents and officials of the United States of America to keep faith, not only with the Indians, but also with their own citizens. For if America broke faith, God would not.

Sir:

The seat you fill places you in a relation of credit and nearness to every citizen. By right and natural position, every citizen is your friend. Before any acts contrary to his own judgment or interest have repelled the affections of any man, each may look with trust and living anticipation to your government. Each has the highest right to call your attention to such subjects as are of a public nature, and properly belong to the chief magistrate; and the good magistrate will feel a joy in meeting such confidence. In this belief and at the instance of a few of my friends and neighbors, I crave of your patience a short hearing for their sentiments and my own: and the circumstances that my name will be utterly unknown to you will only give the fairer chance to you equitable construction of what I have to say.

Sir, my communication respects the sinister rumors that fill this part of the country concerning the Cherokee people. The interest always felt in the aboriginal population—an interest naturally growing as that decays—has been heightened in regard to this tribe. Even in our distant State some good rumor of their worth and civility has arrived. We have learned with joy their improvement in the social arts. We have read their newspapers. We have seen some of them in our schools and colleges. In common with the great body of the American people, we have witnessed with sympathy the painful labors of these red men to redeem their own race from the doom of eternal inferiority, and to borrow and domesticate in the tribe the arts and customs of the Caucasian race. And notwithstanding the unaccountable apathy with which of late years the Indians have been sometimes abandoned to their enemies, it is not to be doubted that it is the good pleasure and the understanding of all humane persons in the Republic, of the men and the matrons sitting in the thriving independent families all over the land, that they shall be duly cared for; that they shall taste justice and love from all to whom we have delegated the office of dealing with them.

The newspapers now inform us that, in December, 1835, a treaty contracting for the exchange of all the Cherokee territory was pretended to be made by an agent on the part of the United States with some persons appearing on the part of the Cherokees; that the fact afterwards transpired that these deputies did by no means represent the will of the nation; and that, out of eighteen thousand souls composing the nation, fifteen thousand six hundred and sixty-eight have protested against the so-called treaty. It now appears that the government of the United States choose to hold the Cherokees to this sham treaty, and are proceeding to execute the same. Almost the entire Cherokee Nation stand up and say, "This is not our act, Behold us. Here are we. Do not mistake that handful of deserters for us;" and the American president and the Cabinet, the Senate and the House of Representatives, neither hear these men nor see them, and are contacting to put this active nation into carts and boats, and to drag them over mountains and rivers to a wilderness at a vast distance beyond the Mississippi. As a paper purporting to be an army order fixes a month from this day as the hour for this doleful removal.

In the name of God, sir, we ask you if this be so. Do the newspapers rightly inform us? Man and women with pale and perplexed faces meet one another in the streets and churches here, and ask if this be so. We have inquired if this be a gross misrepresentation from the party opposed to the government and anxious to blacken it with the people. We have looked at the newspapers of different parties and find a horrid confirmation of the tale. We are slow to believe it. We hoped the Indians were misinformed, and that their remonstrance was premature, and will turn out to be a needless act of terror.

The piety, the principle that is left in the United States, if only in its coarsest form, a regard to the speech of men, forbid us to entertain it as a fact. Such a der-eliction of all faith and virtue, such a denial of justice, and such deafness to screams for mercy were never heard of in times of peace and in the dealing of a nation with its own allies and wards, since the earth was made. Sir, does this government think that the people of the United States are become savage and mad? From their mind are the sentiments of love and a good nature wiped clean out? The soul of man, the justice, the mercy that is the heart's heart in all men, from Maine to Georgia, does abhor this business.

In speaking thus the sentiments of my neighbors and my own, perhaps I over-step the bounds of decorum. But would it not be a higher indecorum coldly to argue a matter like this? We only state the fact that a crime is projected that con-founds our understanding by its magnitude, a crime that really deprives us as well as the Cherokees of a country for how could we call the conspiracy that should crush these poor Indians our government, or the land that was cursed by their parting and dying imprecations our county, any more? You, sir, will bring down that renowned chair in which you sit into infamy if your seal is set to this instru-ment of perfidy; and the name of this nation, hitherto the sweet omen of religion and liberty, will stink to the world.

You will not do us the injustice of connecting this remonstrance with any sec-tional and party feeling. It is in our hearts the simplest commandment of brotherly love. We will not have this great and solemn claim upon national and human justice huddled aside under the flimsy plea of its being a party act. Sir, to us the questions upon which the government and the people have been agitated during the past year, touching the prostration of the currency and of trade, seem but motes in comparison. These hard times, it is true, have brought the discussion home to every farmhouse and poor man's house in this town; but it is the chirping of grasshoppers beside the immortal question whether justice shall be done by the race of civilized to the race of savage man, whether all the attributes of reason, of civility, of justice, and even of mercy, shall be put off by the American people, and so vast an outrage upon the Cherokee Nation and upon human nature shall be consummated.

One circumstance lessens the reluctance with which I intrude at this time on yow attention my conviction that the government ought to be admonished of a new historical fact, which the discussion of this question has disclosed, namely, that there exists in a great part of the Northern people a gloomy diffidence in the moral character of the government.

On the broaching of this question, a general expression of despondency, of disbelief that any good will accrue from a remonstrance on an act of fraud and robbery appeared in those men to whom we naturally turn for aid and counsel. Will the American government steal? Will it lie? Will it kill?—We ask triumphantly. Our counselors and old statesmen here say that ten years ago they would have staked their lives on the affirmation that the proposed Indian measures could not be executed, that the unanimous country would put them down. And now the steps of this crime follow each other so fast, at such fatally quick time, that the millions of virtuous citizens, whose agents the government are, have no place to interpose, and must shut their eyes until the last howl and wailing of these tormented villages and tribes shall afflict the ear of the world.

I will not hide from you, as an indication of the alarming distrust, that a letter addressed as mine is, and suggesting to the mind of the Executive the plain obligations of man, has a burlesque character in the apprehensions of some of my friends. I, sir, will not beforehand treat you with the contumely of this distrust. I will at least state to you this fact, and show you how plain and humane people, whose love would be honor, regard the policy of the government, and what injurious inferences they draw as to the minds of the governors. A man with your experience in affairs must have seen cause to appreciate the futility of opposition to the moral sentiment. However feeble the sufferer and however great the oppressor, it is in the nature of things that the blow should recoil upon the aggressor. For God is in the sentiment, and it cannot be withstood. The potentate and the people perish before it; but with it, and its executor, they are omnipotent.

I write thus, sir, to inform you of the state of mind these Indian tidings have awakened here, and to pray with one voice more that you, whose hands are strong with the delegated power of fifteen millions of men, will avert with that might the terrific injury which threatens the Cherokee tribe.

With great respect, sir, I am your fellow citizen,
Ralph Waldo Emerson

Source: Ralph Waldo Emerson, "Letter to President Van Buren." *Complete Works 11* (Boston: Houghton Mifflin, 1903–4), 89–96.

EXCERPTS FROM A LETTER FROM REVEREND STEPHEN FOREMAN (CHEROKEE) TO REVEREND DAVID GREENE OF THE AMERICAN BOARD OF COMMISSIONERS FOR FOREIGN MISSIONS, BOSTON, 1838

Stephen Foreman was one of the first ordained Cherokee ministers. Affiliated with the influential American Board of Commissioners for Foreign Missions, Foreman was stationed at Candy's Creek in southeastern Tennessee. One can imagine the Reverend in late May 1838, sitting on his porch at dusk each evening as night fell over the mountains in the distance, wondering if tonight would be the last night in his home, the last time he would see these mountains that had been the foundation of the Cherokees for countless generations. The letter indicates the consciousness of the decisions that were made by Cherokees to remain in their homes, not to resist when the soldiers came to take them, but to force that action, which in itself became the supreme resistance.

Candy's Creek, Cher. Nation,
May 31, 1838

Very dear Sir,

As I have no other excuse than that of negligence to offer, for delaying so long to write to you, I believe, I shall not trouble you with any apology at this time in extenuation of my fault. From the date of my letter you will perceive that I am still in the Cherokee Nation East, and still in the neighborhood of Candy's Creek Missionary Station. Indeed, I am now living on the mission premises at C. Creek, and have been since Dec. last. How much longer we shall be permitted [to] remain here in our own lands, to enjoy our rights and privileges, I do not know. From the present aspect of affairs, we shall very soon be without house & (*sic*) home. Indeed, ever since the 23rd of May, we have been looking almost daily for the soldiers to come, and turn us out of our houses. They have already warned us to make preparations, and to come in to camps, before we were forced to do so. But I have stated distinctly to some of the officers at Head Quarters, what I thought of this, so called treaty, and what course I intended to persue (*sic*) in the event no new treaty was made, and see no reasons yet why I should change my mind. My determination, and the determination of a large majority of the Cherokees, yet in the Nation is never to recognize this fraudulent instrument as a treaty, nor remove under it until we are forced to do so at the point of a bayonet. It may seem unwise and hazardous to the fraimers (*sic*) and friends of this instrument, that we should persue such a course, but I am fully satisfied it is the only one we can persue with clear consciences. I am aware some of your missionaries think and act differently on this subject. But this, instead of being any reason why I should persue a similar course, appears to my mind to be the very reason why I should not. And I can say, that I am truly sorry that any of your missionaries have favored in any shape this base instrument, or have felt it their duty to advise the Cherokees to go west. Such a course, in my view is very unwise, and injurious to the cause of missions, and especially to the cause of religion among the Cherokees. If this people are forced under this treaty, I should not at all be surprised if the door should be forever closed against the entrance of missionaries among them, in all time to come. It is almost certain to my mind, that those missionaries who have countenanced this treaty, can never again be useful among the Cherokees. . . . When Mr. Worcester first went from this Nation to the west, the Cherokees were very much surprised, and felt that he was *too* hasty. The consequence was that they looked upon him as a treaty man, though no treaty was yet made. And even now, the Cherokees have less confidence in him than they had previous to his going west . . . in my opinion, the Board would do itself much honor and would render an invaluable service to the missionary cause, if yourself or some one of the Com. would come into the Nation immediately. In the very midst of their sufferings, your presents and your sympathies would make a deep, lasting, and favorable impression upon the minds of this much abused and suffering people. Such a step would give you a good opportunity of conferring with the Nation on the subject of missions among them in future, and of removing any and every unpleasant feeling that may exist toward the Board or any of its missionaries.

I shall also try to send you something every week following in either the shape of a letter or journal, until this critical time with us has passed, or until we arrive at the west, where it has been the wish and policy of the Govt. for a number of years, to deposit us. In the mean time, I hope the Com. and all our friends at the north will remember us constantly at the throne of grace. If any people ever needed the prayers and sympathies of Christians, it is the distressed and oppressed Cherokees.

S. Foreman
June 2

P.S. Five armed soldiers rode up, alighted & (*sic*) came into the house to let us know that we must be ready by Tuesday, the 5th inst. to go to Ross' landing. About all the Cherokees in the limits of Ga. Are now collected into forts. I hope we shall all go peaceably when we are forced away. I hear of none resisting, but some being very much abused.

In haste,
S. Foreman

Source: Papers of the American Board of Commissioners for Foreign Missions (ABCFM), Houghton Library, Harvard University, ABC:18.3.1, V. 10, Item 205.

EXCERPTS FROM THE JOURNAL OF REVEREND
DANIEL BUTRICK, MAY 19, 1838–APRIL 1, 1839

The journal of the Reverend Daniel Butrick is perhaps the most power-
ful primary document of the Cherokee Trail of Tears. Beginning at the
moment when Cherokees were being herded into stockades, continuing
through the internment in camps, and throughout the bitter journey, the
journal ends as Butrick's detachment was disbanded and dispersed after
arriving in the Indian Territory. In between are the riveting, heartfelt
descriptions of despair and faith, anger and grief, illness, new life, and
a lot of death. If one will immerse oneself in the document, it is impos-
sible not to be overcome by the magnitude of the event. As entry after en-
try recounts one death after another, of children in particular, Butrick's
occasional outbursts against the Treaty Party, who he regarded as trai-
tors, are entirely understandable. The building trauma that is sensed as,
over and over, one had to harden oneself to all that was around, carried
through the people and into the Indian Territory. Afterward, the Chero-
kees were of two minds. Some never wanted to talk or think about the
event ever again and as a result, there are very few stories passed down
about the Trail of Tears. But others determined that the event should never
be forgotten and that all the world should know. That YOU should know.

May 26, 1838

This day a number of Georgia citizens of New Echota took sixteen Cherokees
and drove them to the fort and then requested permission of General Scott to
take them out and whip them, though in this they were not gratified. This was
done probably to remind General Scott that no further delay would be made
with regard to collecting the Indians. The soldiers at the various posts now
commenced that work which will doubtless long eclipse the glory of the United
States. . . . Women absent from their families on visits, or for other purposes, were
seized, and men far from their wives and children, were not allowed to return, and
also children being forced from home, were dragged off among strangers. Cattle,
horses, hogs, household furniture, clothing and money not with them when taken
were left. And it is said that the white inhabitants around, stood with open arms
to seize whatever property they could put their hands on . . . the soldiers, it is said
would often use the same language as if driving hogs, and goad them forward
with their bayonets. . . . Those taken to the fort at New Echota, were confined day
and night in the open air, with but little clothing to cover them, when lying on the
naked ground.

July 26, 1838

Let us fancy the feeling of a dear sister, and aged father or mother, or a beloved wife or child, driven by strangers (of adamantine hearts) scorching with fever, under a burning sun, parching with thirst, rendered more tormenting by the heated dust filling the air, see this dear wife of our bosom, languishing, and almost ready to drop to the ground every step, and yet handing to her friends, choosing rather to die in their arms, than be torn from them and thrown into a heated wagon, to be separated forever from all she held dear. See her last despairing look at her husband, as she sinks at his feet and falls in the road. . . . Let us imagine such scenes daily, and for a long time together; and then inquire why the dear Cherokees are doomed to such miseries; have they murdered their white friends? Have they robbed or plundered? Or have they done any wrong to the United States for which that powerful nation is thus putting them to the torture? They have done no wrong to merit any part of this evil, their enemies themselves being judges, but by refusing to acknowledge the justice of that treaty made by a few individuals, in direct opposition to the whole national council and the voice of the people.

Aug. 7, 1838

How does the United States government appease a great nation, laying aside her dignity and with thousands of soldiers, and all her great men, and all her mighty men, and all her powerful generals, with all her civil and military force, chasing a little trembling hare in the wilderness, merely to take its skin, and send it off to broil in the scorching deserts of the West. . . . O how Noble! How magnanimous! How warlike the achievement! O what a conquest! What booty! How becoming the glory and grandeur of the United States! A little hare, a little trembling rabbit, indeed is this poor and afflicted nation, as to power, or a disposition to resist her murderers.

Aug. 8, 1838

Soon in the morning some people came from the camps to dig a grave for a little child who died last night. Soon after a woman came to have a coffin made for another child just over the creek, who died this morning. Thus, the poor little children are almost all dying off. . . . Suppose the President of the United States had ordered his most mighty officers to go to every house and measure every infant under four years of age, and every old person over sixty, in order to make the resident willing to forsake the inheritance of their fathers, and leave it a booty to robbers, how glorious would he appear!. . . . But what crowns the climax is, Go crush the poor Indians almost to death, and then take advantage of that misery, in order to persuade a few confiding individuals to endanger their own lives, by disposing of the country, in violation of a standing law of their nation, making that crime a capital offense.

September 5, 1838

The sickness seems to increase so that in some families, most of the members are sick. When we hear of their sickness, we start as usual for their relief, or comfort, but despair soon checks our zeal. Because, first, they are houseless. They have only a few barks overhead, having them all exposed to damp night air, though they have been accustomed to warm houses. Second. They have no provisions suitable for a sick person. They have only meat and bread, and no bread neither only as they pound it in mortars, which sick women are poorly prepared to do. Third, they are afraid of white people and especially of physicians, so that, in general they had much rather risk themselves with their own doctors; but these are ignorant except in some common familiar complaints, as they formerly appeared in their own healthy retreats, by the cold flowing springs. Fourth, they can be stationary but a short time. The officers are ordering them to their own detachments, and whether sick or well, they must obey these white commanders, unless in some very special cases. And very shortly all must set out on a journey of about 800 miles; and should they live to accomplish that journey, they will arrive in a sickly country, with no houses to shelter them till, with their own hands, they can erect them. And as nearly the whole of the poorer class will be destitute of teams, as will as many who were formerly wealthy, the prospect before them is overwhelming.

There seems to be no place, nor means, nor time, for the recovery of any who are now sick. Their death, of course, seems almost inevitable, unless prevented by a miracle of mercy. I still visit the dear sick people, and try to comfort them.

December 13, 1838

As I was about leaving, Mr. Bushyhead requested me to pray with him, as I was myself desirous to do. Sixty persons had died out of their detachment previous to their arrival at that place.

During the night a Cherokee woman died at the camps. Though she had given birth to a child but a few days before, yet last evening she was up, & (*sic*) no danger was apprehended, but in the morning she was found dead, with the infant in her arms. As the man living near was not willing to have her buried there, and as no plank could be obtained for a coffin, the corpse was carried all day long in the wagon, and at night a coffin was made, and the next morning she was buried near the graves of some other Cherokees who had died in a detachment that had preceded us.

Also on Saturday night of last week an infant, a few months old, died with the bowel complaint. The corpse was interred after meeting on the Sabbath. . . . near the place of the meeting was a man sitting by a fire, afflicted with the bowel complaint. I did not think of his being dangerous, yet yesterday about noon, he died. . . . We learn that the young man burnt on the mountain, when drunk is dead. . . . About sunset, the man who died yesterday was buried near the bank of the creek on which we camped.

December 14, 1838

Last night a child about 12 months old died. This is the 15th death since we crossed the Tennessee River.

December 23, 1838

We have peculiar cause of gratitude for the preservation of the last night. The wind blew a gale nearly the whole night, and seemed to threaten almost certain calamity, both by scattering the fire through the leaves and tents, and also by throwing limbs, trees, etc. upon our heads. But those eyes which never slumber watched over us, and preserved us in safety, though we had but little sleep.

The weather is now piercing cold, so that we despair of holding any public meeting.

December 28 and 29, 1838

Afflicted with a fever afternoons and a cough during the night. . . . It is distressing to reflect on the situation of the nation. One detachment stopped at the Ohio River, two at the Mississippi, one four miles this side, one 16 miles this side, one 18 miles, and one 3 miles behind us. In all these detachments, comprising about 8000 souls, there is now a vast amount of sickness, and many deaths. Six have died within a short time in Maj. Brown's company, and in this detachment. Of Mr. Taylor's there are more or less affected with sickness in almost every tent; and yet all are houseless & (*sic*) homeless in a strange land, and in a cold region exposed to weather almost unknown in their native country. But they are prisoners. True, their own chiefs have directly hold of their hands, yet the U. (*sic*) States officers hold the chiefs with an iron grasp, so that they are obliged to lead the people according to their directions in executing effectually the Schermerhorn treaty.

March 23, 1839

After early breakfast, we proceeded to Mr. Woodalls's, 8 miles. This is the place of deposit, & (*sic*) also the place where Mr. Taylor is to deliver the detachment over to the U. (*sic*) States officers, who are to supply them with provisions one year. We arrived about noon and made arrangements for a meeting tomorrow.

April 1, 1839

We made arrangements to send Jonas, the little boy who came with us, to his father; gave our tent to an old Cherokee woman, who had none, & (*sic*) took our leave of the dear detachment, with whom we had been wandering these five months past.

Source: *The Journal of Rev. Daniel S. Butrick*. Monograph One. Park Hill: The Trail of Tears Association, Oklahoma Chapter, 1998. Used by permission of the Oklahoma Chapter, Trail of Tears Association.

Glossary

Allotment: In the American Indian context, an "allotment" refers to a section of land that is designated to be owned by an individual, rather than collectively owned by the tribal government as was the practice among most tribes. Allotment was forced on Indians as an aspect of federal assimilation policy between 1887 and 1934, even though most Indians deeply opposed it. Its impacts were devastating to most tribes, who lost significant portions of their land bases as a result. It also struck a blow against the communitarian traditions of Indian peoples. Most tribes have never recovered from the detrimental impacts of land allotment, either territorially or culturally, and regard it as the most destructive aspect of federal policies ever enacted upon them. Cherokee lands in the Indian Territory were allotted between 1898 and 1906.

Ani Giduwagi: The name by which Cherokees call themselves in their language. "Ani" is the noun, meaning people, and "Giduwa" is a descriptive adjective, meaning "on a high place" or something similar. The suffix "gi" agrees with the noun and indicates a plural.

Assimilation: A federal policy enacted in the late 19th and early 20th centuries that had two major components: (1) the removal of Indian children from Indian homes to be educated and acculturated in boarding schools and (2) the allotment of land into individual parcels to be given to individual Indians. The effort to create an individualistic ethic within communitarian peoples was determined as necessary for success in the American economic landscape, as well as separating Indians from their cultures so they could more easily "melt" into the American melting pot. Similar to earlier notions of "civilizing" Indians, assertions that Indian cultural beliefs and practices are detrimental to Indian success have never disappeared from the American popular psyche.

Civilization Policy: First federal Indian policy focused on extending European norms of civilization into Indian cultures and lifeways. Indian men were to become yeoman farmers and herdsmen, and women were to be schooled in the domestic arts, and all were to be Christianized. The policy was most prominent in the late 18th and early 19th centuries, but came gradually to be replaced by the idea that Indians should be removed to areas west of the Mississippi River. However, notions of "Europeanizing" Indians have never entirely abated.

Colonization: The process of a more powerful entity occupying one less powerful in territorial, cultural, linguistic, social, and economic spheres. Hallmarks of colonization may include the creation of economic dependency, disallowing native language usage, disparaging or criminalizing native cultural and religious practices, territorial encroachment, military subjugation, cultivating native informants and overseers, controlling native women and children, and enslavement. Aspects of these characteristics can be seen in the Cherokee experience with the British and, later, the United States.

Consensus: A process of collective decision making in which high levels of agreement must be reached before collective action is sanctioned. Usually works best in smaller groups as it involves much discussion and compromise, thus becoming unwieldy and difficult to achieve in larger bodies. The Cherokees relinquished their consensus style of governing when they began to engage in a centralization of governmental authority in the early 1800s, but aspects of consensus-oriented worldview can still be seen among contemporary Cherokees.

Doctrine of Discovery: A European legal doctrine developed to resolve competing claims of colonizers to the same territories in the Americas. It acknowledges Indian occupancy rights, but denies Indian titles, which are reserved to the "discovering" European nation. Initially implemented between Spain and Portugal, Britain never adhered strongly to the precept, but the Supreme Court made some concessions to the concept in the *Johnson v. McIntosh* case (1822).

Domestic Dependent Nation: A legal category created in the 1831 *Cherokee Nation v. Georgia* case, that recognized the tribal governments in the United States as having distinct governmental existence within the United States separate from state or federal government. The legal refining of the jurisdictional parameters of being a "domestic dependent nation" has occupied the courts and federal Indian law to the present day.

Egalitarian: Anthropological term describing a society in which all persons within it have equal access to resources and power. The Cherokees have been described as historically a very egalitarian society.

Ethnic Cleansing: The attempt to make a region racially, ethnically, culturally, religiously, socially, and linguistically homogenous by removing or killing persons whose languages, races, and cultural beliefs and practices do not adhere to the desired homogeneity. Indian removals have been viewed by many as instances when the United States enacted ethnic cleansing on indigenous peoples within its borders.

Fee Simple Patent: Land grant given to each of the "Five Civilized Tribes" for the lands they received in exchange for their removal to the Indian Territory (presently Oklahoma). The grants conveyed the land titles as private property owned by the tribal governments and insured that their titles were more than occupancy rights, but actual legal ownership of their lands. For many decades in the middle and late 1800s, fee simple ownership was a strong barrier to the United States' ability to take the land the Cherokees had been ceded in the Indian Territory, but ultimately, it too was taken by questionable methods.

Genocide/Genocidal: The attempt to eradicate a people, usually on the basis of their race, religious practices, cultural beliefs and practices, or nationality. The campaigns of warfare against the Cherokees by the British in the French and Indian War and by Americans in the Revolutionary War are accurately described as genocidal campaigns because of the tactics that were employed, including scorched earth destruction of the food supply and the ability to produce food.

Indian Agents: Federal commissioners established in the 18th and 19th centuries to oversee federal–tribal interactions in a region. Appointed by the president, they often were some of those charged with implementing federal policy objectives toward the tribes. Indian agents among the Cherokees were often embroiled in tribal intrigue and fostered tribal divisions.

Indian Territory: Generally regarded historically as encompassing the present-day state of Oklahoma, but which has also been used more broadly to include much of the Plains area of the United States. The Cherokees and 34 other tribes were removed from their homelands to the Indian Territory.

As a result, Oklahoma is today the home of 39 tribes, only 4 of which are indigenous to the area.

Indigenous: Original or aboriginal to an area.

Kanati: Mythic hunter figure in Cherokee cosmology that represents roles of masculinity and indicates identity and an integral component of concepts of balance in the Cherokee world.

Matrilineal Clan: A corporate kinship group that counts as its members the individuals whose lineages are derived through the women of the family. The Cherokees are a matrilineal people who group themselves by clans.

Moravians: A Germanic Christian denomination that established two bases of missionizing operations in the United States at Salem, North Carolina, and Bethlehem, Pennsylvania. Moravians were the first missionaries to work among the Cherokees.

Mother Town: One of several preeminent towns that were regarded as the original and most symbolically meaningful settlements among the Cherokees.

Nation-state: Describes a governing system that exercises centralized and coercive control over its members or citizens, and often over others outside their own citizenry. Most of the developed world is structured as nation-states; most tribal nations that have existed in human history have not created centralized state apparatuses, but are "nations" only in the senses of shared language, kinship systems, and religious beliefs and practices, for instance. The Cherokees may have fit the definition of a nation-state in the 19th century, although a weak one, as they had little ability to employ coercive power beyond their own society.

Nationalism/Nationalist: The particular devotion to one's own political and cultural governing systems and the strong promotion of its interests; one who holds that sensibility. Many people exhibit nationalist sentiments, but in extreme forms, nationalism can result in ethnocentrism to the point of oppression and even ethnic cleansings and genocides against other nationalities. The Cherokees evidenced what has been called "indigenous nationalism" in the 19th century, as they attempted to develop a nation-state apparatus, but also to integrate many tribal characteristics into its new national systems.

Nunnehi: Mythic warrior-like apparitions believed by many Cherokee people to appear in times of need and desperation to assist the Cherokees to success, particularly military success.

Oconoluftee Cherokees: Named for Cherokees who, in the mid- and early 1800s, resided in regions surrounding the Oconoluftee River in present-day North Carolina. These communities were granted reserves in ceded territory in 1819, exempted from removal, and became the nucleus for the government later known as the Eastern Band of Cherokees Indians.

Old Settlers (Western Cherokees): Specifically referred to Cherokees who emigrated from the Cherokee Nation and settled in Arkansas Territory in 1817, but evolved as a reference to all Cherokees who voluntarily resettled to Arkansas and/or the Indian Territory at any time prior to the federally mandated removal.

Per Capita Payments: An equal distribution of funds to individual recipients of a group that may occur once or periodically. Historically, federal annuities have been made in this fashion. In contemporary times, gaming and other revenues are sometimes made in this manner. In the 19th and early 20th centuries, the federal government and the Cherokee Nation both made some per capita distributions, but such distributions are rare or nonexistent within the contemporary Cherokee Nation.

Plenary Rights: The legal rights established in both the U.S. Constitution and federal statute, and affirmed by the federal courts that convey to Congress the exclusive authority to regulate by policy or statute the governmental relationships with the tribes. Effectively excludes the states from such regulatory authority unless granted to them by Congress.

Prophetic Movement: Described by anthropologists as a charismatic movement, often focusing on an individual or event, which emerges to inspire a group to action in response to a vision of the future. Often arises within a people in times of extreme social stress. Such movements arose among the Cherokees in the late 18th and early 19th centuries, and among the "Red Stick" Creeks and other followers of Tecumseh during the War of 1812.

Protectorate: A smaller community, cultural group, nation, etc. that has entered into an agreement to accept protection, military, economic, etc. from a larger group or government. The Cherokees were, by treaty, a protectorate of the United States.

Reservation: A parcel of land that is held in a legal trust status by the U.S. government on behalf of the Indian tribe that inhabits the land. Although the tribe is considered the legal owner of the property, the United States is regarded analogously as the "equitable" owner of the property, since it is holding the property as a trust. Therefore, the United States is considered to have a legal right to assert its interests within the property. The property is nontaxable and cannot be used as collateral, and cannot be leased, sold, or otherwise transferred without the permission of the United States, specifically the Bureau of Indian Affairs. The Cherokee Nation never had a reservation, as it held its land in fee simple.

Reserve: A section of land, usually ranging from quarter section (160 acres) to a full section (640 acres), that was withheld from a land cession and granted to an individual or family. It is usually "restricted," meaning exempt from property taxes. The Oconoluftee Cherokees were initially granted reserves by treaty in 1819.

Scorched Earth: Tactic of warfare by which an aggressor attacks its foe by burning critical structures and resources, such as homes and towns, woods, orchards, fields, food stores, etc., often leaving a region completely devastated from fire. Such tactics were employed against Cherokees in both the French and Indian Wars and the Revolutionary War.

Second Trail of Tears: Informal reference among contemporary Cherokees to emigrations away from northeastern Oklahoma in the 20th century. Resulting from economic marginalization in the region of their former collective landholding in the northeastern part of the state, it has resulted in the dispersal of over two-thirds of the Cherokee Nation's citizens from the center of tribal government and the cultural communities of their people.

Self-determination: In the context of tribes in the United States, refers to the ability to make administrative decisions on their own behalf. As a federal policy, "self-determination," implemented since approximately 1975, allows tribes to contract with agencies of the federal government to administer the programs they have designated for tribes using federal funds. The contemporary Cherokee Nation operates almost entirely on self-governance contracts for virtually all of its programs.

Selu: The Cherokee word for corn, Selu is the mythic premier woman in Cherokee cosmology. She represents feminine labor, feminine roles, and the feminine energy that balances the masculine energy of the hunter figure, Kanati, in the egalitarian worldview of the Cherokees.

Sovereignty: The ability and the right of a government or organization to make decisions for itself about its own systems, structure, and future. In the tribal context, sovereignty is applied not only in the political/governmental sphere, but also addresses the ability and the right to make decisions about one's own cultural and social practices and development, which have frequently been constrained or prohibited through federal policies. Most contemporary tribes are said to be "quasi-sovereign" politically/governmentally, meaning that while still exercising aspects of sovereign powers, other aspects have been taken away by treaty, statutes, or court federal decisions. Tribes in a state of military powerlessness and economic dependency may have little ability to prevent or protest the reduction of their own sovereign powers.

Syllabary: Describes the writing system of the Cherokees' language, which is comprised of symbols that represent combinations of sounds (syllables), rather than specific sounds, as are represented by the symbols of an "alphabet." Invented by the native genius, Sequoyah, the Cherokee syllabary is believed to be the only language from which a written version was created after having been exclusively an oral expression throughout the entirety of its previous existence.

Symbiotic: A term borrowed from evolutionary biology to describe interdependent relationships in complex ecosystems and to describe similar interdependency between components of human social and/or cultural systems or networks. For example, in the Cherokee context, the two houses of the general council—the National Council and the National Committee—had duties assigned exclusively to each that insured that each house had to consult and work with the other in order for legislation to be developed and passed. Neither house could function without the other.

Syncretism: The meshing of two or more different social or cultural systems into a new expression containing elements of each. For instance, among the Cherokees, aspects of Christian beliefs and practices were often infused with the long-standing traditional beliefs and practices, resulting in a religious expression that adapted cosmological understandings from each system into a new system that reconciled most or all previously existing conflicts.

Trust Responsibility: A fundamental tenet of federal Indian law that derived from the 1831 Supreme Court case *Cherokee Nation v. Georgia*. The court set a precedent that established the federal government as the "guardian" or trustee of the Indian nations within its boundaries, which resulted in the concept that the United States bears a responsibility to the tribes as their trustee.

Tseg'sgin: The Cherokees' name for Andrew Jackson in their own language. The moniker is a pun on "Tseg'sin," which was the pronunciation of "Jackson," and "sgin," a word for "devil" in the Cherokee language. Thus, Andrew Jackson became "Jack the Devil" in Cherokee story.

Uktena: A mythical creature in Cherokee cosmology described as a giant serpent with a crystal embedded in its forehead. The figure of the Uktena conveys many messages to Cherokees about anomalies and oppositions— that positive elements may be encased in the negative, etc.—that formed the framework for Cherokee action and behavior in their older social and spiritual systems.

Worldview: The shared construction of their reality by a cultural group, most deeply embedded and conveyed through language usage, but exemplified in virtually every aspect of that people's social and cultural life. Extreme clashes in worldviews between peoples, such as Native Americans and the European colonizers, have often not been reconciled in human history, but instead have resulted in attempts, often successful, by one or both groups to eradicate either the worldview or the people themselves of the other.

Annotated Bibliography

Primary Source and Reference

Conley, Robert J. 2007. *A Cherokee Encyclopedia*. Albuquerque: University of New Mexico Press. Guide to Cherokee cultural and historical references.

Crewes, Daniel and Richard W. Starbuck. 2010. *Records of the Moravians among the Cherokees, Volume One, Early Contact and Establishment of the First Mission 1752–1802*. Tahlequah, OK: Cherokee National Historical Society. Journal entries of the Moravian missionaries to the Cherokees provide insights into daily life at the mission and surrounding communities in 1752–1802.

Crewes, Daniel and Richard W. Starbuck. 2010. *Records of the Moravians among the Cherokees, Volume Two, Beginnings of the Mission and Establishment of the School, 1802–1805*. Tahlequah, OK: Cherokee National Historical Society. Journal entries of the Moravian missionaries to the Cherokees provide insights into daily life at the mission and surrounding communities in 1802–1805.

Crewes, Daniel and Richard W. Starbuck. 2011. *Records of the Moravians among the Cherokees, Volume Three, the Anna Rosina Years, Part 1, Success in School and Mission, 1805–1810*. Tahlequah, OK: Cherokee National Historical Society. Journal entries of the Moravian missionaries to the Cherokees provide insights into daily life at the mission and surrounding communities in 1805–1810.

Crewes, Daniel and Richard W. Starbuck. 2012. *Records of the Moravians among the Cherokees, Volume Four, the Anna Rosina Years, Part 2, Warfare on the Horizon, 1810–1816*. Tahlequah, OK: Cherokee National Historical Society. Journal entries of the Moravian missionaries to the Cherokees provide insights into daily life at the mission and surrounding communities in 1810–1816.

Evans, E. Raymond, ed. 1981. "Jedediah Morse's Report to the Secretary of War on Cherokee Indian Affairs in 1822." *Journal of Cherokee Studies* 6, no. 2 (Fall): 60–78. Primary account of the man commissioned to report to the secretary of war on Indian Affairs throughout the United States and its territories.

Gaul, Theresa Strouth, ed. 2005. *To Marry an Indian, the Marriage of Harriett Gold and Elias Boudinot in Letters, 1823–1839*. Chapel Hill: University of North Carolina Press. Primary documents and interpretation of Boudinot relationship within context of Cherokee crisis and of gender and racial dynamics within the American nation.

Hoig, Stanley W. 1996. *Night of the Cruel Moon: Cherokee Removal and the Trail of Tears*. New York: Facts on File. Narrative history of the removal.

Kilpatrick, Jack and Anna Gritts. 1968. *New Echota Letters*. Dallas: Southern Methodist University. Writings of Samuel A. Worcester, missionary to the Cherokees, particularly in the *Cherokee Phoenix*.

King, Duane and E. Raymond Evans, eds. 1979. "History in the Making: Cherokee Events as reported in Contemporary Newspapers." *Journal of Cherokee Studies, Special Issue* 4, no. 2 (Spring): 64–66, 68–117. Selected newspaper accounts, more than half of which are from the pre-removal, removal, and post-removal eras.

King, Duane and E. Raymond Evans, eds. 1978. "The Trail of Tears: Primary Documents of the Cherokee Removal." *Journal of Cherokee Studies, Special Issue* 3, no. 3 (Summer): 131–189. Collection of 14 personal, social, military, and official documents, both Cherokee and federal.

King, Duane and E. Raymond Evans, eds. 1979. "Tsali: The Man behind the Legend." *Journal of Cherokee Studies, Special Issue* 4, no. 4 (Fall): 197-204. Primary documents around the incident of Tsali and the roundup in North Carolina.

Lumpkin, Wilson. 1907. *The Removal of the Cherokee Indians from Georgia*. New York: Dodd, Mead & Co. Perspective of Governor Wilson Lumpkin of Georgia on Cherokee removal.

McClinton, Rowena. 2007. *The Moravian Springplace Mission to the Cherokees*, Vols. I and II. Lincoln: University of Nebraska Press. Translations of Moravian diaries from the Springplace Mission.

Mooney, James. 1982. *Myths of the Cherokee and Sacred Formulas of the Cherokees*, from the 19th and 7th Annual Reports Bureau of American Ethnology (1900 and 1891, respectively). Nashville: Charles and Randy Elder—Booksellers. Anthropological cataloguing of observed customs and collected stories and oral traditions.

Perdue, Theda, ed. 1996. *Cherokee Editor, the Writings of Elias Boudinot*. Athens: University of Georgia Press. Selected writings from the *Cherokee Phoenix* and other sources chronicle Boudinot's development as an author and the transition in his sentiments concerning removal.

Perdue, Theda. 1979. "Letters from Brainerd." *Journal of Cherokee Studies* 4, no. 1 (Winter): 4–9. Short collection of letters from the Brainerd Mission, written by children being schooled there in the early 1800s.

Perdue, Theda and Michael Green, eds. 1995. *The Cherokee Removal: A Brief History with Documents*. Boston: Bedford Book of St. Martin's Press. Contains many of the significant primary documents of the removal era.

Peterson, Herman A. 2011. *The Trail of Tears, an Annotated Bibliography of Southeastern Indian Removal.* Carbondale: Southern Illinois Press. Extensive bibliography of the removals of the Five "Civilized" Tribes.

Phillips, Joyce B. and Paul Gary Phillips. 1998. *The Brainerd Journal, a Mission to the Cherokees, 1817–1823.* Lincoln: University of Nebraska Press. Journal from the primary mission of the American Board of Commissioners for Foreign Missions (ABCFM).

Royce, Charles C. 2006 (reprinted). *The Cherokee Nation of Indians* (Fifth Annual Report of the Bureau of Ethnology, Smithsonian Institution, 1883–1884). Whitefish, MT: Kessinger Publishing. Meticulous study of the historic context, terms, and impacts of Cherokee treaties.

Rozema, Vicki. 2002. *Cherokee Voices, Early Accounts of Cherokee Life in the East.* Winston-Salem, NC: John F. Blair. Collection of primary documents from late 18th- and early 19th-century life among the Cherokees.

Rozema, Vicki. 2003. *Voices from the Trail of Tears.* Winston-Salem, NC: John F. Blair. Collection of primary documents pertaining to Cherokee removal.

Shadburn, Don. 1990. *Cherokee Planters in Georgia, 1832–1838.* Cumming, GA: Don L. Shadburn. Contains genealogical information and historic plats.

Shadburn, Don. 1993. *Unhallowed Intrusion, a History of Cherokee Families in Forsyth County, Georgia.* Cumming, GA: Don L. Shadburn. Contains genealogical information and historic plats.

Sturtevant, William C. 1981. "John Ridge on Cherokee Civilization in 1826." *Journal of Cherokee Studies* 6, no. 2 (Fall): 79–91. Essay to linguist Albert Gallatin on the progress of "civilization" among the Cherokees.

Trail of Tears Association, Oklahoma Chapter. 2002. *1835 Cherokee Census.* Park Hill, OK: Trail of Tears Association. Census of the Cherokee population in the southeast in 1835, including information about their households.

Trail of Tears Association, Oklahoma Chapter. 1998. *The Journal of Rev. Daniel S. Butrick, May 19, 1838–Apr. 1, 1839.* Park Hill, OK: Trail of Tears Association. One of the best firsthand accounts of the experience of Cherokees on the Trail of Tears.

Walker, Charles O. 1988. *Cherokee Footprints, Volume I.* Canton, GA: Industrial Printing Services, Inc. Local history through newspaper and firsthand accounts.

Secondary Sources: Surveys

Adair, James. 1930. *History of the American Indians,* edited by Samuel Cole Williams. Johnson City, TN: Watauga Press. As constructed by a trader among the Cherokees in the mid-1700s.

Brown, John P. 1938. *Old Frontiers: The Story of the Cherokee Indians from Earliest Times to the Date of Their Removal to the West, 1838.* Kingsport, TN: Southern Publishers, Inc. Well-documented and readable history of the era.

Conley, Robert J. 2005. *The Cherokee Nation, a History*. Albuquerque: University of New Mexico Press. Enjoyable overview of the general history.

Cotterill, R. S. 1954. *The Southern Indians: The Story of the Five Civilized Tribes before Removal*. Norman: University of Oklahoma Press. Extensive and well documented.

Hoig, Stanley W. 1998. *The Cherokees and Their Chiefs, In the Wake of Empire*. Fayetteville: University of Arkansas Press. General history constructed around Cherokee leadership.

Malone, Henry. 1956. *Cherokees of the Old South, a People in Transition*. Athens: University of Georgia Press. Survey of social history through the removal era.

McLoughlin, William G. 1993. *After the Trail of Tears, the Cherokees' Struggle for Sovereignty, 1838–1880*. Chapel Hill: University of North Carolina Press. Very detailed and well-documented early chapters about immediate aftermath of removal.

McLoughlin, William G. 1986. *Cherokee Renascence in the New Republic*. Princeton, NJ: Princeton University Press. Very detailed and well-documented social and political history focusing on national development.

Mooney, James. 1975. *Historical Sketch of the Cherokees*. Chicago: Aldine Publishing Company. Overview developed by late 19th-century anthropologist among the Cherokees.

Starkey, Marion. 1946. *The Cherokee Nation*. New York: Alfred A. Knopf. Not documented, but charming and intuitive work.

Starr, Emmett. 1921. *History of the Cherokee Indians*. Oklahoma City: Warden. Reprint edited by Jack Gregory and Rennard Strickland. Fayetteville, AR: Indian Heritage Association, 1967. Reprinted Muskogee, OK: Hoffman Printing Co., Inc., 1984. Exhibits gaps in the chronology, but significant as one of the first renderings of their own history by a Cherokee.

Thornton, Russell. 1990. *The Cherokees: A Population History*. Lincoln: University of Nebraska Press. A unique method of recounting Cherokee history through population losses and increases through time. Author is a Cherokee.

Wardell, Morris L. 1938. *A Political History of the Cherokee Nation, 1838–1907*. Norman: University of Oklahoma Press. Second printing, 1977. First chapters concern the aftermath of the Trail of Tears. Meticulously documented.

Woodward, Grace Steele. 1963. *The Cherokees*. Norman: University of Oklahoma Press. Considered a standard, but should be read as an ethnocentric production of its time.

Secondary Sources: Specific Eras

Carter, Samuel III. 1976. *Cherokee Sunset, a Narrative of Travail and Triumph, Persecution and Exile*. New York: Doubleday. Popular general history focusing on the removal era in particular.

Corkran, David H. 1962. *The Cherokee Frontier: Conflict and Survival, 1740–62*. Norman: University of Oklahoma Press. Well documented and focusing on the complex era preceding and during the French and Indian Wars.

Ehle, John. 1988. *The Trail of Tears, the Rise and Fall of the Cherokee Nation*. New York: Anchor Books. Written in a popular journalistic style and taking some literary license, but poorly documented and difficult to reference.

Foreman, Grant. 1932. *Indian Removal, the Emigration of the Five Civilized Tribes of Indians*. Norman: University of Oklahoma. 11th printing, 1989. Meticulous work focusing specifically on removal.

Hatley, Thomas. 1993. *The Dividing Paths: Cherokees and South Carolinians through the Era of Revolution*. New York: Oxford University Press. Brings forth complexities of Cherokee frontier existence and trading relationships previous to and during Revolutionary War era. Scholarly and well documented.

Hicks, Brian. 2011. *Toward the Setting Sun, John Ross, the Cherokees, and the Trail of Tears*. New York: Atlantic Monthly Press. Newer popular work focusing on removal era. Written in novelistic style, some documentation.

Perdue, Theda and Michael D. Green. 2007. *The Cherokee Nation and the Trail of Tears*. New York: Viking. Well-documented and interesting survey of the removal era.

Reid, John Philip. 1976. *A Better Kind of Hatchet: Law, Trade, and Diplomacy in the Cherokee Nation during the Early Years of European Contact*. University Park: Pennsylvania State University Press. Political and economic history of 18th-century Cherokees.

Smith, Daniel Blake. 2011. *An American Betrayal, Cherokee Patriots and the Trail of Tears*. New York: Henry Holt and Co. Popular history providing new interpretations of internal divisions within Cherokee political society during removal era.

Wilkins, Thurman. 1986. *Cherokee Tragedy, the Ridge Family and the Decimation of a People*. Norman: University of Oklahoma Press. Popular, but well-documented history of the removal era focusing on the Ridge family. Provides a balanced interpretation of internal Cherokee divisions.

Biography

Andrew, John A. 2007. *From Revivals to Removal: Jeremiah Evarts, the Cherokee Nation, and the Search for the Soul of America*. Athens: University of Georgia Press. Well-documented and insightful biography of one of the Cherokees greatest advocates.

Bass, Althea. 1936. *Cherokee Messenger*. Norman: University of Oklahoma Press. Classic biography of Reverend Samuel Worcester, missionary to the Cherokees and plaintiff in Supreme Court case.

Corn, James F. 1978. "Conscience or Duty: General John E. Wool's Dilemma with Cherokee Removal." *Journal of Cherokee Studies* 3, no. 1 (Winter): 35–39. Short examination of the internal conflict within the general first assigned to enact the removal.

Eaton, Rachel Caroline. 1914. *John Ross and the Cherokee Indians*. Menasha, WI: Bantam Publishing Co. Early biography, interesting as one of the first produced by a Cherokee author.

Evans, E. Raymond. 1977. "Notable Persons in Cherokee History: Stephen Foreman." *Journal of Cherokee Studies* 2, no. 2 (Spring): 230–239. Brief biographical sketch, but with good information on Foreman's preremoval and removal era activities.

Faulkner, Cooleela. 2006. *The Life and Times of Reverend Stephen Foreman*. Tahlequah, OK: Cherokee Heritage Press. Biography of one of the first Cherokee ministers of the ABCFM and a captain on the Trail of Tears. First sections of the book are about removal.

Foster, George Everett. 1885. *Se-quo-yah, the American Cadmus and Modern Moses*. Tahlequah, Cherokee Nation: H. B. Stone. Reprinted New York: AMS Press, 1979. Early classic work about Sequoyah, inventor of the Cherokee syllabary.

Gabriel, Ralph Henry. 1941. *Elias Boudinot, Cherokee, and His America*. Norman: University of Oklahoma Press. Early popular work about the first editor of the *Cherokee Phoenix*.

Hoig, Stanley W. 1995. *Sequoyah: The Cherokee Genius*. Oklahoma City: Oklahoma Historical Society. More recent popular biography of Cherokee genius Sequoyah.

Lowery, George. 1835, 1977. "Notable Persons in Cherokee History: Sequoyah, or George Gist." *Journal of Cherokee Studies* 2, no. 4 (Fall): 385–393. Interesting account of Sequoyah and his invention of the syllabary as told by his contemporary, George Lowrey, second chief of the Cherokee Nation in 1835. Introduction by John Howard Payne.

Moulton, Gary. 1978. *John Ross, Cherokee Chief*. Athens: University of Georgia Press. Considered the premier biography of John Ross, derived from the extensive collection of Ross's papers collected during his 38 years as principal chief of the Cherokees.

Essays

Anderson, William L., ed. 1991. *Cherokee Removal, Before and After*. Athens: University of Georgia Press. Collected essays on events and social processes leading to Cherokee removal, as well as impacts of the removal, even to the present day.

Evarts, Jeremiah and Francis Paul Prucha. 1981. *Cherokee Removal: The "William Penn" Essay and Other Writings*. Knoxville: University of Tennessee Press. Compilation of the essays of Jeremiah Evarts of the ABCFM with interpretation of contemporary significance in the context of Indian rights.

Hudson, Charles M. 1975. *Four Centuries of Southern Indians*. Athens: University of Georgia Press. Essays on social aspects of southeastern Indian cultures and history.

Johoda, Gloria. 1975. *The Trail of Tears, the Story of the American Indian Removals 1813–1855*. New York: Wings Books. Each chapter addresses in a very popular style different tribal groups that experienced removal in different eras and geographic regions.

King, Duane, ed. 1979. *The Cherokee Indian Nation: A Troubled History*. Knoxville: University of Tennessee Press. Essays by scholars on social and political aspects of Cherokee society, with several essays specifically concerning the removal era.

McLoughlin, William G. 1995. *Cherokees and Missionaries, 1789–1839*. Athens: University of Georgia. Essays focusing on the aspects of mission work among the various denominations among the Cherokees.

McLoughlin, William G. 1994. *The Cherokees and Christianity, 1794–1870, Essays on Acculturation and Cultural Persistence*. Athens: University of Georgia Press. Essays on Cherokee reaction to Christianizing efforts.

McLoughlin, William G., Walter H. Conser, and Virginia Duffy. 1984. *The Cherokee Ghost Dance: Essays on the Southeastern Indians, 1789–1861*. Macon, GA: Mercer. Essays on cultural pressures and change in the critical era of the new United States and its first policy of "civilization" of the Indians, as well as tribal cultural resistance and revitalizations.

Perdue, Theda. 2003. *"Mixed Blood" Indians: Racial Construction in the Early South*. Athens: University of Georgia Press. Three essays on the subject of racial construction among southeastern Indians in the late 18th and early 19th centuries.

Social, Legal, and Political Processes

Campbell, Janet and David G. 1981. "Cherokee Participation in the Political Impact of the North American Indian." *Journal of Cherokee Studies* 6, no. 2 (Fall): 92–105. Analysis of impacts of Cherokee political advocacy on tribes throughout the country from 18th to early 20th centuries. It includes the preremoval and removal eras.

Champagne, Duane Willard. 1992. *Social Order and Political Change: Constitutional Governments among the Cherokee, the Choctaw, the Chickasaw, and the Creek*. Palo Alto: Stanford University Press. Scholarly work examining political and economic change within southeastern tribes in the context of 18th- and 19th-century global economy.

Champagne, Duane. 1983. "Symbolic Structure and Political Change in Cherokee Society." *Journal of Cherokee Studies* 8, no. 2 (Fall): 87–96. Scholarly interpretation of social conditions and institutions that contribute to Cherokee political and economic adaptability.

Christiansen, James R. 1985. "Removal: A Foundation for the Formation of Federalized Indian Policy." *Journal of Cherokee Studies* 10, no. 2 (Fall): 215–29. Examines the impetus over decades for removal as a federal policy.

Fiorato, Jacqueline. 1978. "The Cherokee Mediation in Florida." *Journal of Cherokee Studies* 3, no. 2 (Spring): 111–19. Account of little known mediation engaged in by Cherokees between United States and the Seminoles in 1837, indicating that on the eve of their own removal, the Cherokees continued to test the parameters of Indian sovereignty.

Horsman, Reginald. (1967) 1992. *Expansion and American Indian Policy.* Norman: University of Oklahoma Press. Federal Indian policy in the context of the federalism–states' rights struggle and in response to American humanitarianism.

Hutchins, John. 1977. "The Trial of Samuel Austin Worcester." *Journal of Cherokee Studies* 2, no. 4 (Fall): 356–74. Overview of the trial of the missionaries in both state and federal courts. Many newspaper accounts of the events.

Norgren, Jill. 1996. *The Cherokee Cases, the Confrontation of Law and Politics.* New York: McGraw-Hill. Excellent presentation for the layperson of the meanings of the Cherokee cases for the Cherokees in the removal era and tribes in contemporary times.

Reid, John Philip. 2006. *A Law of Blood, the Primitive Law of the Cherokee Nation.* DeKalb: University of Northern Illinois Press. Excellent and scholarly analysis of original Cherokee concepts of law within the context of their own system and in relation to colonial misunderstandings.

Sheehan, Bernard W. 1973/1974. *Seeds of Extinction: Jeffersonian Philanthropy and the American Indian.* Chapel Hill: University of North Carolina Press/New York: W.W. Norton & Company, Inc.(reprinted). Analysis of the paradoxes between the reform instincts of Americans in the Jeffersonian era and their actual impacts on Indians.

Strickland, Rennard. 1975. *Fire and the Spirits, Cherokee Law from Clan to Court.* Norman: University of Oklahoma Press. Traces the evolution of Cherokee understandings of law, particularly in the 19th century. Development of the Cherokee court system is emphasized.

Vipperman, Carl J. 1978. " 'Forcibly If We Must': The Georgia Case for the Cherokee Removal, 1802–1832." *Journal of Cherokee Studies* 3, no. 2 (Spring): 103–10. Analysis of the state's perspective of Cherokee removal.

Place and Places

Butler, Brian M. 1977. "The Red Clay Council Ground." *Journal of Cherokee Studies* 2, no. 1 (Winter): 140–53. Brief history and archaeology of the council ground used by the Cherokees during the removal era after being forced from their capital of New Echota.

Calloway, Brenda C. 1989. *America's First Western Frontier: East Tennessee, a Story of the Early Settlers and Indians in East Tennessee.* Johnson City, TN: Overmountain Press. Focuses on area west of the Appalachias and peoples interacting therein, including Cherokees and other Indians, from 1600 to 1839.

Duncan, Barbara and Brett Riggs. 2003. *Cherokee Heritage Trails Guidebook.* Chapel Hill: University of North Carolina Press. Guide to Cherokee sites remaining in the southeast, with historical contexts.

Evans, E. Raymond. 1977. "Fort Marr Blockhouse: Last Evidence of America's First Concentration Camp." *Journal of Cherokee Studies* 2, no. 2 (Spring): 256–63. Brief account of Fort Marr as a removal stockade.

Evans, E. Raymond. 1977. "Highways to Progress: Nineteenth Century Roads in the Cherokee Nation." *Journal of Cherokee Studies* 2, no. 4 (Fall): 394–400. Analysis of roads through the Cherokee Nation and the impacts of travelers through their country in the early 1800s.

Gilbert, Joan. 1996. *The Trail of Tears across Missouri.* Columbia: University of Missouri Press. Specific historic and geographic information about the removal as it passed through Missouri. Generally good but questionable in its uncritical repetition of family legends.

Hill, Sarah H. 2005. *Cherokee Removal: Forts along the Georgia Trail of Tears.* National Park Service and the Georgia Department of Natural Resources/ Historic Preservation Division. Recommendations to the National Park Service of military sites to be designated as part of the National Trail of Tears.

Hudson, Charles M. 1976. *The Southeastern Indians.* Knoxville: University of Tennessee Press. Chapters on the various tribes inhabiting the region, including Cherokees.

McEwan, Bonnie G., ed. 2000. *Indians of the Greater Southeast, Historical Archaeology and Ethnohistory.* Gainesville: University Press of Florida. Archaeological and ethnohistorical survey of the tribes in the south, from Texas to Florida, at the time of European contact, including the Cherokees.

Milling, Chapman J. 1969. *Red Carolinians.* Columbia: University of South Carolina Press. Overview of the Indian presence in the Carolinas in the 18th century, including the Cherokees.

Rozema, Vicki. 2013. *Footsteps of the Cherokees: A Guide to the Eastern Homelands of the Cherokee Nation,* 3rd ed. Winston-Salem: John F. Blair. Travel guide of historic Cherokee sites, with interpretation.

Snell, William R. 1977. "The Councils at Red Clay Council Ground, Bradley County, Tennessee, 1832–1837." *Journal of Cherokee Studies* 2, no. 4 (Fall): 344–55. Historical account of councils held during removal era.

Cherokee Oral, Rhetorical, and Literary Traditions

Bender, Margaret. 2002. *Signs of Cherokee Culture: Sequoyah's Syllabary in Eastern Cherokee Life*. Chapel Hill: University of North Carolina Press. Social impacts of the development of a Cherokee writing system.

Cushman, Ellen. 2011. *The Cherokee Syllabary: Writing the People's Perseverance*. Norman: University of Oklahoma Press. Interesting study of the creation and spread of the syllabary, and the potentials for subsequent generations of Cherokee speakers even into the modern age. Author is a Cherokee.

Denson, Andrew. 2004. *Demanding the Cherokee Nation, Indian Autonomy and American Culture, 1830–1900*. Lincoln: University of Nebraska Press. Cherokee political rhetoric and its usage to demand and define rights within and in relation to the American nation. First chapter establishes removal as the basis for all future rhetorical arguments and claims throughout the remainder of the 19th century.

Duncan, Barbara, ed. 1998. *Living Stories of the Cherokee*. Chapel Hill: University of North Carolina Press. Collection of Cherokee oral tradition as told by contemporary members of the Eastern Band of Cherokees.

Galloway, Mary Regina Ulmer, ed. 1990. *Aunt Mary, Tell Me a Story, a Collection of Cherokee Legends and Tales as Told by Mary Ulmer Chiltoskey*. Cherokee, NC: Cherokee Publications. Contemporary Cherokee author's account of stories heard in her family from the Eastern Band of Cherokees.

Justice, Daniel Heath. 2006. *Our Fire Survives the Storm, a Cherokee Literary History*. Minneapolis: University of Minnesota Press. Interpretation of the Cherokee textual literary tradition as identity, consciousness, and resistance. Author is a Cherokee.

Kilpatrick, Jack and Anna Gritts. 1995. *Friends of Thunder, Folktales of the Oklahoma Cherokees*. Norman: University of Oklahoma Press. Collected stories from the Oklahoma Cherokees, the descendants of those who experienced the removal. Authors are Cherokees.

Maddox, Lucy. 1991. *Removals, Nineteenth-Century American Literature and the Politics of Indian Affairs*. New York: Oxford University Press. Rereading texts by prominent American authors (e.g., Melville, Hawthorne, and Thoreau) in the context of removal and the "Indian question" that occupied the American consciousness in the early 1800s.

Monteith, Carmelita. "Literacy among the Cherokee in the Early Nineteenth Century." *Journal of Cherokee Studies* 9, no. 2 (Fall): 56–75. Examines factors in the early 1800s that influenced the Cherokees to become literate.

Strickland, William. 1977. "Cherokee Rhetoric: A Forceful Weapon." *Journal of Cherokee Studies* 2, no. 4 (Fall): 375–84. Well-researched article containing many examples of strategic uses of Cherokee political rhetoric in preremoval era.

Underwood, Thomas Bryan and Moselle Stack Sandlin. 1956. *Cherokee Legends and the Trail of Tears.* Cherokee, NC: Cherokee Publications. Cherokee stories for younger readers.

Wiget, Andrew. 1983. "Elias Boudinot, Elisha Bates, and *Poor Sarah*: Frontier Protestantism and the Emergence of the First Native American Fiction." *Journal of Cherokee Studies* 8, no. 1 (Spring): 4–21. Literary criticism of influences and impacts of Boudinot's novel.

Cherokee Arts and Culture

Adair, James. 1930. *Out of the Flame, Cherokee Beliefs and Practices of the Ancients*, edited by Willena Robinson. Tulsa, OK: Cherokee Language and Culture. Observations and interpretations of Cherokee beliefs and practices by a trader who lived among them and intermarried into them in the mid-1700s.

Fitzgerald, David, Duane King, and Principal Chief Chadwick Smith. 2007. *The Cherokee Trail of Tears.* Portland, OR: Graphic Arts Books. Beautiful photographic collection of the places and people of the Trail of Tears, with accompanying text by scholar Duane King and Cherokee Principal Chief Chad Smith.

Fundaburk, Emma Lila and Mary Douglass Fundaburk Foreman. 2001. *Sun Circles and Human Hands, the Southeastern Indians—Art and Industry.* Tuscaloosa: University of Alabama Press. Comprehensive work on southeastern symbology and its meanings in traditional arts and material production.

Gaillard, Frye. 1998. *As Long as the Waters Flow, Native Americans in the South and the East.* Winston-Salem, NC: John F. Blair. Photography of the southeastern sites that were and remain important to Cherokee history and cultural beliefs.

Hill, Sarah H. 1995. *Weaving the Worlds: Southeastern Cherokee Women and Their Basketry.* Chapel Hill: University of North Carolina Press. Extraordinary work tying Cherokee history and evolutions in basketry in style, material, and design and the resulting social meanings.

Hudson, Charles. 1978. "Uktena: A Cherokee Anomalous Monster." *Journal of Cherokee Studies* 3, no. 2 (Spring): 62–75. Exploration of the Cherokee cultural meaning of the mythic Uktena.

Reed, Marcelina. 1993. *Seven Clans of the Cherokee Society.* Cherokee, NC: Cherokee Publications. Short introduction to the clans of the Cherokees and their meanings, produced by the Eastern Band of Cherokee Indians.

The Eastern Band of Cherokee Indians

Bridges, Ben Oshel. 1979. "A Legal Digest of North Carolina Cherokees." *Journal of Cherokee Studies* 4, no. 1 (Winter): 10–20. An overview of the legal status of the Oconoluftee Cherokees, later known as the Eastern Band of Cherokees, including the preremoval and removal eras.

Finger, John. 1984. *The Eastern Band of Cherokees, 1819–1900.* Knoxville: University of Tennessee Press. Most comprehensive work on the complexity and evolution in the 1800s of the people known as the Eastern Band of Cherokees.

Frizzell, George E. 1982. "Remarks of Mr. Thomas, of Jackson." *Journal of Cherokee Studies* 7, no. 2 (Fall): 64–68. Brief account of William Holland Thomas, advocate for the Oconoluftee Cherokees on their rights.

Missions and Missionaries

Higginbotham, Mary Alves. 1976. "Creek Path Mission." *Journal of Cherokee Studies* 1, no. 2 (Fall): 72–86. Documented article about the Creek Path Mission in the years previous to and during the removal era.

Snell, William. 1979. "Candy's Creek Mission Station." *Journal of Cherokee Studies* 4, no. 3 (Summer): 163–84. Brief account of life at the mission in the early 1800s, with some primary documents and appendices.

Walker, Robert Sparks. 1931. *Torchlight to the Cherokees: The Brainerd Mission.* New York: Macmillan. Heartfelt history of the Brainerd Mission of the ABCFM to the Cherokees from someone who has lived in the region and felt its influences throughout his life.

Slavery

Miles, Tiya. 2010. *The House on Diamond Hill: A Cherokee Plantation Story.* Chapel Hill: University of North Carolina Press. Historical account of the Vann plantation, home of the most notorious of Cherokee slaveowners.

Miles, Tiya. 2006. *Ties That Bind: a Story of an Afro-Cherokee Family in Slavery and Freedom.* Berkeley and Los Angeles: University of California Press. Historical account of Shoe Boots (Chulio), a member of the Cherokee National Council in the early 1800s, and his wife, Doll, his former slave.

Perdue, Theda. 1979. *Slavery and the Evolution of Cherokee Society.* Knoxville: University of Tennessee Press. Traces the meaning and development of slavery among the Cherokees from systems of exchange and/or incorporation of prisoners to chattel.

Women

Johnston, Carolyn Ross. 2003. *Cherokee Women in Crisis, Trail of Tears, Civil War, and Allotment, 1838–1907.* Tuscaloosa: University of Alabama Press. Analysis of roles and pressures on Cherokee women of different strata under federal civilization policy. First section of the book focuses on the removal era.

Perdue, Theda. 1998. *Cherokee Women: Gender and Culture Change, 1700–1835.* Lincoln: University of Nebraska Press. Outstanding and very well-documented ethnohistorical treatment of the roles and power of women in Cherokee society in the 18th and early 19th centuries.

Gold

Williams, David. 1993. *The Georgia Gold Rush: Twenty-Niners, Cherokees, and Gold Fever.* Columbia: University of South Carolina Press. Excellent work focusing on gold and the interstices between Georgia greed and Cherokee rights. Places the Cherokees at the center of the story.

Epidemics

Kelton, Paul. 2007. *Epidemics and Enslavement: Biological Catastrophe in the Native Southeast, 1492–1715.* Lincoln: University of Nebraska Press. Well researched and documented, unique exploration of the subject.

Novels about the Trail of Tears

Conley, Robert J. 1995. *Mountain Windsong, a Novel of the Trail of Tears.* Norman: University of Oklahoma Press. Romantic and tragic tale of lovers separated by the removal. Well researched and placed into the larger context of the historic event and its meaning. Author is a Cherokee.

DVDs

National Park Service, US Department of the Interior. 2009. *The Trail of Tears,* 23 minutes. Produced in conjunction with the Cherokee Nation and the Eastern Band of Cherokees. Producers, writer, and actors are Cherokees, including children from the Cherokee Language Immersion School. In English and Cherokee with subtitles.

Rich-Heape Films. 2006. *The Trail of Tears: Cherokee Legacy,* 115 minutes. Starring Cherokee actor Wes Studi and including many historians and researchers providing context.

Websites

http://historyproject.ucdavis.edu/lessons/view_lesson.php?id=11. Dr. Roland Marchand's lesson on "The Removal of the Cherokee Nation." It includes background information, task assignment, investigative question, and 47 primary documents.

www.coretexts.org/old/cherokeelessons/unit4/index.htm. Dr. Julia Coates's two lessons on "The Legal and Political Struggle Over Cherokee Removal." It includes guiding questions, learning objectives, historical overview, textual sources, questions for analysis, discussion topics, optional question to tie the lessons together, suggested papers, and supplemental reading.

http://www.nps.gov/nr/twhp/wwwlps/lessons/118trail/118trail.htm. National Park Service lessons are derived from the sites on the actual Trail of Tears. It includes inquiry questions, historical context, maps, images, readings, activities, and table of contents.

Index

ABCFM. *See* American Board of Commissioners for Foreign Mission

Act of Reform of 1817, 50–51

"Act of Union," 135

Agriculture, 5

Alcohol abuse, 136

American Board of Commissioners for Foreign Mission (ABCFM), 147, 148, 152, 199; Cherokees and, 79; education and, 64; Evarts as director of, 149; missionaries arrested by Georgia, 78–79; Worcester and, 158–59

"Ani Giduwagi," 4

Arkansas, 46; Cherokees in, 50, 56

The Articles of Agreement and Cession Between the United States and the State of Georgia. *See* Georgia Compact

Battle of Horseshoe Bend, 47, 153; pensions promised to Cherokee veterans of, 100

Bell, John, 123

Blackburn, Gideon, 154

Black Fox, 44–45

Blood law, 7–8; abolition of, 31–32; Ridge Treaty Party killings and, 136–37; Treaty of Hopewell and, 23

Boudinot, Elias (Buck Oo-watie), 64, 90, 147–48; death of, 131–32, 148;

Indian Removal Act and, 69, 71–72, 179–81; Indian removal treaty support and, 91, 102; intermarriage, 64–65; land cession advocated by, 89–90; move to Indian Territory, 112–14; Treaty of New Echota, 104; *Worcester v. Georgia* and, 82, 87–88, 184

Brainerd Mission, 152

British, 9; Cherokees and, 12–14, 21; French tensions with, 13–14; trade embargo, 12–13

Butler, Elizur: arrest of, 79; imprisonment of, 92–93, 148–49; Ross Party and, 93–94; on Trail of Tears, 93–94, 123–24, 149

Butrick, Daniel, 123–24, 149; journal excerpts, 201–4

Byrd, Joe, 142

Calloway, Colin, 20

Carroll, William, 99, 101

Catawba, 4

Cherokee council, 7. *See also* General Council; Grand councils; National Council of the Cherokee Nation

Cherokee folklore, 2; migration story, xi–xii; technology and, 19–20

Cherokee Golden Age, 139

Cherokee lands, 65–66, 148; boundaries of, 22–24; collective tribal landholdings and, 168; frontiers people

About the Author

JULIA COATES is the lead instructor for the award-winning Cherokee Nation History Course. She holds a PhD in American Studies from the University of New Mexico, has been an assistant professor of Native American Studies at the University of California, Davis, and a visiting professor at Northeastern State University in Tahlequah, Oklahoma, capital of the Cherokee Nation. She presently works for the American Indian Studies Center at UCLA. She is a citizen of the Cherokee Nation and serves on its Tribal Council.